The SPIRIT *of* NEW ORLEANS

& the Characters Who Live There

Christopher Briscoe

The Spirit of New Orleans & the Characters Who Live There

Published by: Shifting Gears Publications, Ashland, Oregon
www.ShiftingGearsPub.com
Interior & Cover Design by: Jeff Altemus, Align Visual Arts

ISBN: 978-1-7339584-0-0

Printed in the United States of America

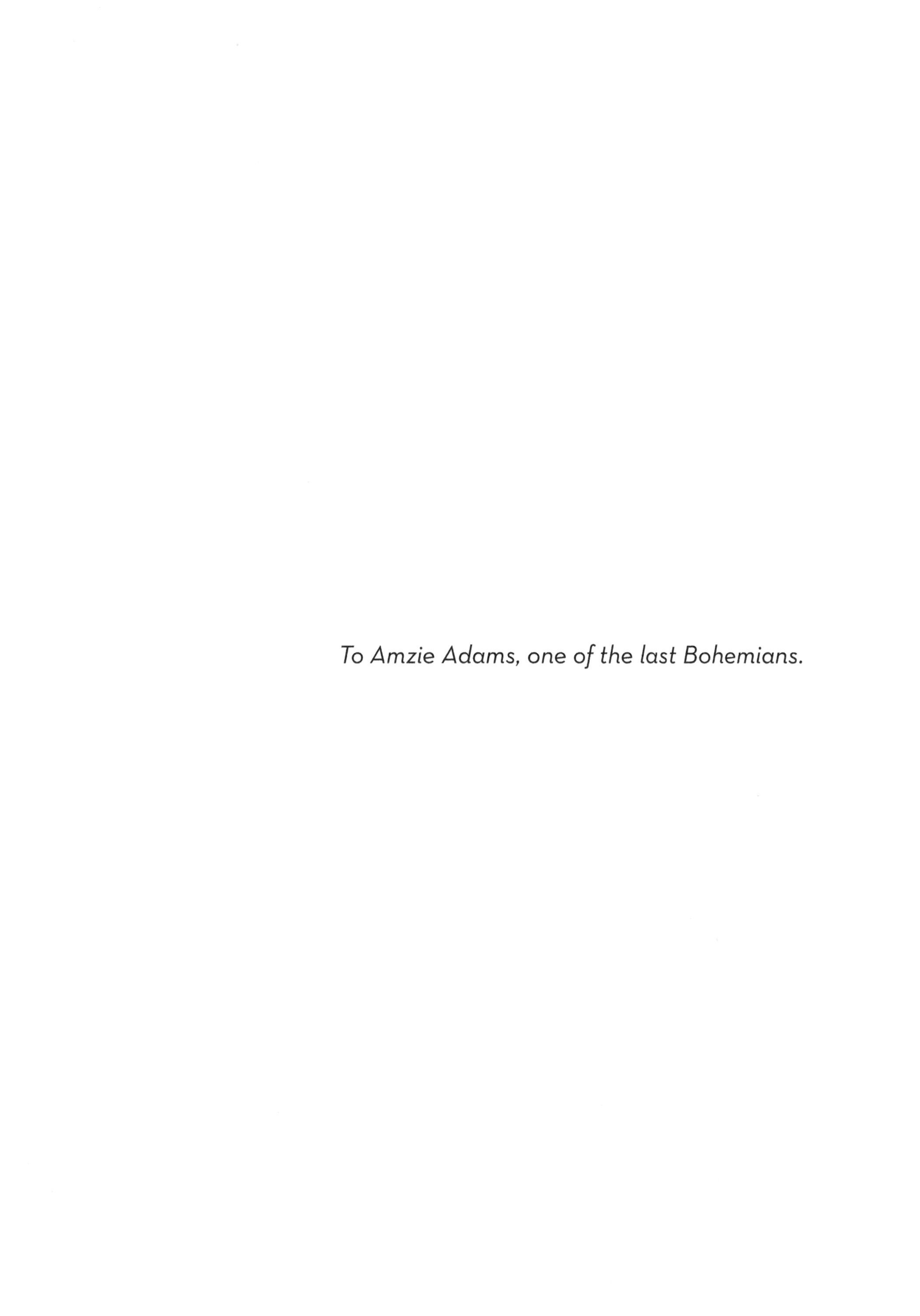

To Amzie Adams, one of the last Bohemians.

The Work of Christopher Briscoe

BIG events, natural and otherwise, are quickly documented by the image makers of our times; the photojournalists, the paparazzi, the curious onlookers with their ubiquitous digital instruments. Next, the artists weigh in, adding meaning and defining the zeitgeist. The news cycle moves on. What's left behind is a slightly changed world, unnoticed by most. For people like Christopher Briscoe, however, these new landscapes are opportunities to explore and redefine.

Briscoe is a special breed of photographer, operating in the indefinable area between fine art and commercial photography. In order to succeed in this world, he needs to serve two masters. On the photographic side, he needs to capture an image that is narrative and personal. It must define the time and explore the person. It must grab the eye. It must be a solid composition. It must look good on the printed page. On the fine art side, the body of work needs to represent a unique worldview. It must have a tone. It must contribute to a greater idea. It must contain and demonstrate the mystery of visual art.

From Southeast Asia to New Orleans, Briscoe embeds himself into the culture he documents. He discovers photographic opportunities that lead to narratives and eventually to the essence of a place and its people.

In his newest book, The Spirit of New Orleans, *Briscoe documents the people and musicians of a post-Katrina New Orleans. While the accompanying text is critical to the book's story, this is essentially a visual record of encounter and acculturation. The photographs tell their own story. The portraits of the individual musicians are intimate, technically masterful and warmly personal, but the street scenes are the heart of this work. One of these photographs is of a young girl with an umbrella looking at the camera as mourners walk away behind a horse-drawn hearse. The image creates a sense of poignancy combined with a day-to-day realism that firmly anchors the event in a world we recognize, but, for many of us, regretfully never know.*

Briscoe's humanity, sensitivity and involvement play out in every shot, from the rain-soaked funeral procession to the man in the teal-colored Mardi Gras Indian costume. In this last photograph, a youthful bicyclist dodges in front of the costumed man. The careful cropping of this image, where the faces of both men are hidden from view, is a perfect example of intuitive artistic storytelling. This whole book is a major artistic accomplishment.

John Davis, Davis & Cline Gallery

The Spirit of New Orleans

New Orleans is a blend of cultures that flows from a long history of talented characters. They dance and drink at funerals. They close up shop, taping a note on the door explaining how they cut their finger and have a gig to play that night. A stripper may see herself as a healer, a burglar considers himself a collector, a lawyer gives bicycle tours. Locals view outsiders as unfortunates who are missing the big party. New Orleans is a place where you can sit on the banks of the whiskey-brown Mississippi River all day long, watching its secrets float by without feeling guilty about anything.

For centuries, New Orleans has been a gumbo of unique creativity. For starters, the city is built on land that continually sinks, refuses to solidify, washes away, is rebuilt, then sinks again. The creative juices there run deep, just like the never-ending Mississippi that flows past. Century-old buildings pop with the color of tiny courtyard gardens, wrought-iron railings wrap-around balconies, and restaurants are steeped in history, like the one that Napoleon frequented. All are expressions of a city as unique in its crazy, creative wholeness as the characters who call it home.

Arron Washington, a New Orleans drummer, tells a colorful story about when he was a boy, sitting near the trolley car tracks, listening to the clickity-clack of the train rolling past, then pedaling home so he could replicate what he just heard on his drum set. More on that later, plus what happened when he was inspired by a cockroach.

Hoping to earn some extra cash, Tutu Lulu (a guy named Curtis), dances in a bright yellow tutu and sparkling red high heels, spinning in the middle of Bourbon Street during a morning drizzle. He says, "New Orleans is the only place where I truly feel at home. And it's the only place where broken people can come to live in peace and be themselves."

Musician Deacon John and his brother Charles talk about playing with Little Richard and Carlos Santana. Harold Battiste remembers when he helped Cher get started.

Goddess Celeste describes creating intimacy during her mystical sessions and "going to the other side."

Other residents tell stories about "the storm" and their struggles to survive. Each tale carries a common thread of passion and creativity as bold and deep as the mighty Mississippi. That river—that deep, ever changing, winding mass that is so muddy a cupful looks like a truck-stop cup of joe—is surely the perfect metaphor for this city and its people. It symbolizes their own enduring power, and their suffering at the hands of life's unpredictability. The folks who live here flow just like that river, each character is a tributary and they all converge to produce something unique in the world. Most of these artists do not create in order to make a living. Creativity has claimed them, just like the river chooses its own course, dancing to the music echoing from the French Quarter.

Christopher Briscoe

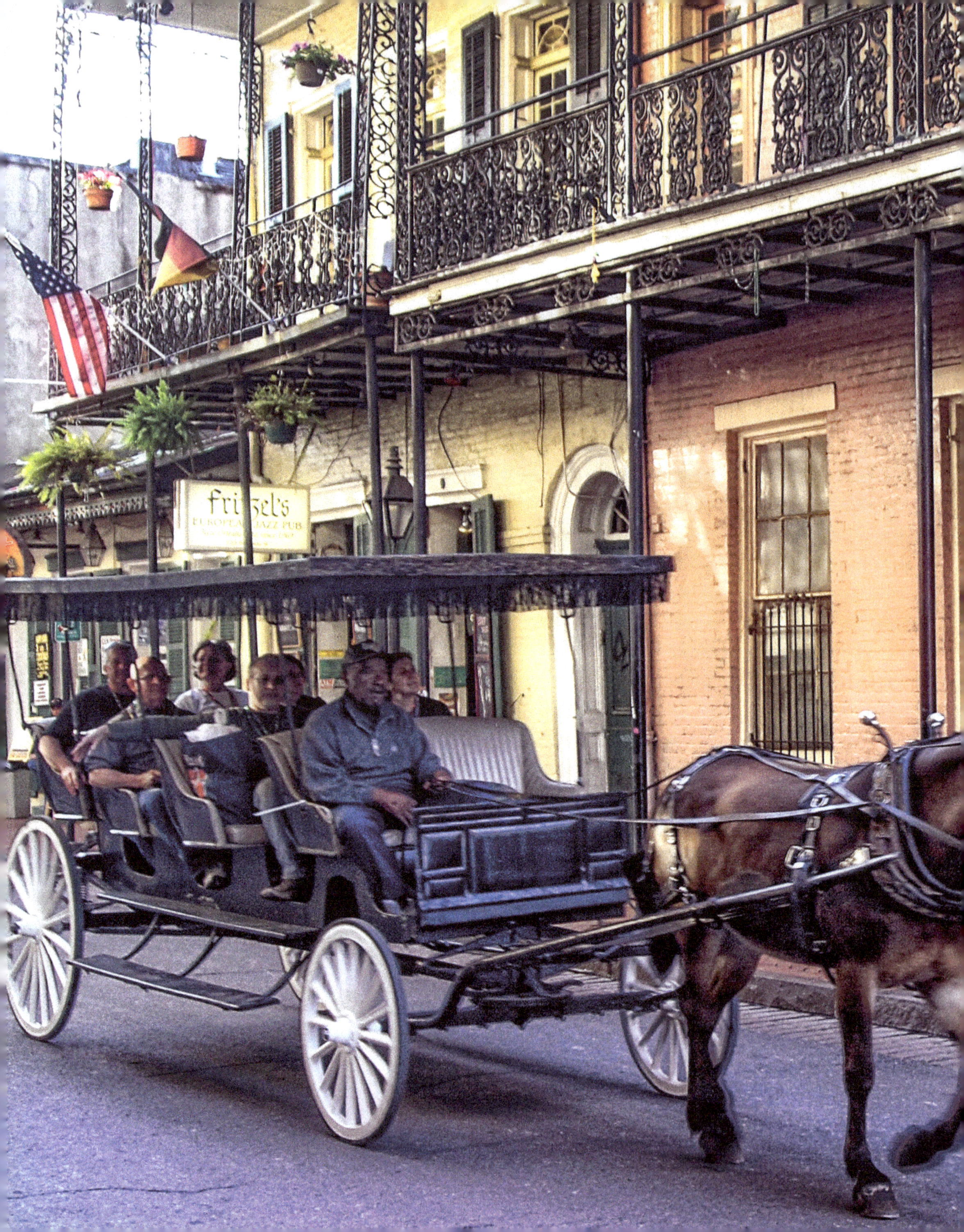
fritzel's
EUROPEAN JAZZ PUB

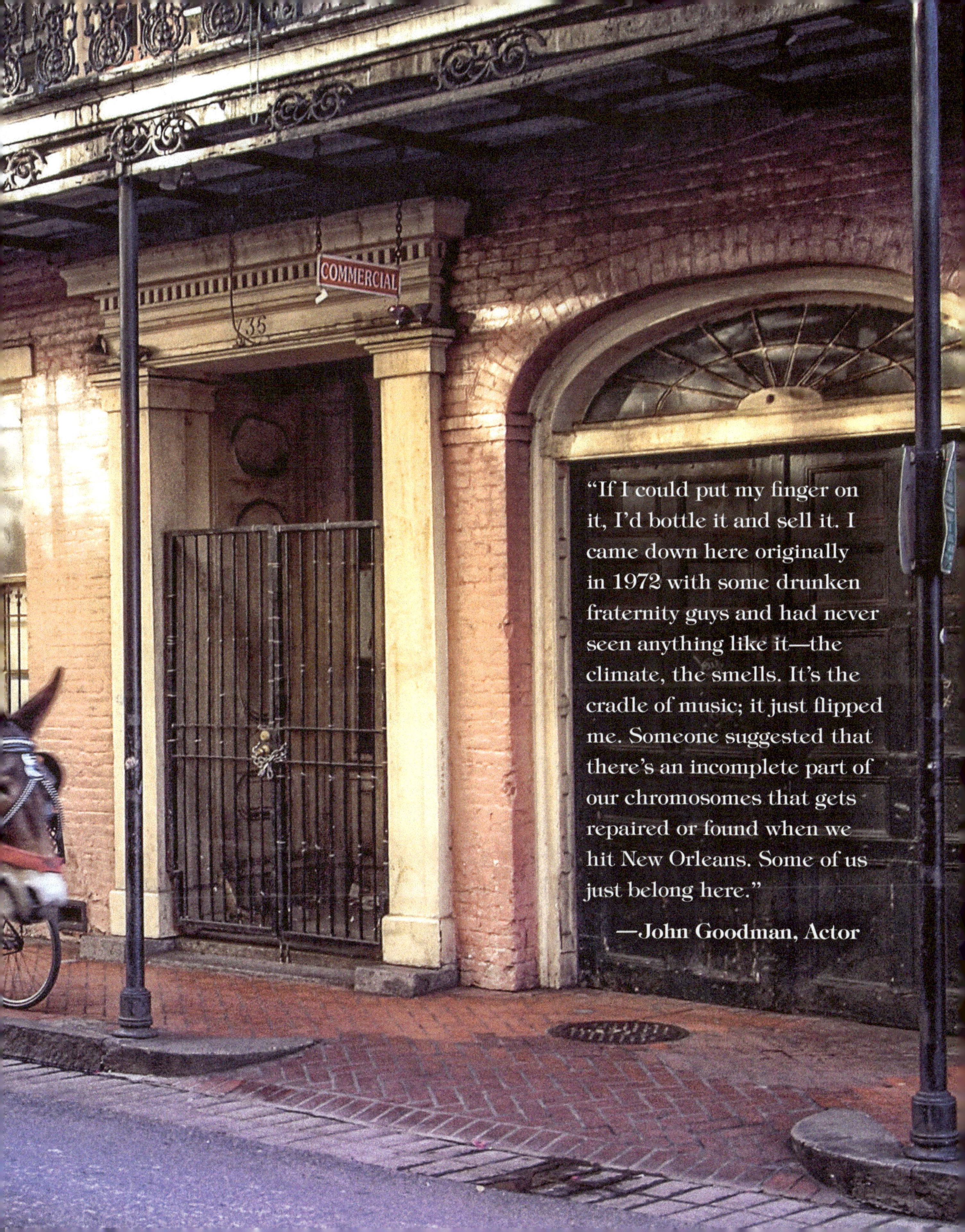

"If I could put my finger on it, I'd bottle it and sell it. I came down here originally in 1972 with some drunken fraternity guys and had never seen anything like it—the climate, the smells. It's the cradle of music; it just flipped me. Someone suggested that there's an incomplete part of our chromosomes that gets repaired or found when we hit New Orleans. Some of us just belong here."

—John Goodman, Actor

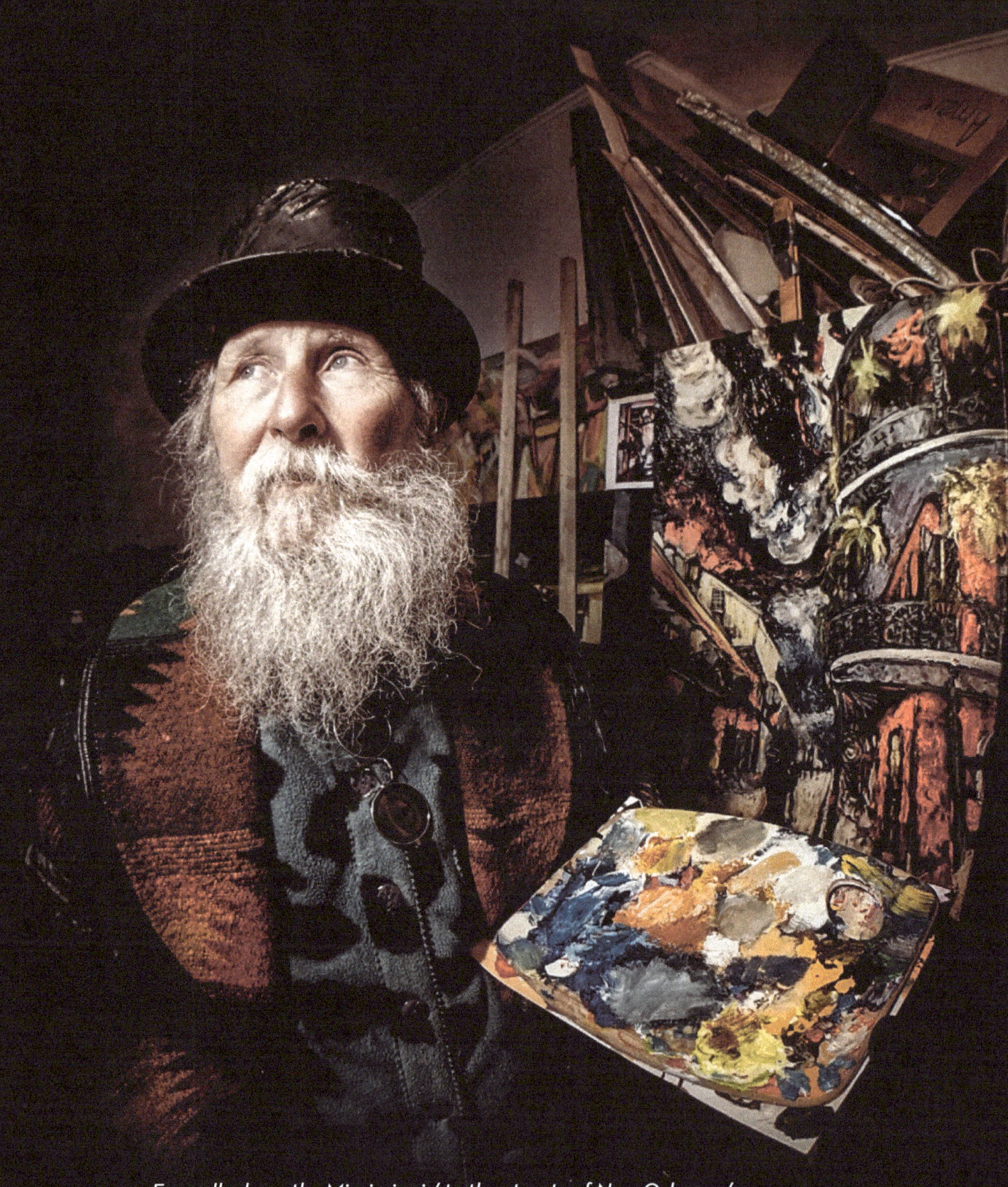

Fog rolls down the Mississippi / to the streets of New Orleans /
crawls through the Old Quarter / and carries the ghosts that feed my dreams.
—Amzie Adams

Amzie Adams
In Search of the Psychic Signposts

ON ANY GIVEN DAY, you might spot Amzie in the French Quarter, jamming with other musicians, perhaps with his hand-made electric voodoo stick or on one of his cigar box guitars. He'll be dressed in one of his carefully collected outfits; a gaucho vest, hand painted leather pants, white boots with tips that curl forward like the top of two Dairy Queen frosted cones. You immediately notice his glasses. They're round, perched on top of his high cheek bones and both lenses have green, holographic eyes embedded in the glass. His white beard is streaked with wisps of gray, peeking out from under a well-worn black top-hat that features a fully illuminated inset of a tiny dollhouse. Peer inside and you'll find a tiny figurine of Amzie himself relaxing in an easy chair. He's a walking work of art.

How old is that guy? And who is that pretty young woman with him? If you're a tourist from the Midwest you might stare, family in tow, then keep on walking. You might steal a glance, wishing you could snap a quick photo, then scurry away. But you'll have missed meeting one of the most interesting characters in New Orleans.

Poet, musician, painter, photographer, philosopher, inventor, historian; Amzie embodies them all. A local gallery owner once called Amzie "the last of the real bohemians," to which he retorted, "I don't want to be the last one. I want there to be a million more Boho's. We come from all over the world and New Orleans is the place for us."

If you stop and listen, you'll hear some improvised music unlike anything you've ever heard back home. If you venture closer and introduce yourself, you'll likely be surprised by Amzie's polite, articulate, matter-of-fact nature. If you can engage him, you may find yourself heading down a rabbit hole with many twists and turns. And the next time you inhale, you may lean back, wondering what that smell is. It's not cologne. That musky scent is pure Amzie, as complex as the man himself.

If you're lucky and adventuresome, you might even walk with Amzie through
the French Quarter. After a few blocks, you'll wonder if you're with the Mayor
or some kind of royalty. Amzie will be leading the way with measured strides,
his tall swamp-wood walking stick in hand. It's more of a staff, with ruby colored
blown glass on the top that sparkles like cosmic rays of sunshine.

EVERYBODY KNOWS AMZIE. "Dr. A! You gonna be at that party in Voodoo
Alley tonight?!" "Dude, where is Chicken Girl? I heard she OD'd." "Amzie,
you killed it at the club last night. You should do a new CD." He'll often stop to
shoot the shit. Other times, he just responds with a respectful nod and keeps
on walking.

"There's a musical vibe here and our connections are incredible," he says.
"Most of the musicians in New Orleans have played together at one time or
another. I'll walk by the Spotted Cat in the dark and if my drummer is playing
inside, he'll feel my presence, turn, and tap on the window with his stick, just to
say 'hi.'

"When you're with musicians and really rock'n, it's almost as if a higher power
or source takes hold. Nobody knows where it comes from. It's an energy blend
of all the musicians. The creative synergy in New Orleans is stronger than
anywhere else in the Universe. It's unique. It's as though we're in a creative
Petri dish together. You know, we're below sea level and it might be 100
degrees with 100% humidity. Toss the right elements into that Petri dish and
you get a mix of music that never existed before and may never exist again."

Amzie's has an office. It's a wobbly two-person table inside Envie, a sidewalk

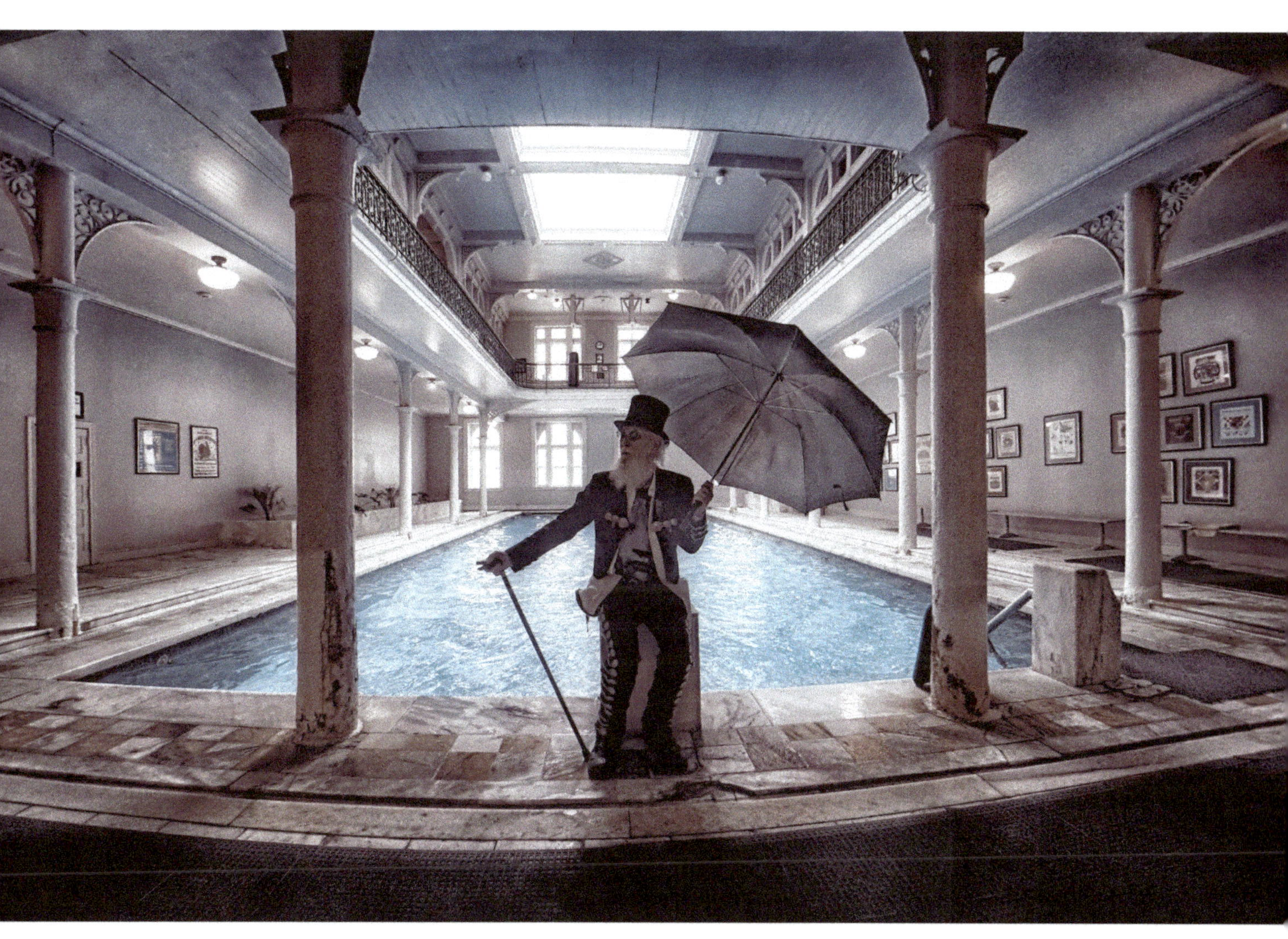

cafe at the edge of the French Quarter that rounds the corner of Decatur Street. Envie is popular with locals and tourists alike who flow in through the front door which is always open. Amzie takes his place in the short line, standing on the well-worn white tile floor in front of a glass food case. The overhead chalk-smeared menu board offers breakfast: gluten-free pastries to accompany your morning coffee topped off with whatever booze you need. A barista with long dreads surveys Amzie with a soulful smile. She already knows his order: scrambled eggs, toast, and his special blend of half coffee and half tea. She'll punch the key labelled "Amzie" on their cash register. That's for him alone; others have tried to order the same thing and use that key. No way. It's Amzie's key.

> *"In my neighborhood, it gets so hot during the summer that people shoot at each other just to keep the air moving."*

From his table, he can see into the tiny back room, which is a kind of Amzie gallery, adorned with electric-bright Amzie paintings, their colorful, wild, brush strokes reminiscent of Van Gogh. A tattered life-size cardboard cutout of Amzie is propped in the corner, perhaps a precursor to a statue in the park, honoring a guy who—if Facebook "likes" were cash—would be a millionaire.

Sit with Amzie for long enough and you'll by wading through endless stories about his early life: driving tanks in the Marine Corp, the time he lived with a wealthy heiress in New Jersey, and when he recorded music on John Lennon's studio bus. Later, Amzie is likely to shift into his hair-raising, bad-ass tales, like the time a guy tried to break into his house. Amzie grabbed a shotgun and pumped it loudly to scar the burglar off. All that did was provoke the guy. "I'll be back!" he yelled. Amzie deadpans, "In my neighborhood, it gets so hot during the summer that people shoot at each other just to keep the air moving."

Throughout the conversation, you may notice that he is a slow eater. Amzie only has a few teeth left and has to carefully mash his food, taking his time to slowly butter the toast. He rarely finishes his meal, usually asking for a to-go container. This will be his next meal too.

Amzie's mental library is vast. Ask him any historical question about New Orleans and he will suddenly become as articulate as he was when he was interviewed for the PBS's *American Experience*. Or, you could ask him about the mystical third eye that shows up in many of his paintings. He even might elucidate about how back in the 1700's, people wore aromatic sachets around their necks when they walked through the garbage strewn streets.

The twists and turns through the depths of your conversation will push you to your limits and beyond, making you wish you were taking notes. Throughout his narratives, Amzie often weaves a continuous thread about the loves of his life. Brian, another local character once told me, "Amzie and I were in a Mardi-Gras parade when a woman on a distant balcony leaned over the railing and yelled down, 'Amzie! Amzie! 1974, remember me? Call me!' He just turned away and muttered, 'Oh shit, I have no idea who she is. Just keep walk'n.'"

ONE EVENING, I WENT TO AN ART SHOW of Amzie's paintings and watched an elementary school teacher from Ohio—dressed as though she was ready for a PTA meeting—slowly circle him. Once sucked into the Amzie vortex, seduced by his one-of-a-kind charm, she was quickly primed to buy his $4,000 paintings and also ready to follow him back to his place. This is what she came to New Orleans for, to finally venture out of her life-long conservative comfort zone and peek over the cliff into the abyss of possibilities.

According to Amzie, the schoolmarm did go home with him. I tried to imagine what she thought as she walked into his tiny place, cluttered with decades of towering, precarious piles of random stuff. I pictured her turning sideways to maneuver toward a small bed area, framed by several layers of mosquito netting like a tiny treehouse. A less adventurous newcomer might hesitate at the doorstep and wonder, "Where's the hazmat suit?"

His anthology of stories continues to bubble in a steady stream, as if they are flowing out of the nearby Mississippi. If you are new to the Amzie show, you will probably we wondering, "Did that really happen to him? Is this all bullshit?" But anyone lucky enough to know Amzie for a long time realizes that these stories are true and that he's the real-deal.

AMZIE GREW UP IN NEW JERSEY. "All the towns around me were the same. Orange, South Orange, West Orange, East Orange. You might as well call them all 'Fred.' He escaped to the Marine Corps and lasted until 1964 when he hitched his way to New Orleans for Christmas. When I arrived in the French Quarter, there must have been 22 hippie bars. Hippies everywhere. You could get beans and rice for a quarter and rent was $35 a month. My first place to sleep was under someone's covered kitchen table.

"Most bars were kind of post-Beatnik. As a musician, you could play at any of these bars, 24 hours a day, 7 days a week. It was like heaven for a musician. I often jammed with Babe Stovall who played a Steel National guitar behind his head. That's when I learned how to play music. Babe and I would go down to Jackson Square and he would start playing his guitar, 'Oh when the saints, go marching in...' Tourists would be walking in the square by the fountain and they'd see us, me, a hippie dude playing dulcimer, and him, a cool old black guy with a guitar behind his head. The minute a good crowd gathered, he'd smack hi guitar down at his feet and say, 'My name is Babe Stovall. This is a steel guitar. If I hit you with it, it's gonna hurt.' And he'd continue, 'We take anything from a penny on up. We take food stamps, too, cause we likes to eat.' When he started to play again the crowd would start to clap and he'd yell out, 'Don't

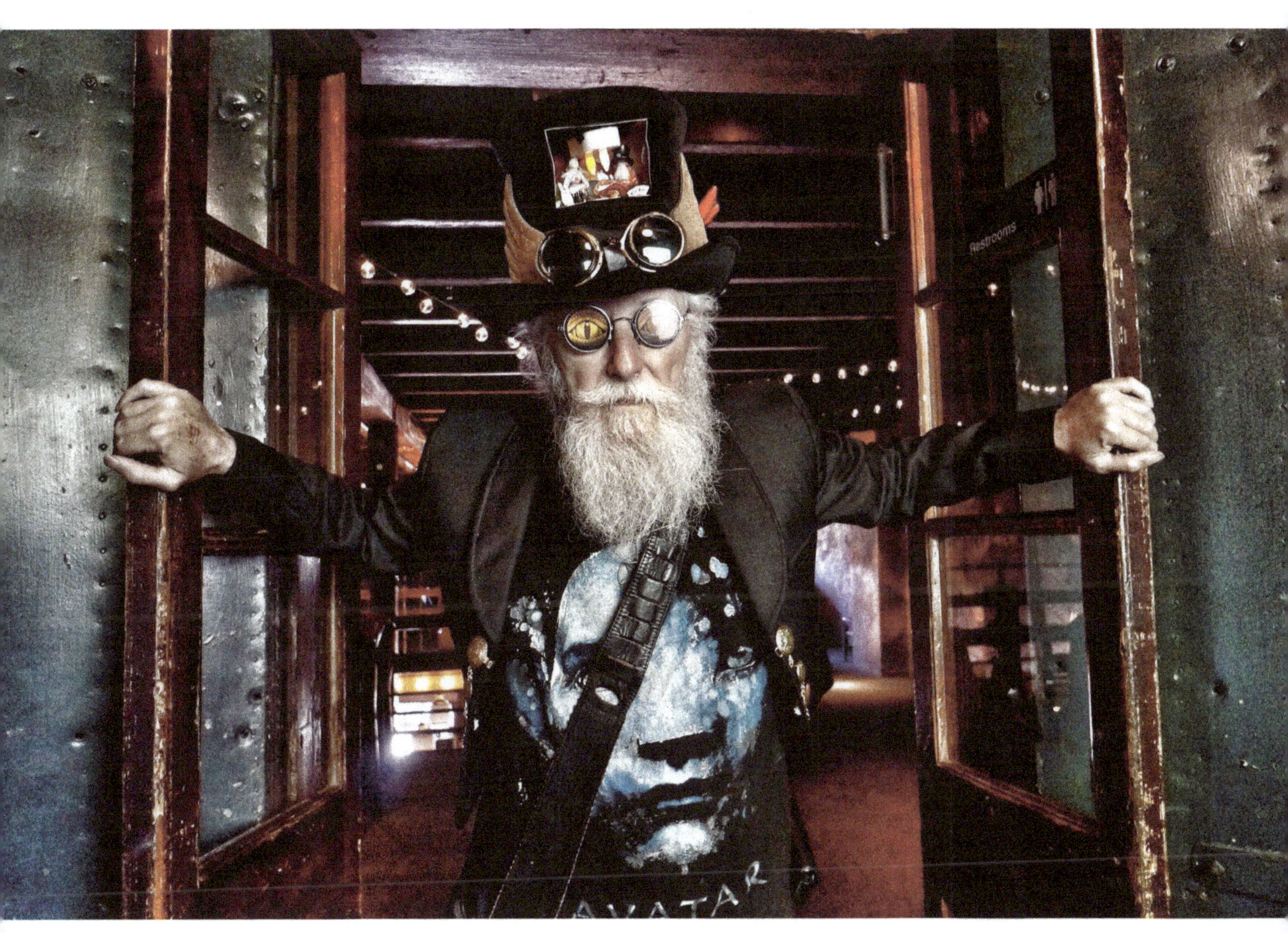

Restrooms
AVATAR

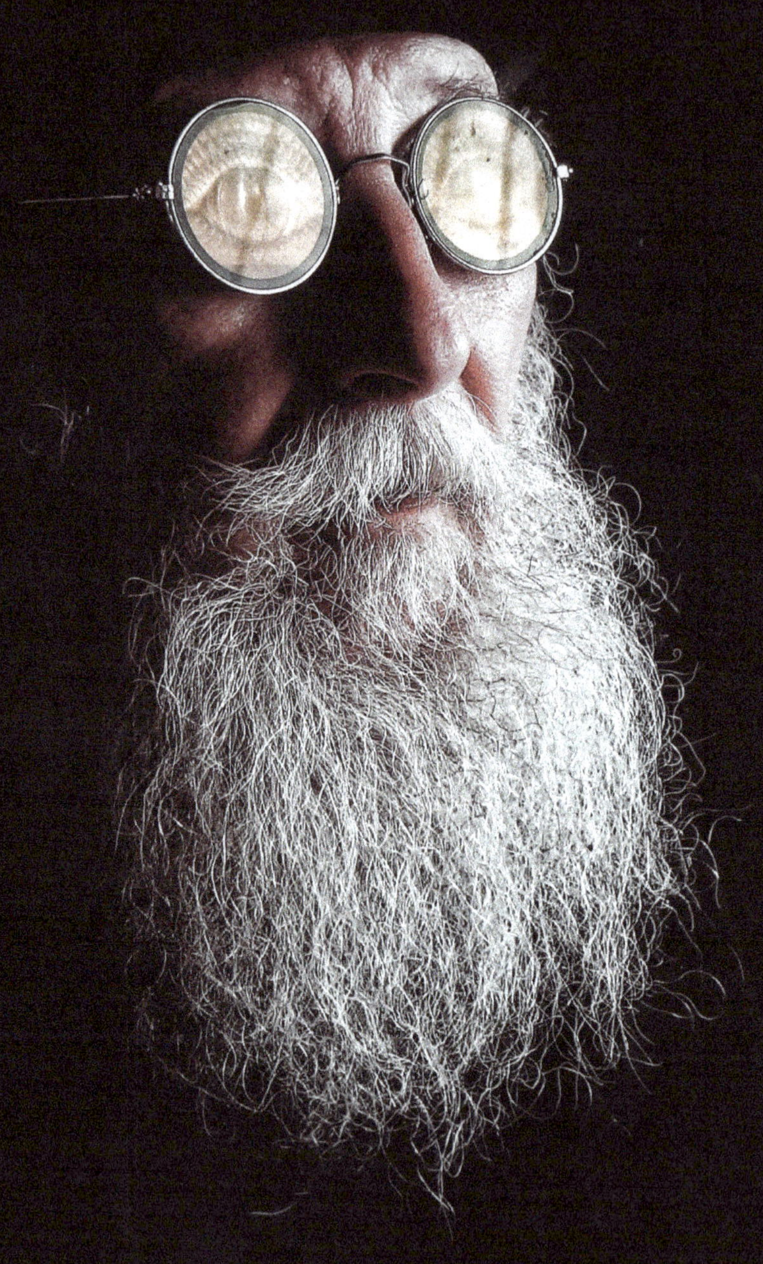

clap!' And everybody would go, 'Huh?' Then he'd say, 'Throw money.' And I'm think'n, 'Man, this guy's got it wired.'"

"I lived next door to Tennessee Williams for a while. He was always trying to pick us up, 'Hey, boys, you want to go swimming? It's hot outside.' Tennessee was funny.

"Back then, the police in New Orleans acted as if we all had parked our spaceships behind the French Quarter and snuck into town. They had a tactical squad that would—if you were a freak—just jack you up and take you to jail. So, the only thing we had was the A.C.L.U. and underground newspapers that developed throughout America. There was The Great Speckled Bird in Atlanta. There was The Oracle in San Francisco. In New York, there was a bunch of different ones like The Village Voice and The East Village Other. Besides providing a way for the counter culture to communicate, these newspapers became an integral part of the economic system for hippies. We could buy one for a quarter and then resell it for 50 cents. And our rights were protected by the First Amendment, guaranteeing us free speech and freedom of the press, at least theoretically.

"Now everybody's screaming about gentrification and condominiums. I understand their point of view, but hey, it's better than sleeping under a table… with no air conditioning… in August… with mosquitoes. But now we are being pushed out toward the Bywater. We're moving into the Marigny. Soon, we're gonna be moving into St. Holy Cross, and all the way to Delacroix and even out to the Lakefront. We're gonna to take that place over. The way I see it, even though it is gentrification with this condominium thing and the arrival of the squares—and maybe the French Quarter is done for—this change is both good and bad.

"I used to live in a neighborhood where a lot of folks got shot and stabbed. Seriously. People I knew, bleeding on the floor from knife wounds, because they fell asleep in the wrong spot on Decatur Street, on Frenchman Street, or made the mistake of knocking over some guy's beer at a bar. One dude stumbled into my place and said, 'I been shot.' I went, 'Ha ha, that's funny,' but he fell down. He had been shot. I got him over to Cherry Hospital and he survived but was discharged with Hepatitis 2. So, would you rather have a crack-head living next to you, shooting your old lady in the head, or would you rather have a hipster living next door in a condo who might buy your paintings?

"As I grew older, I started looking at everything in a different way, with a different perspective. You know, I always liked the idea of having signposts on the psychic highway. Like: 'Don't go here,' 'Don't park here,' 'Wrong Way', and all that stuff. I guess what's really worked for me has been chanting, meditating and fasting—and especially music. With music, you get into a certain space in your head and your mind and your spirit, as if you're spirit-walking. The voodoo in Africa, and the Aborigines in Australia, they have something similar. American Indians too, they go on a spirit quest.

"In Australia, they do a walkabout. When a person reaches a certain age, they go off by themselves to make a connection with God and the great spirit, the universe. In India, they have the yogis and they also have the sadhus. When those sadhus near the end of their life they leave their family. They get a bowl and make a one-stringed instrument out of it and walk around India. Everybody feeds them. What they're doing, with their one-stringed instrument, is trying to find a single sound that's uniquely them.

"It's all about trying to make that connection with the signposts on the psychic highway and reading those messages through your life. Catholics even have it. They have a thing called the state of grace, where they try to connect with the whole of the universe. Myself, I make that connection through art, through music, through poetry, through writing, through all the ways that God created us. We're his paintbrushes. If you don't do what you're supposed to do while you're here, it's a big deal. That's why I keep looking for those psychic signposts along the way."

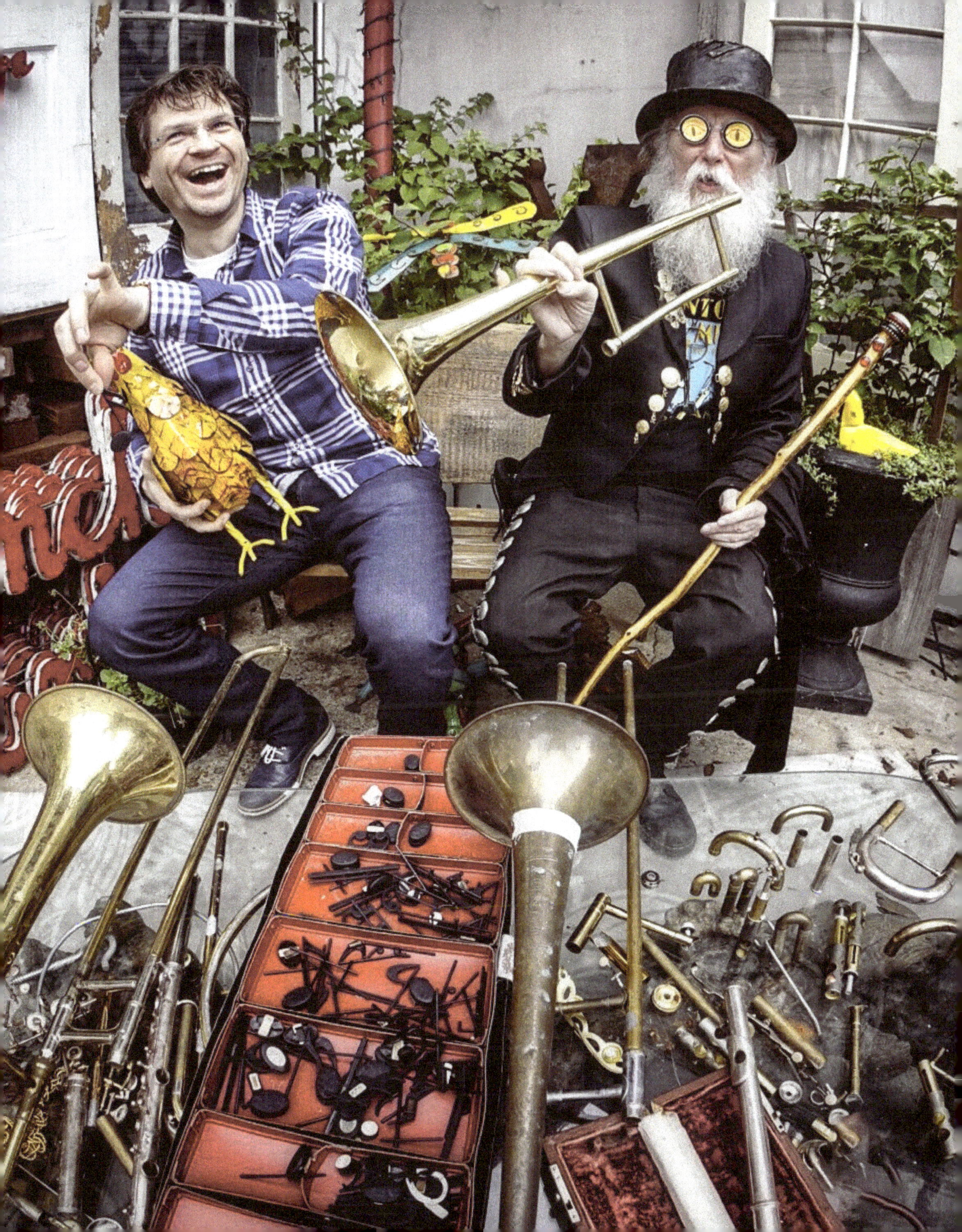

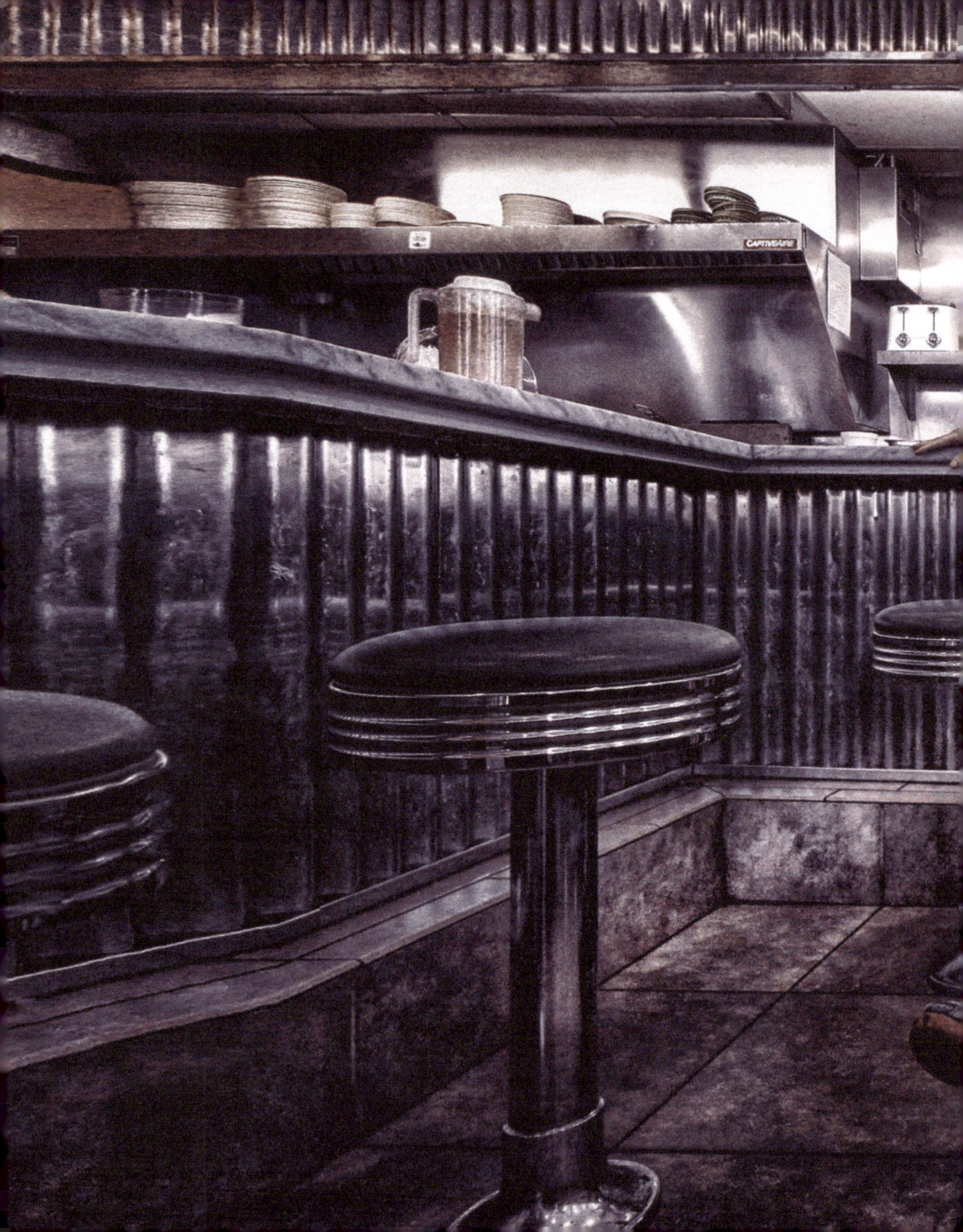

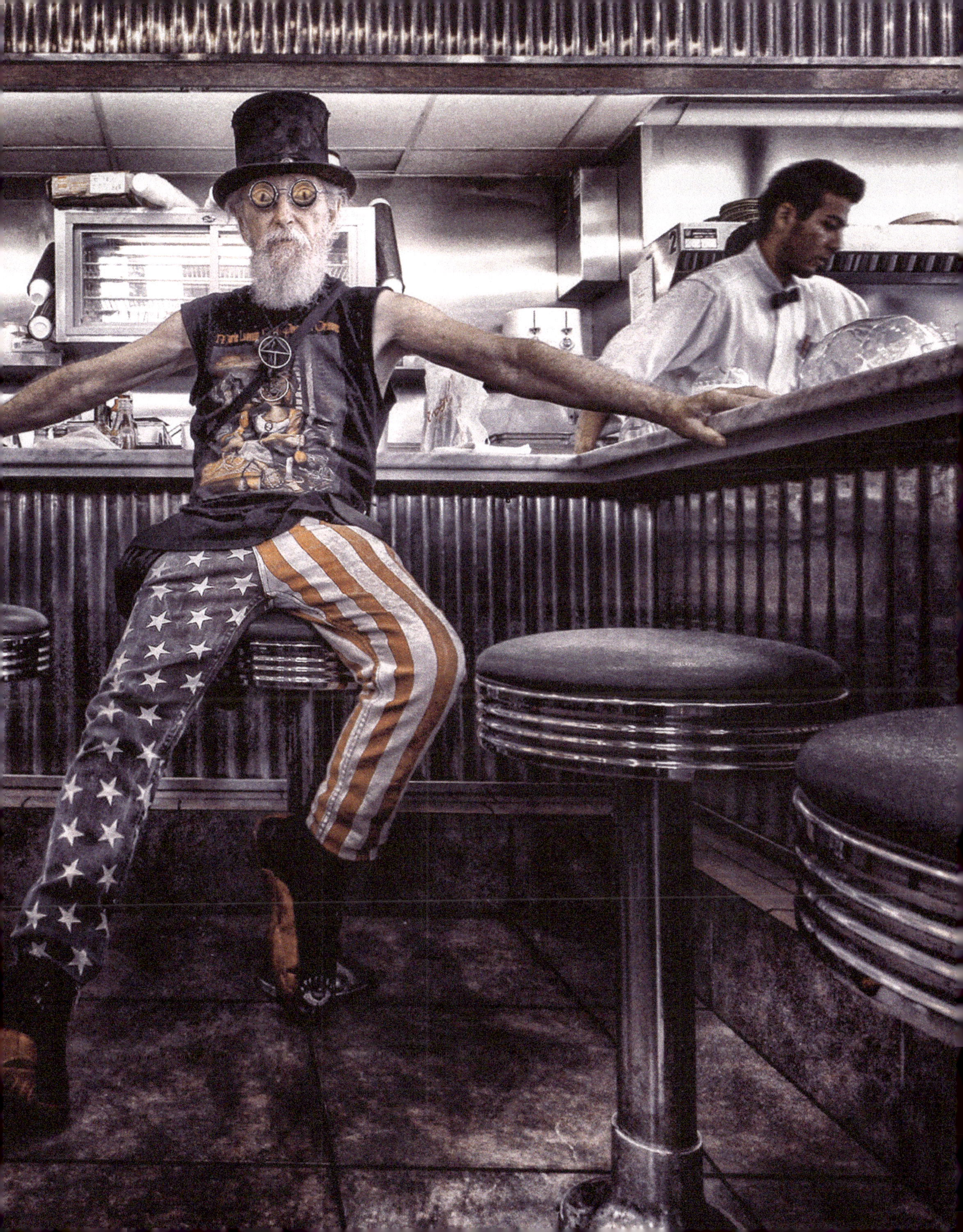

People Watching

Who needs reality TV when there's New Orleans? The city's humanity is spellbinding, with an incredible variety of music and food, creating a local rhythm, style, and attitude of freewheeling fun. This is where Hurricanes, Big Ass Beers, and Hand Grenades were invented, all poured into red go-cups for wandering the streets. Every dawn, street sweepers spray a soapy foam to flush away the latest onslaught in 300 years of spilt beer and urine.

New Orleans is like no other place in the world. As they say, "Laissez les bon Temps Rouler!" Or, in English: "Let the good times roll!"

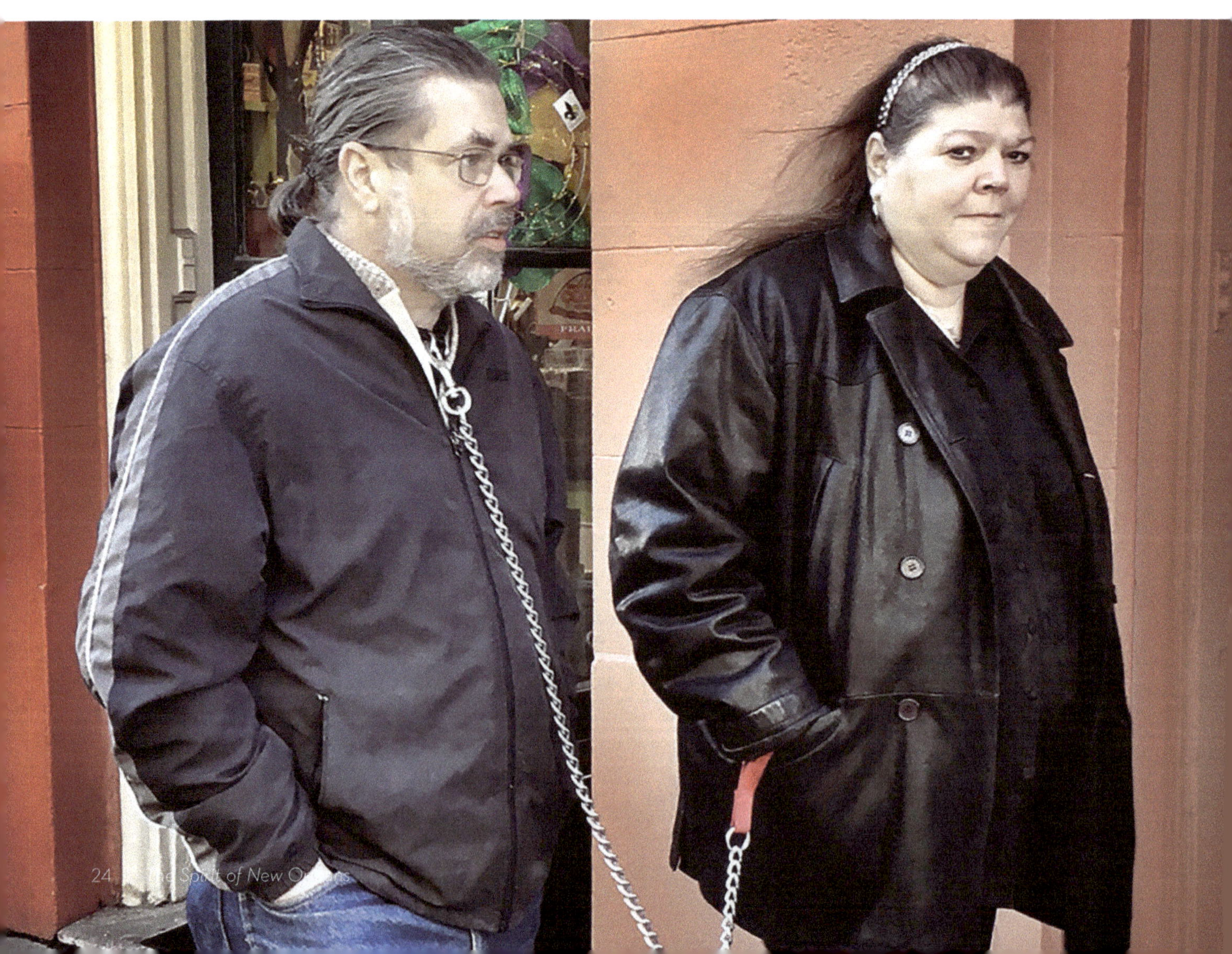

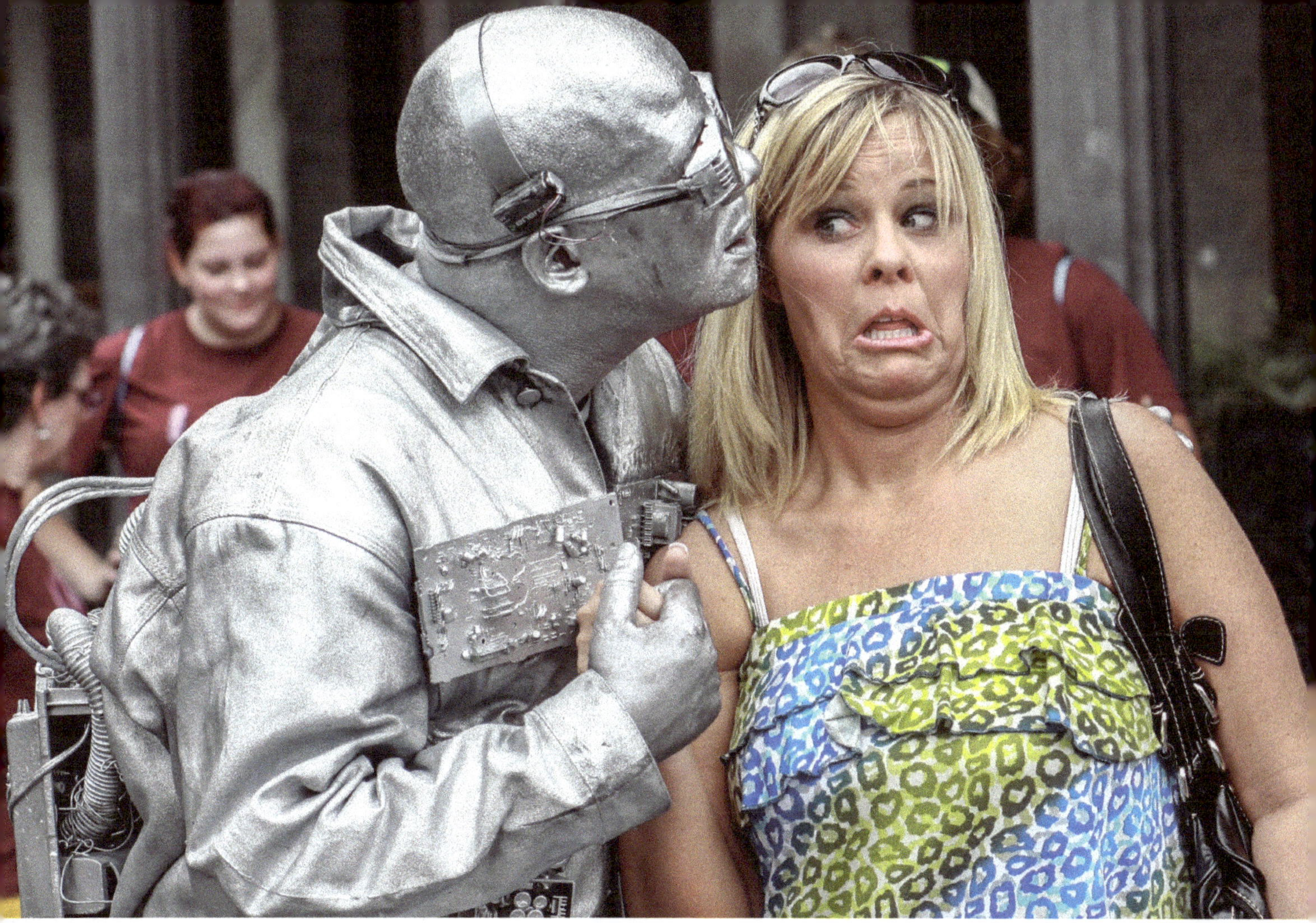

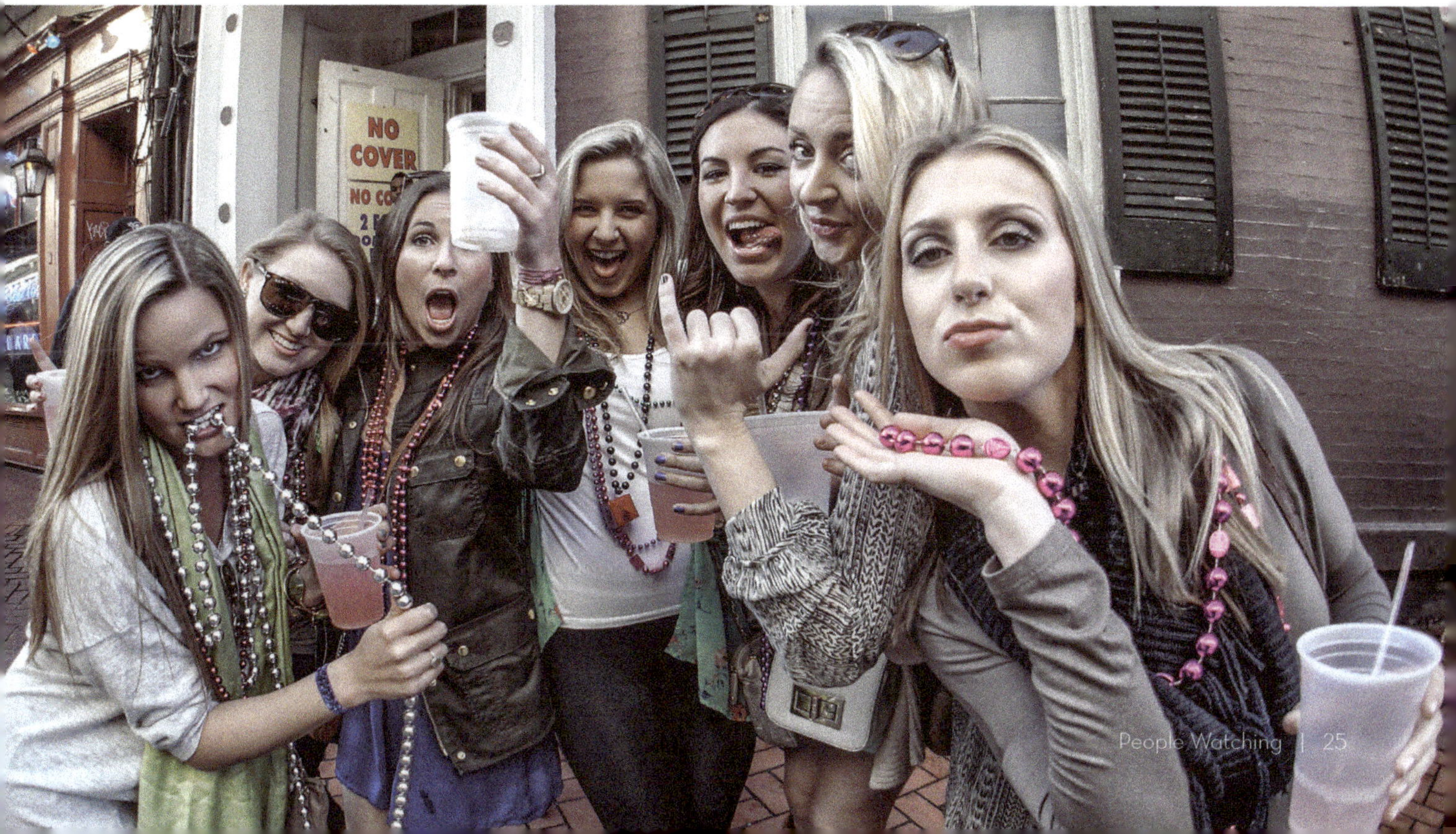

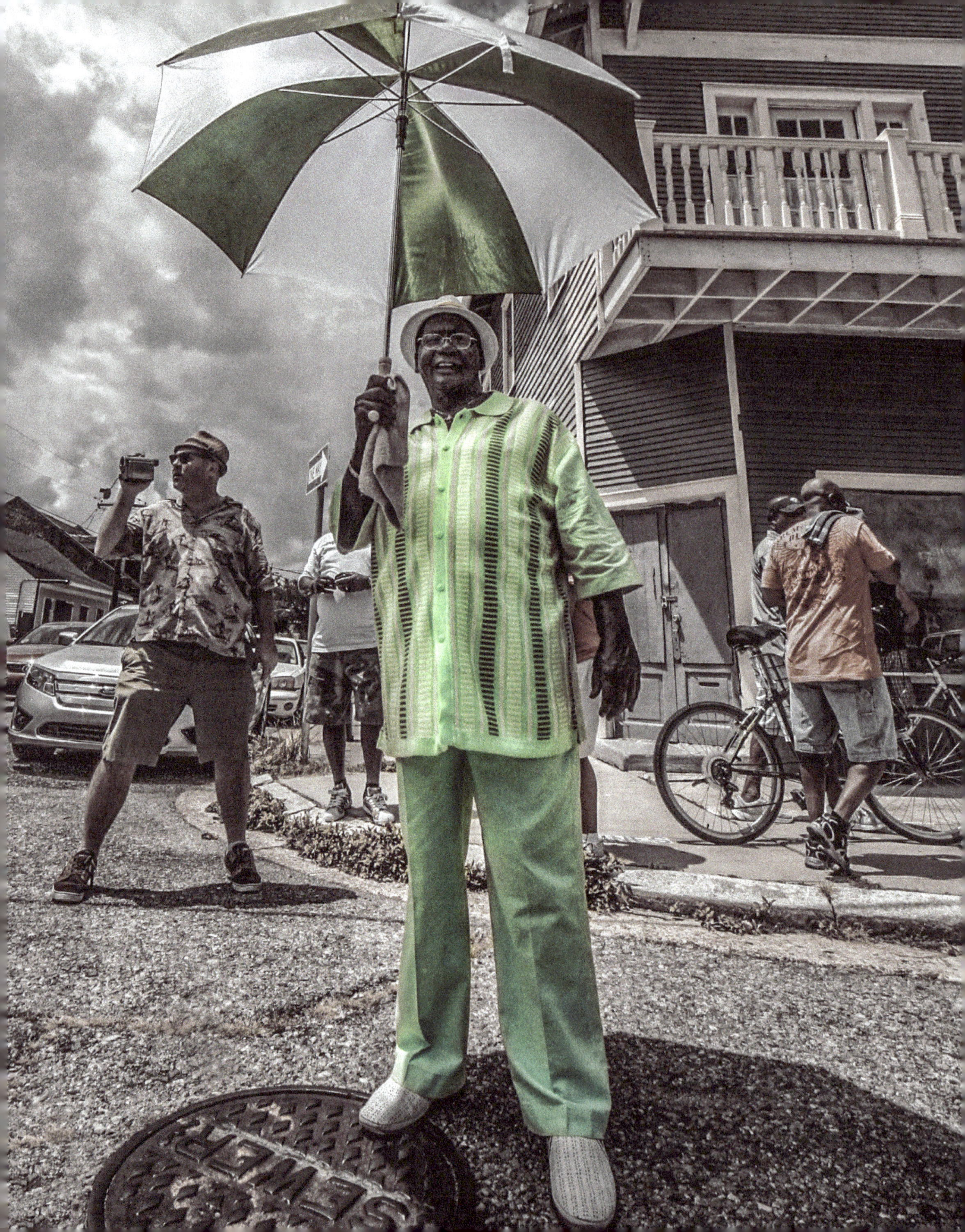

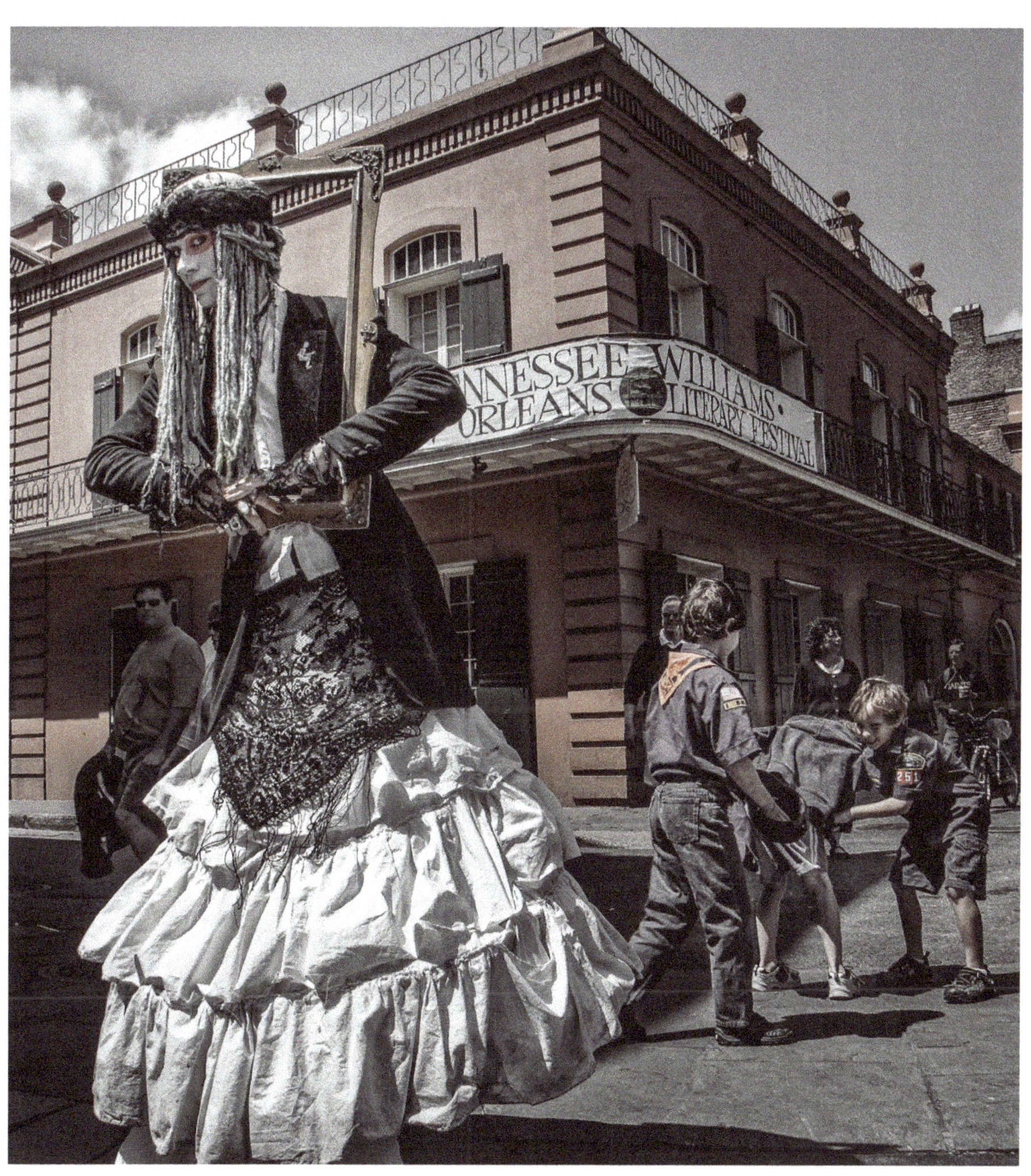
TENNESSEE WILLIAMS
ORLEANS LITERARY FESTIVAL

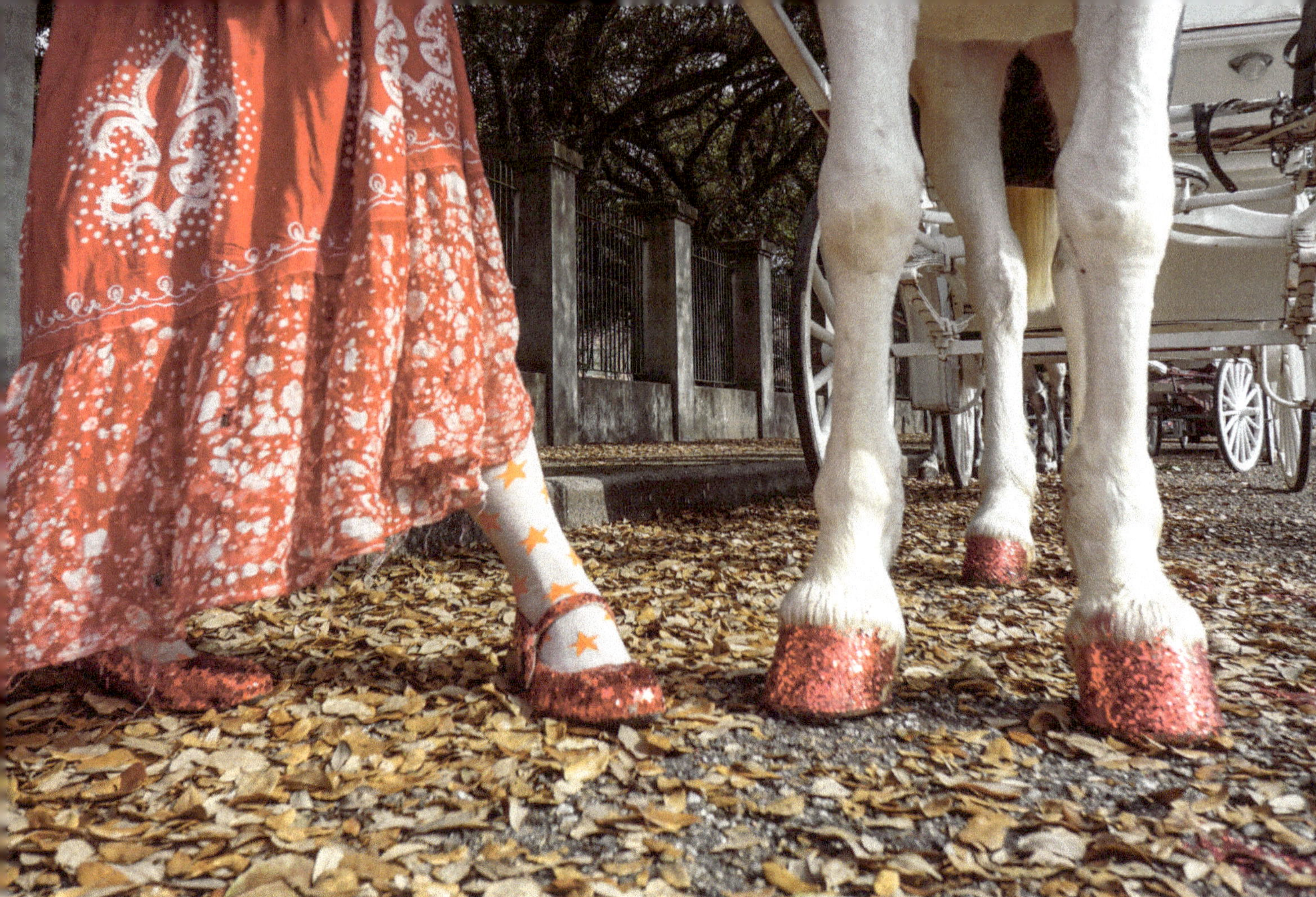

Kaliecia Smith

Every night, Kaliecia Smith—AKA "Sparkles the Tour Guide"—shepherds tourists through the French Quarter in a buggy pulled by a mule named Claudia. "I always wanted my own unicorn so I decorated my favorite mule with a horn, angel wings and sparkling hooves.

"I am a singing, artist, buggy driver," says Sparkles. "Everything in my life comes down to the little moments: sunlight coming through leaves, love's first kiss or gazing into the deep brown eyes of my dog."

Most evenings you can find Sparkles and Claudia lined up with other carriages in front of Jackson Square.

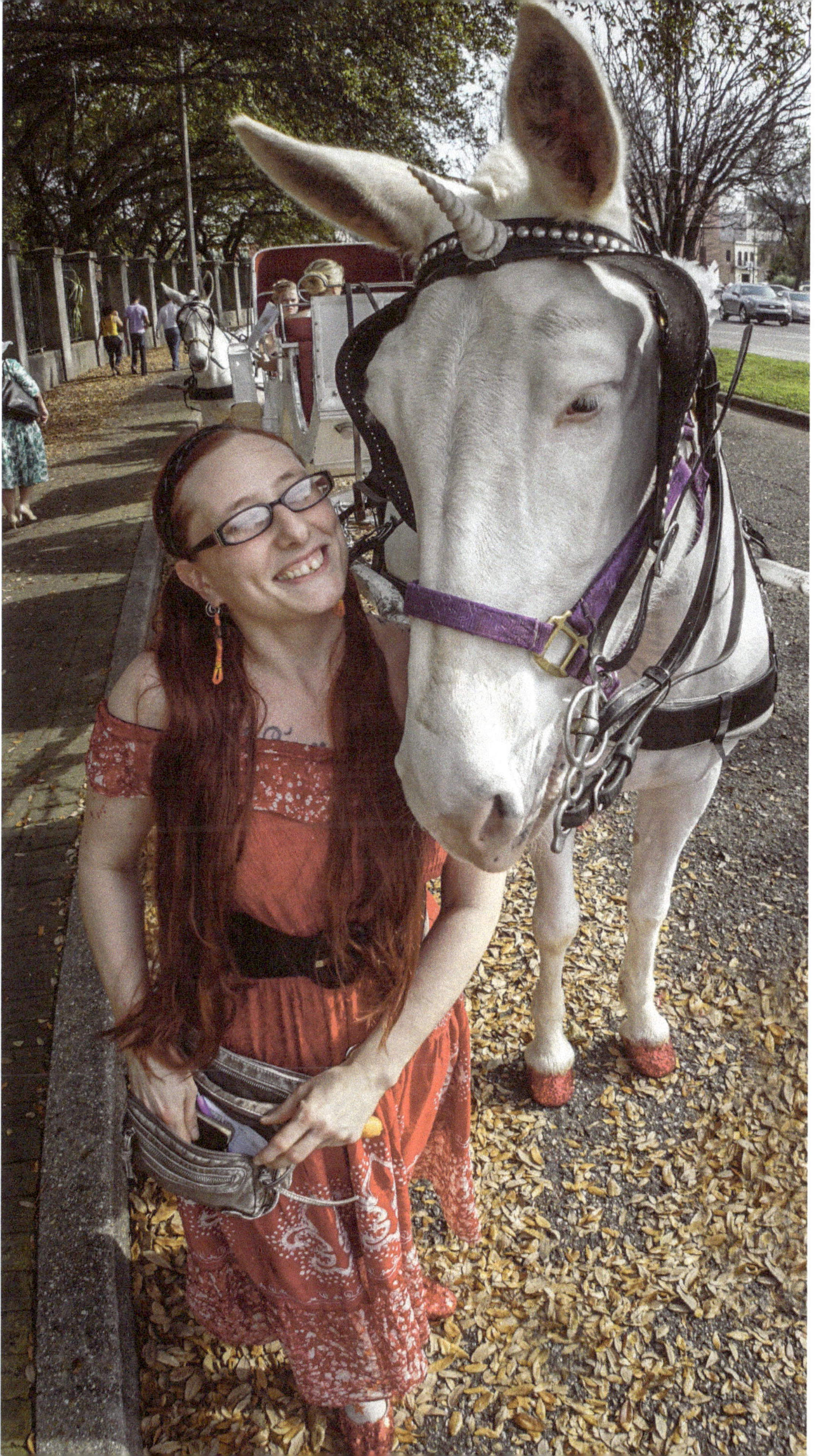

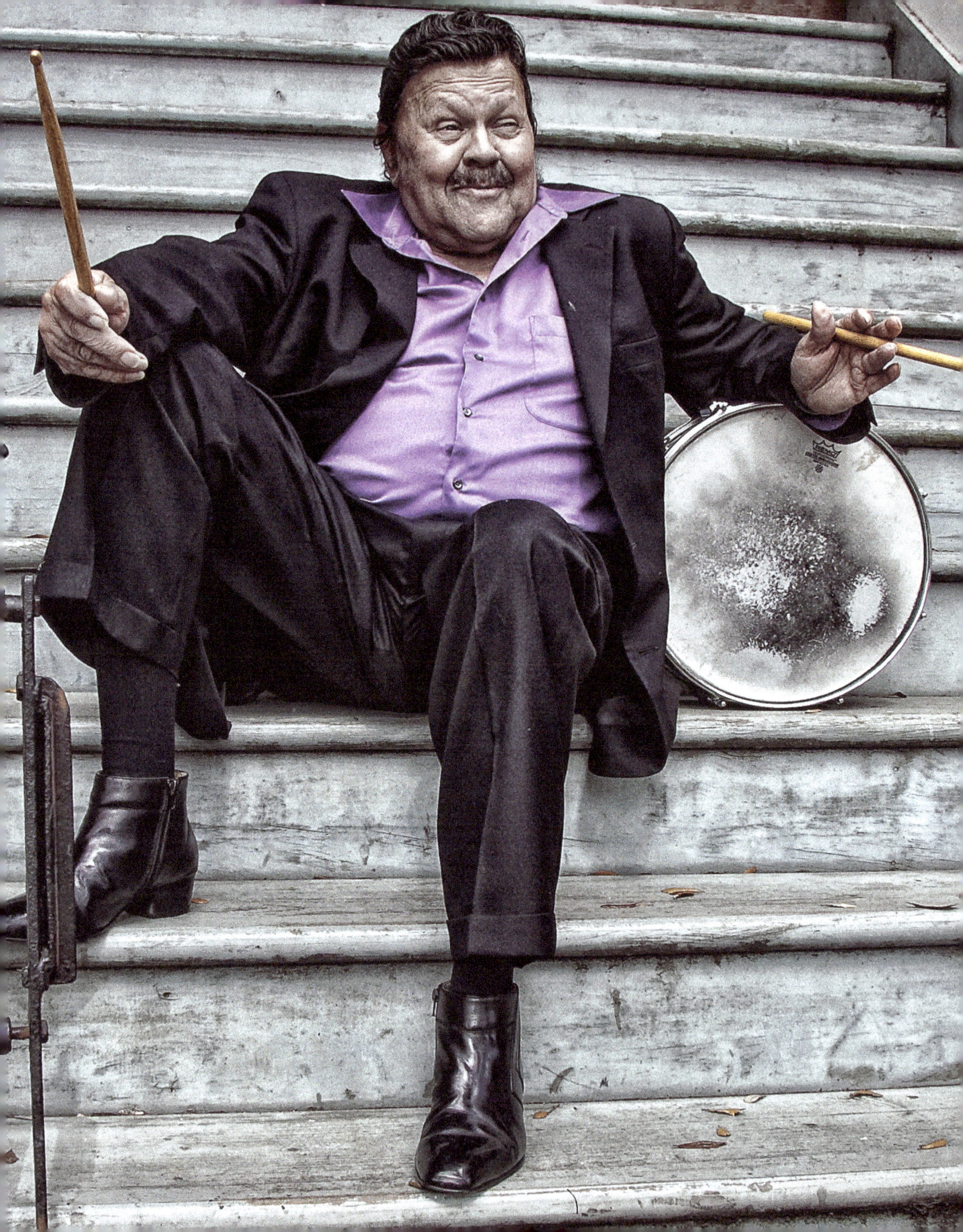

Aaron Washington

"I have rhythm. When I was seven, they had a train—musicians are kind
of weird, you know—they had a train that would cross Carrington Avenue
and they had some loose tracks as the train would cross. And I'd get up
on my bicycle and just wait. The people never knew what I was waiting for,
but this train at five o'clock would cross Carrington Avenue and hit those
tracks and was going, 'Be-rump-ba-ba-de-bum-da pop-bam,' and they was
just going on. And I would go home and practice what I heard. And I would
do things; they would think it was weird. But then I would play it and they
would say, 'Where'd you get that at?' And I would say, 'Ah, from the train.'

"I would get a tape recorder, one of the reel-to-reel ones, and this is going
to really blow your mind. I'd get a cockroach and put him on a sand paper
and the little mic would pick it up. He would walk across the sand paper
and he would cross the sand paper like, 'Shu, shu, shu,' and then I would
play that with my brushes and they would say, 'You gotta be crazy,' and I
say, 'No, most musicians are the way they are.' When I was studyin' music
when I was in school we would all do things like that and they would say,
'They do all kinds of strange things.'

"They would say, 'You sure you hittin' the right licks, five-stroke roll? Prove
it.' I took a carbon sheet of paper and another piece of paper and hit one,
two, three, four, five ba-ba-ba-ba-ba, and raise it up and there were five
little marks... That's a five-stroke roll, you can count 'em if you want to, but
that's what it was.

"I would travel—I went to Montego Bay in the Bahamas and different parts
of the islands—and I would listen to different rhythms. I found that in
the Bahamas the beat was on the down beat, like, 'Chicka, chicka-boom,
chicka-chicka-boom,' but when you got to Montego Bay, 'Chicka-chicka-um,

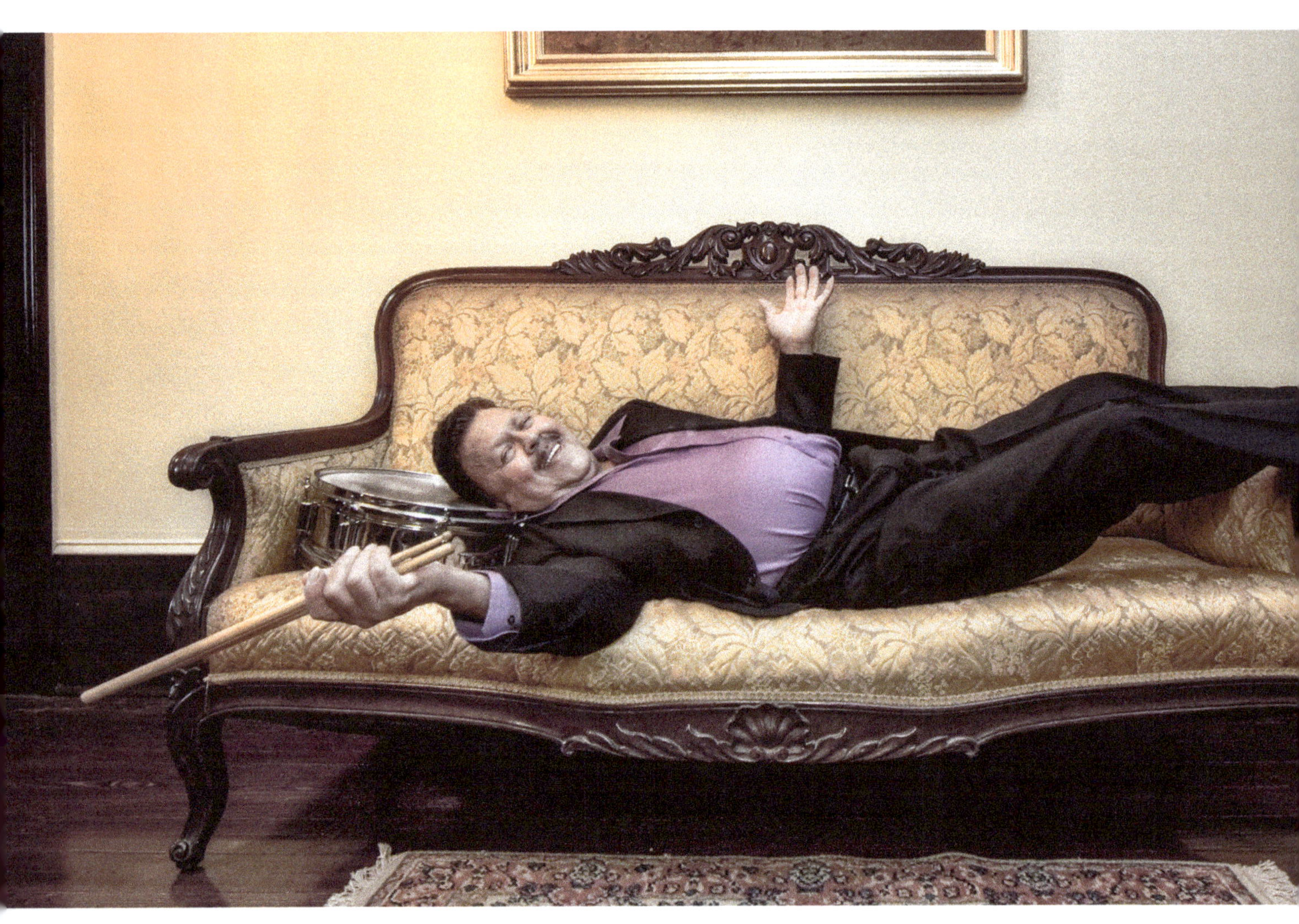

chicka-chicka-um,' like an upbeat, so ya see, these different rhythms. It's like a bird chirpin'. He never chirped like tweet, tweet, tweet. He doesn't do that, he say like, 'Dud-uh-la-dup-durp-du.' And this is how rhythm is taken from whatever you can get. There is rhythm in everything! You walk, you talk. It's like a person.

"In English you have dynamics. In music, you have dynamics. In English, you have iambics. Okay, so in English [when] I'm talking with you, it's like, 'Hey, this is what's happening,' or, 'Hey, what did you do yesterday?' It makes sense, doesn't it? [He repeats the sentences in monotone.] Well, you don't play music that way! [Laughter.] You want to make sense, anything you do.

"And this is how Jazz is. Jazz is the type of thing where it's an 'answer and call' thing. I'll give you a good example. [Sings] 'Oh when the saints [Pause], go marching in.' Whatever is done [with] the instrument or voice is Jazz, Blues [and] improvising. This is what Jazz is about. It's a simple phrase, not goin' into a lot of musical.... You can identify by 'answer and call.' Whatever you hear, it's the same thing, you can't get away from it. As a Jazz musician, you build on that...

"Create!"

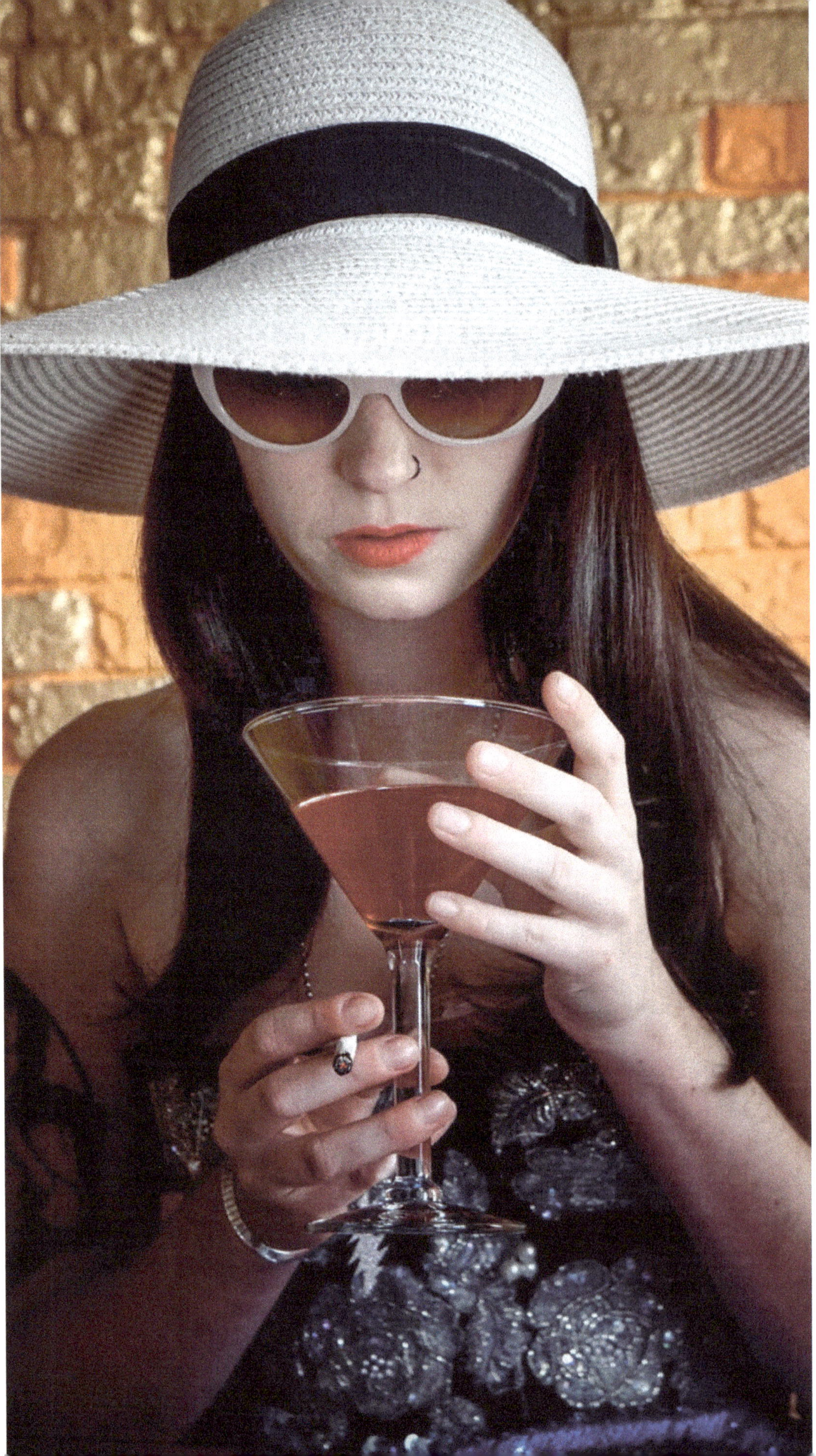

Reyes Sunshine

"I grew up on the road. I was just six when my Dad's band, The Grateful Dead, broke up. He and I went to Indonesia and Thailand and India, collecting music and instruments to add to his own music for a huge collection he was building for the Smithsonian.

"In the spring of 2009, the Dead got back together so I went on tour with them. After that, I got into an art school in San Francisco and moved in with all my crazy friends. We'd have drag parties and open mics and everyone got naked and painted each other. It was a mad scene. Picture it: sixteen year-olds living in a penthouse with graffiti everywhere; total chaos every day.

"I was working at the Fillmore back then, holding the puke bucket for the bands. The day after I graduated from art school I went to New York to do an internship with Rolling Stone but I hated New York so I went to London where I could go to school without having to take the SAT's. I got into film and learned how to present myself as a writer; I got published.

"But, I really wanted to go back to New Orleans. I'd been here once before during Jazz Fest and had a series of bizarre, magical experiences. Some roadie invited me on stage for Tom Petty. Someone gave me $100 for a cigarette. Someone gave me a $20 ticket to a Dr. John show but someone else gave me a pass to that show so I sold the ticket for another hundred dollars.

"It was amazing. Like, talking to this guy who said, 'Don't freak out. My name is Boz Skaggs.' He gave me a list of all the greats to meet in New Orleans if I moved there. Everything just rolled out in front of me, so easy. I was 19.

"I went on tour again with the Dead last summer. Our manager quit in Sonoma County, stranding my Dad with this album-in-progress of all the sounds we had gathered on the road when I was six years old, including music from my godfather, Jerry Garcia, who had passed away. I've been working with my Dad on it for the past year and a half now, producing the album and working with the band.

"Dead and Company is a whole new group of awesome musicians. I've been really lucky to live with them. We have a studio that runs 24/7 throughout the year. Managing that is the real challenge!

"So, looking back, I'd say that the best part of growing up with the band and living on the road are all the people you get born with. My family is so fucking beautiful. They're so incredible. They have totally changed my life.

"The worst part of growing up that way? It's very hard when you're super young. There's a learning curve with self-control that is much harder when you're a kid with endless possibilities. And I was with adults so much that it became difficult for me to relate to anyone my own age. To this day, except for the kids I lived with in San Francisco many years ago, I don't have anyone that's my age very close to me. All of my friends are 20 years older than me. My best friend is 78 and I relate to him better than anyone.

"I have to say that New Orleans music has always been my favorite. It's everything to me. I get to live inside of this whole New Orleans fantasy with my musical heroes. I have Woody Guthrie tattooed on my back and Patty Smyth is on my arm.

"It's been the craziest adventure."

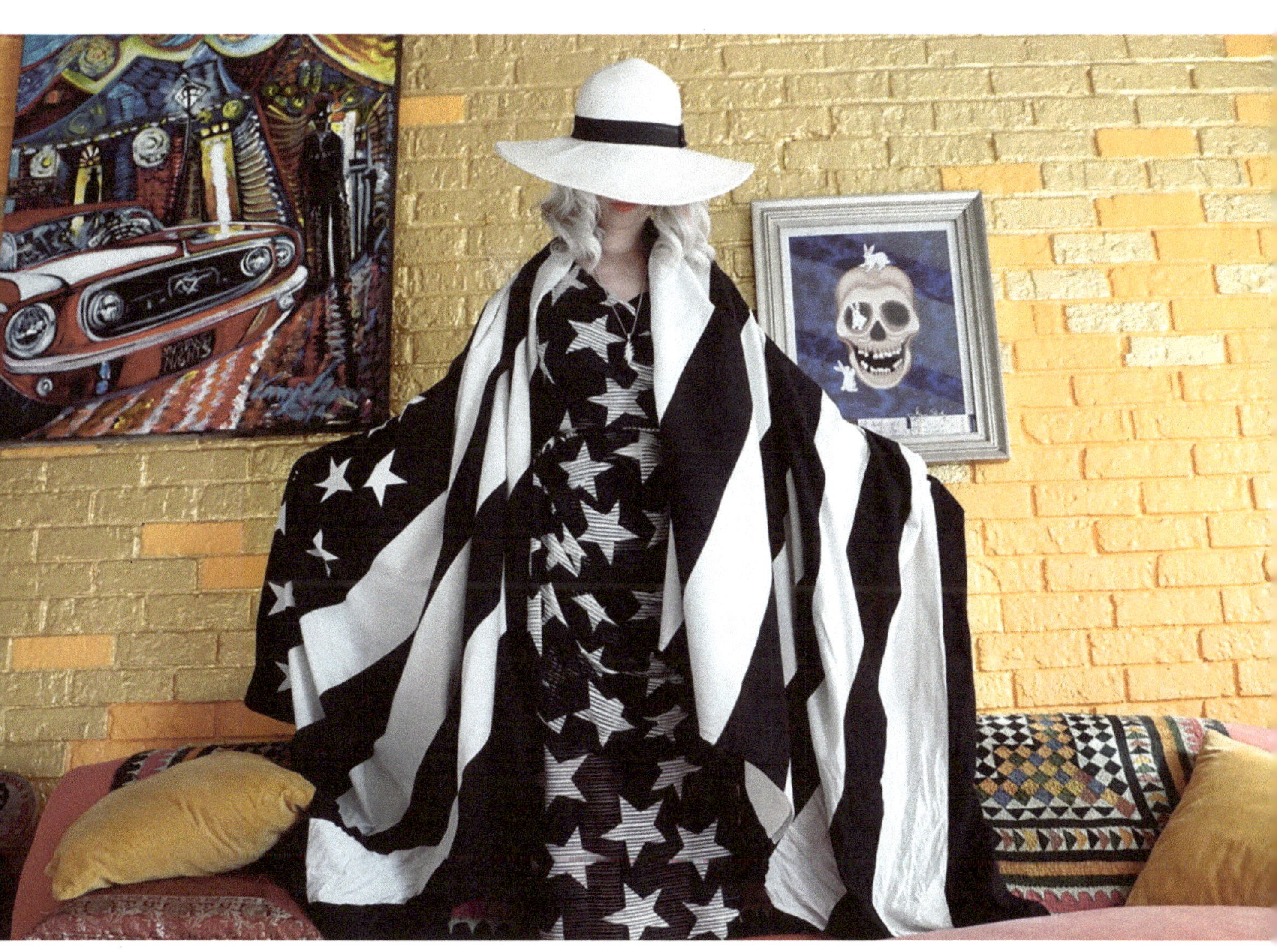

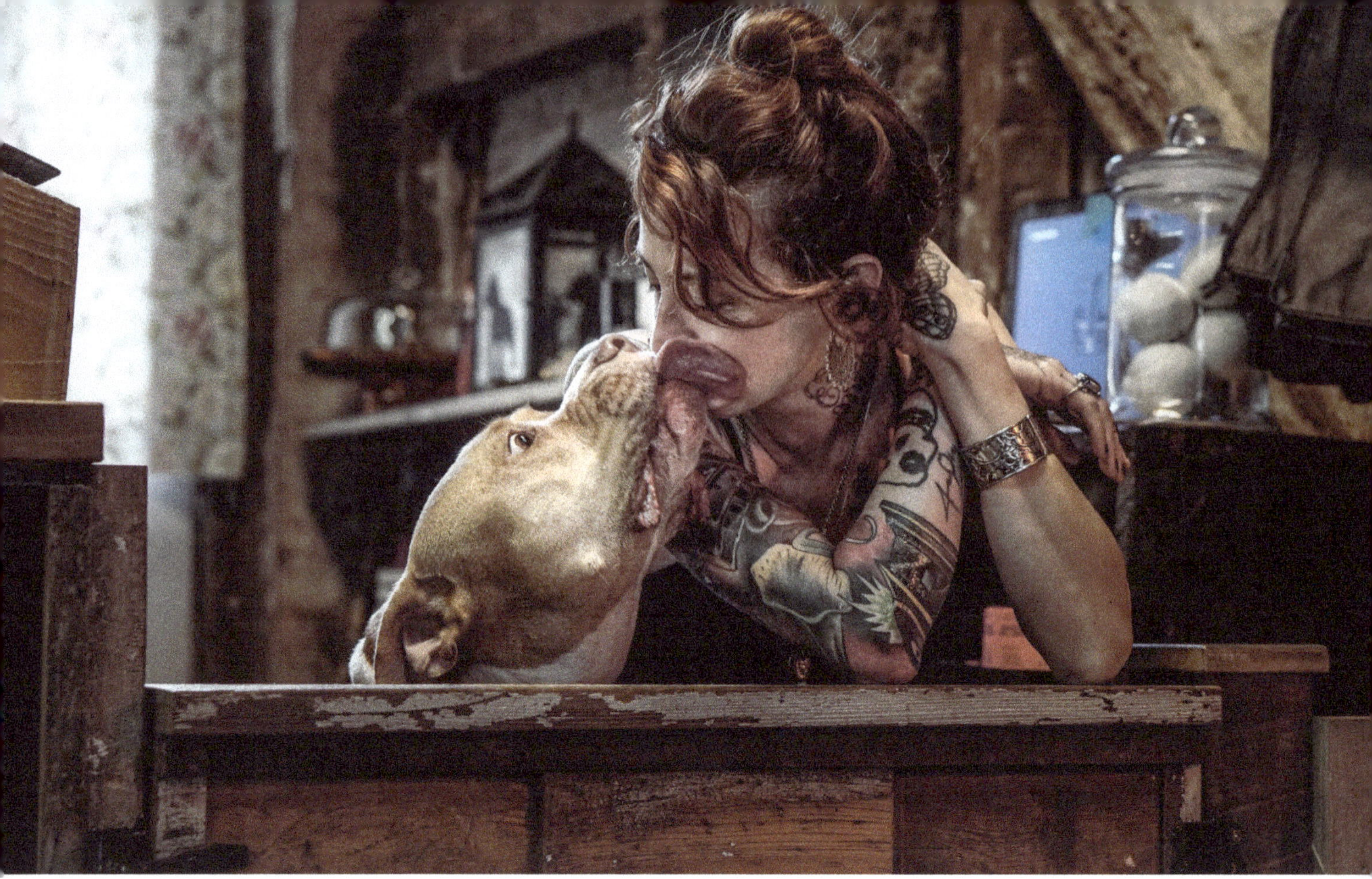

Mariah Harmony

Known as the 'old soul' who keeps things grounded and organized, always figuring out new ways to help the homeless: dogs, ex-cons, and children.

"I came here from Southern California to rescue a dog hanging from a tree. Then I moved all of my rescue dogs here—shuttling 200 of them in my old school bus. When the hurricane came, folks left dogs at my doorstep, sometimes tied up to my front fence. This area is really bad for heart worm. One mosquito bite can infect a dog. We have so many dogs now that sometimes our annual vet bill is $500k at my family's Villalobos Rescue Center."

Eric Ogilvie

When I first approached Eric, a sword-swallower, his head was snapped back as he guided two long chrome blades on their way down his throat. In the background, a woman came out of a restaurant and stood on the sidewalk, stunned, her own mouth open, watching in disbelief. The swords slid back up out of his tattooed face. Eric shared with me:

"I was drawn to New Orleans. I really feel at home here. There's a lot more opportunity for someone who does performing like I do. I can walk out in the street and make a few bucks or book a few gigs on a weekly basis. That can't be said for most of the country."

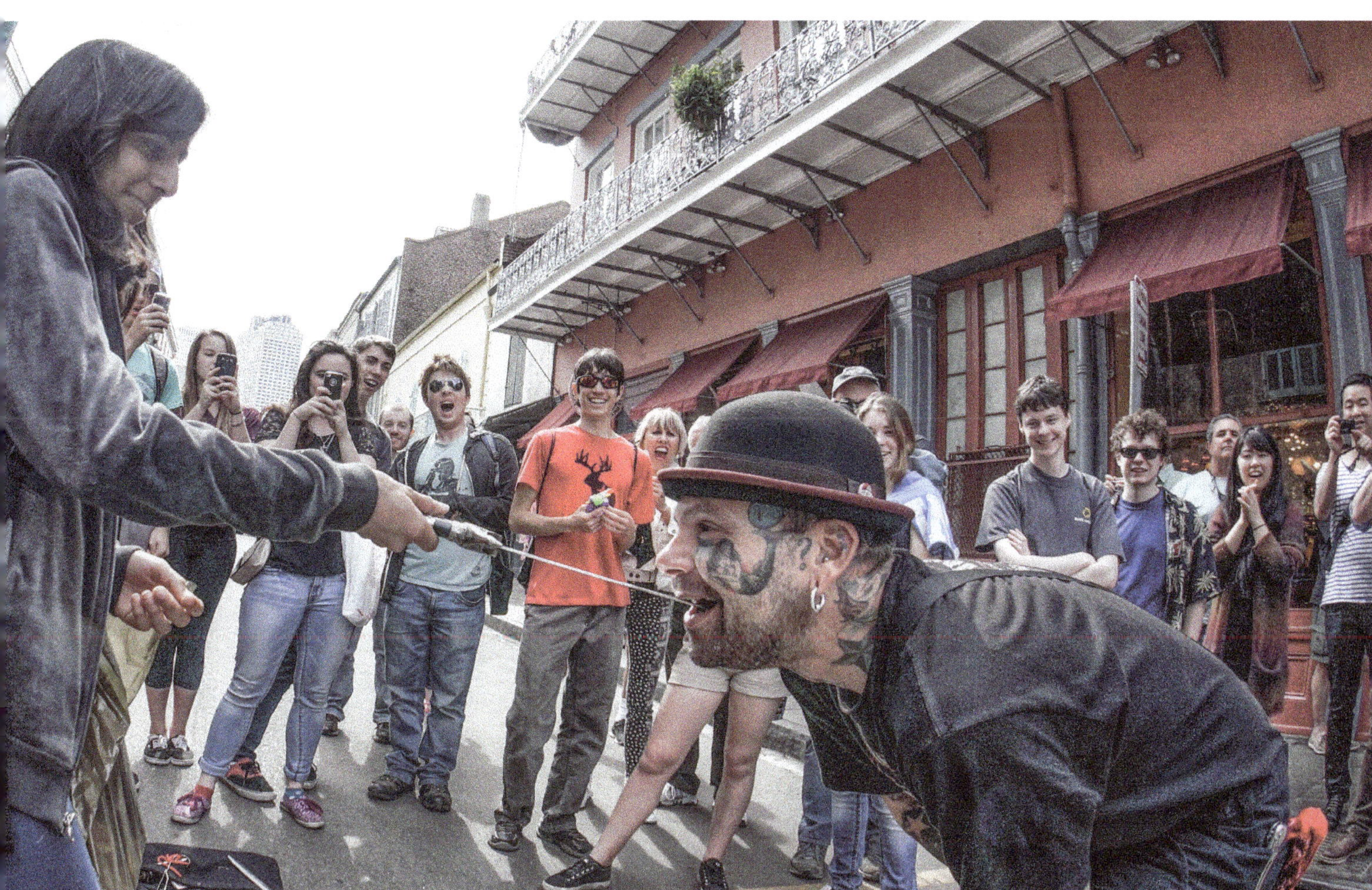

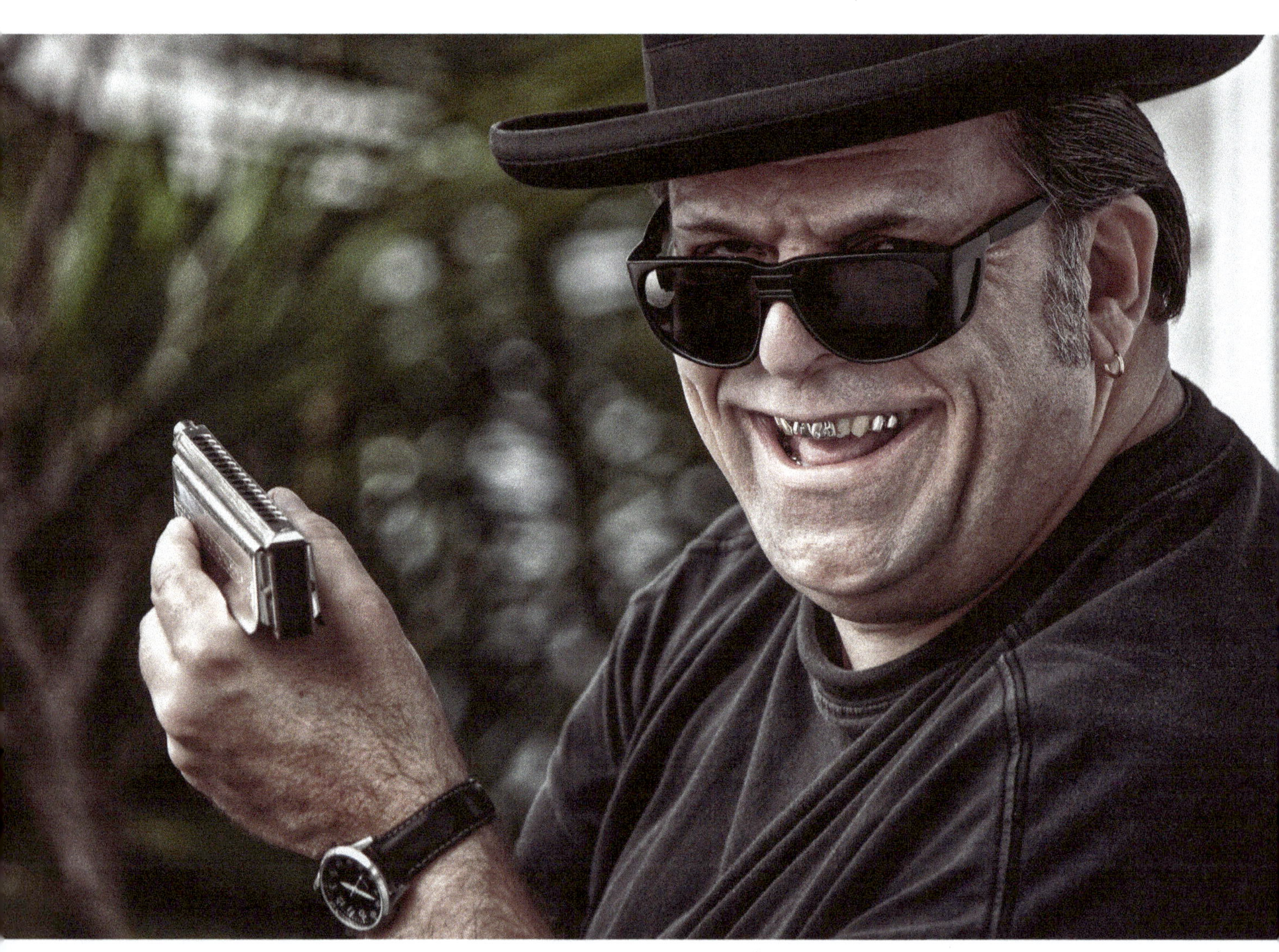

James Monque'D

"Everyone calls me Jay. I've been blowin' the harmonica since I was four years old. I learned from my grandmother, who was a great harmonica player. My daddy played the harmonica too. There have been a bunch of harmonica players in my family: my daddy, a couple of my uncles, my grandmother and two of her brothers. A couple of her uncles played, too. In my family, harmonica players go way back.

"My grandmother liked to play Creole songs. My grandfather didn't speak English, never learned to read or write his own name. He just spoke French. My grandmother spoke English with a very thick Creole accent. She had started playing harmonica when she was four years old. When I was getting on her nerves, she'd say, "Here, go play with this," and that was it. When I was seven years old, me and my cousins would play: Barbara on guitar, Juanita on piano.

"Barbara was 11 and Juanita was 13. We started a band. Me and my cousins played on the TV. It was during the early morning show, five o'clock in the morning... on a show called Jambalaya, during *The Farm Market Report*. Me and my cousins, we got to be on TV with their house band that backed us up. They had to stand behind a curtain because they couldn't be seen on TV. It was Clifton

Chenier and his band. It was in the days of segregation. It was sad at the time. Even 10 or 11 years later, when I understood what it was all about, it bothered me.

"Then when I was 13, I put together my own band. We used to play at a skating rink in the Ninth Ward. I been at it ever since. I played in junior high school and during high school. When I was 17, in 1963, the principal of the school—I went to Catholic school—and our principal, Brother Timothy, agreed to let me take a 15-day leave of absence to play on the road all over Texas, blowin' harmonica for Mr. Lightnin' Hawkins. It was still in the days of segregation. We played with Mans Liscolm and played with all kinds of musicians from here in New Orleans. I was a member of Frogman Henry's band for a while.

"Then I went into the Navy. After my second trip to Vietnam in '67 I started playing with Johnny Hooker's band. I moved back home to New Orleans in '72, right here into my same neighborhood. I had only been home for 10 days when Frogman Henry found out. I went right back to work, blowin' harmonica. I've been doin' it ever since.

"The Blues is what I do. All sorts of blues...Delta Blues, Chicago Blues, West Coast Blues...To me it's all just Blues."

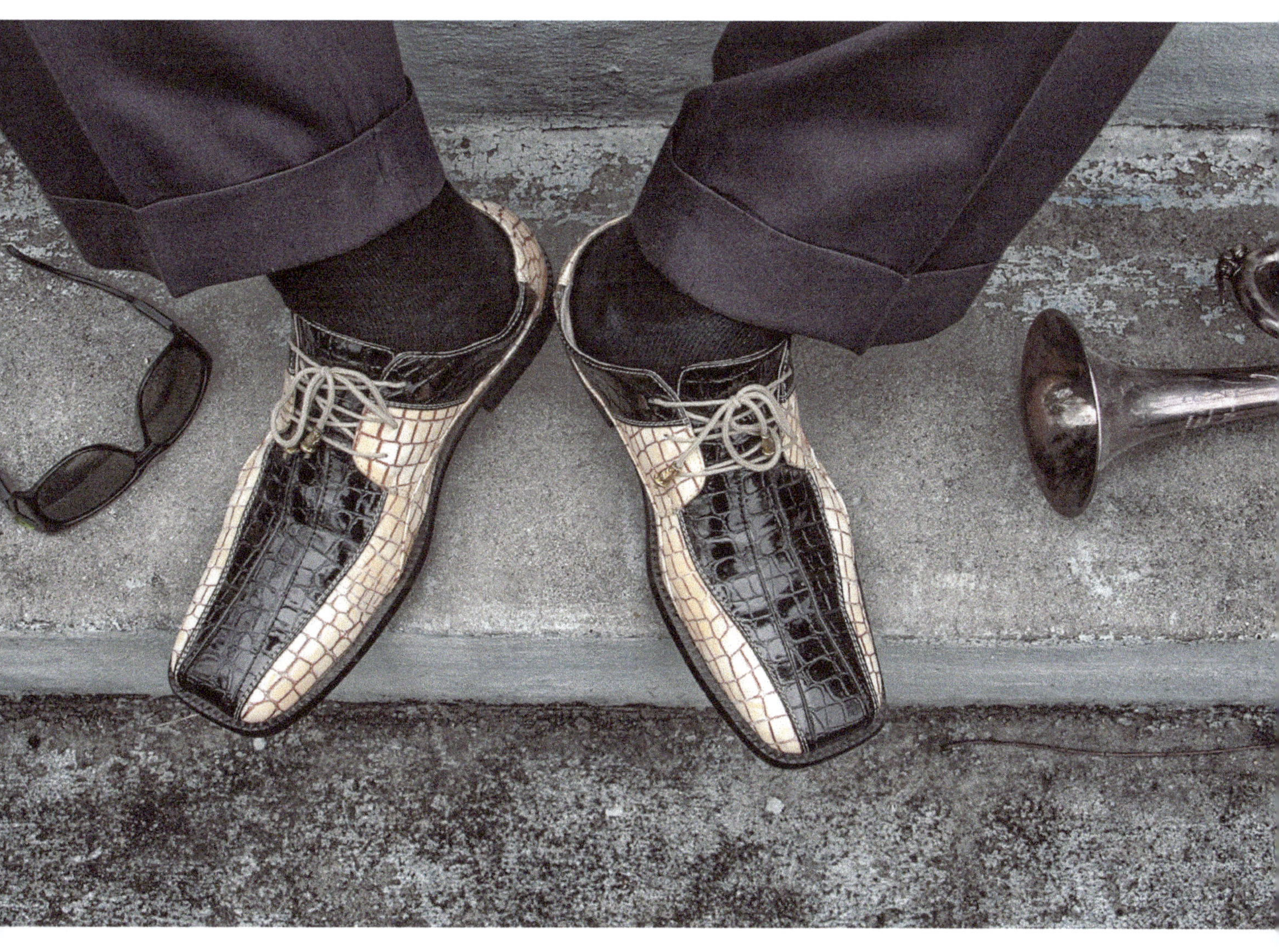

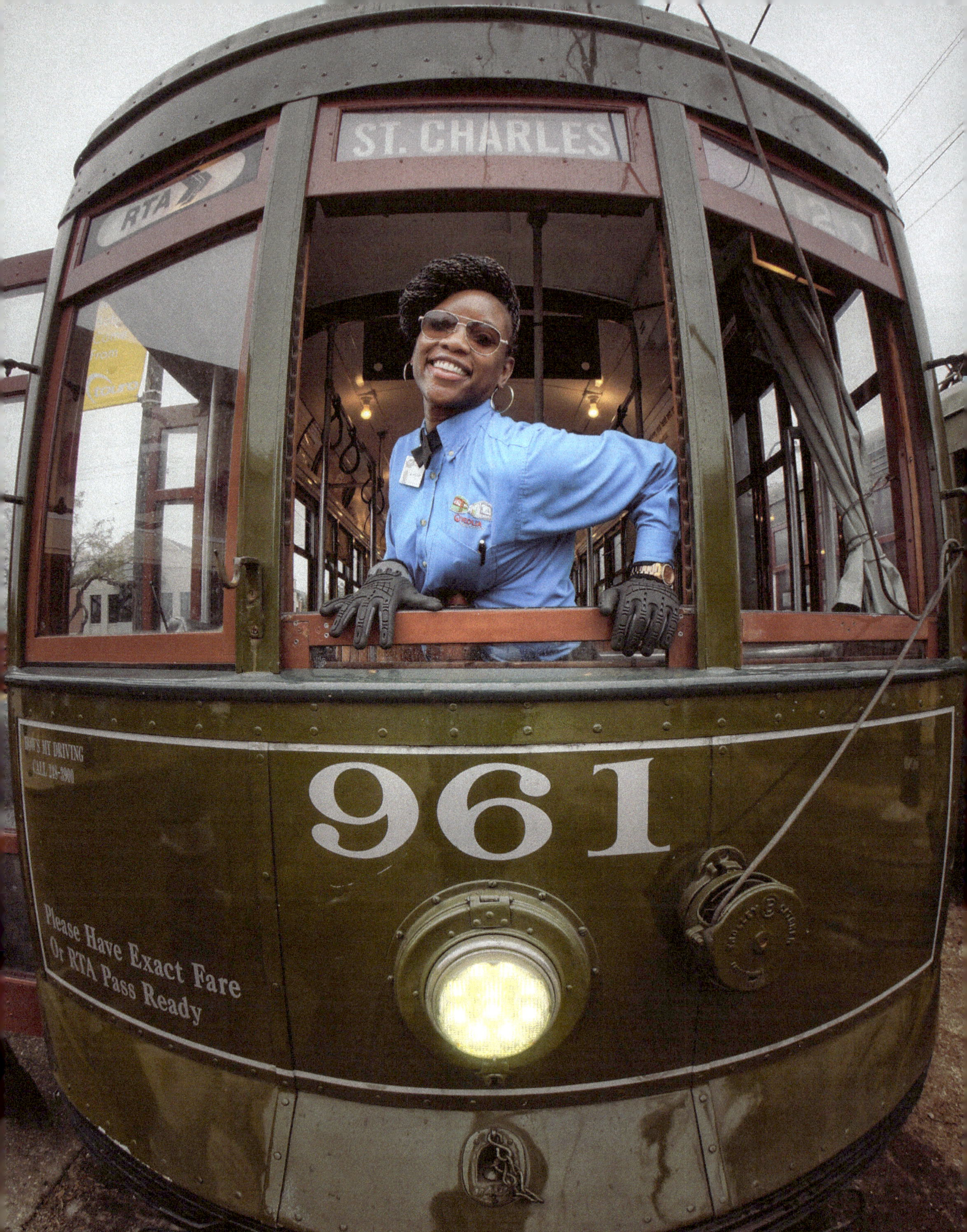

ST. CHARLES
RTA
961
Please Have Exact Fare
Or RTA Pass Ready

Streetcars

Tennessee Williams wrote *A Streetcar Named Desire* in 1947, immortalizing the New Orleans street car as a symbol of charm and romance.

The dark green St. Charles streetcar is the oldest continuously operating streetcar line in the world, still rumbling down the middle of St. Charles and Carrollton avenues as it has for more than 150 years.

Vintage streetcars built by the Perley A. Thomas Company traverse the six-mile crescent from Carondelet at Canal Street, through the oldest and most majestic section of Uptown, around the Riverbend, through a tunnel of live oaks, past dozens of antebellum mansions, Loyola and Tulane universities, Audubon Park, and fine hotels, restaurants and bars.

Hurricane Katrina and subsequent floods knocked all the streetcar lines out of operation and damaged many of the streetcars, but all services were restored by 2008. Today, New Orleans' three streetcar lines provide service 24-hours a day. A pass costs $1.25. Exact change is required.

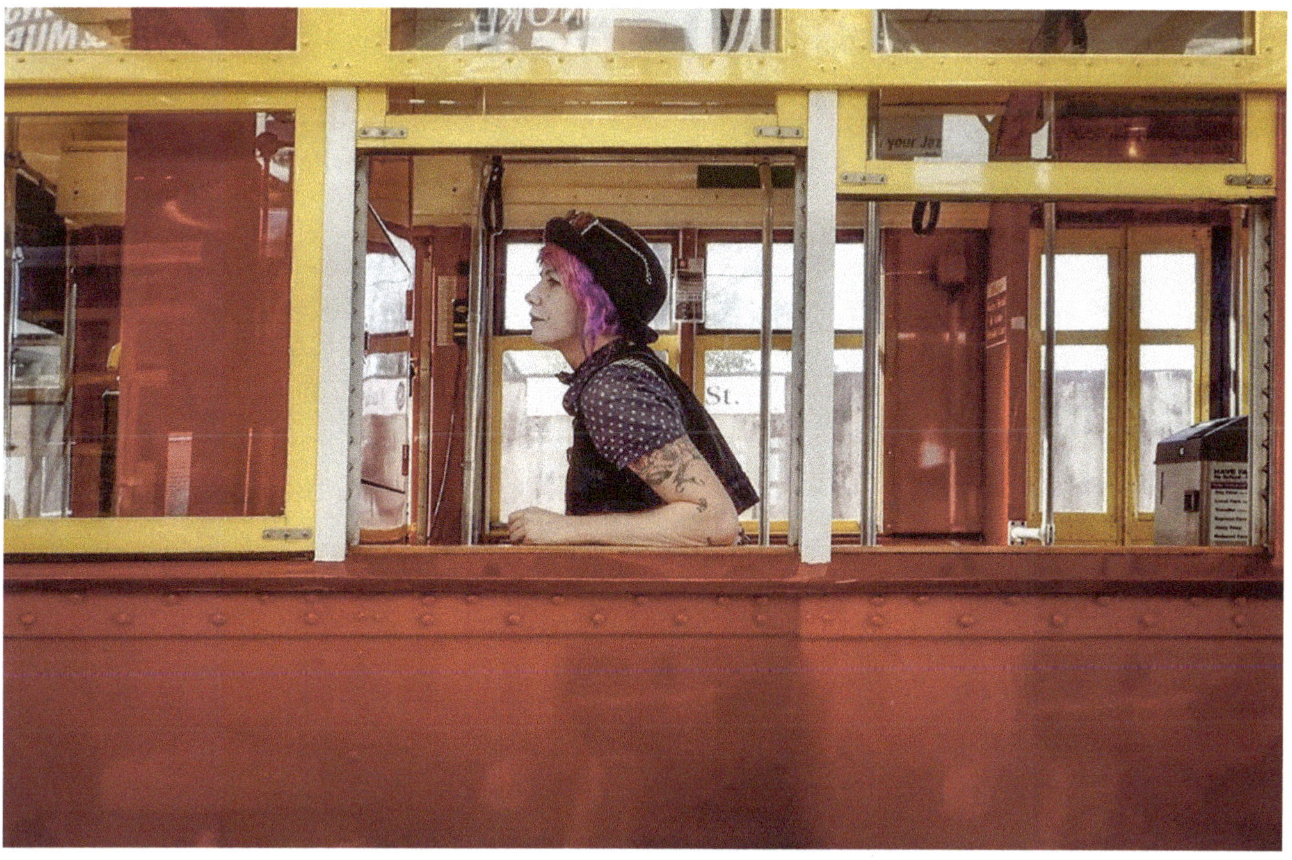

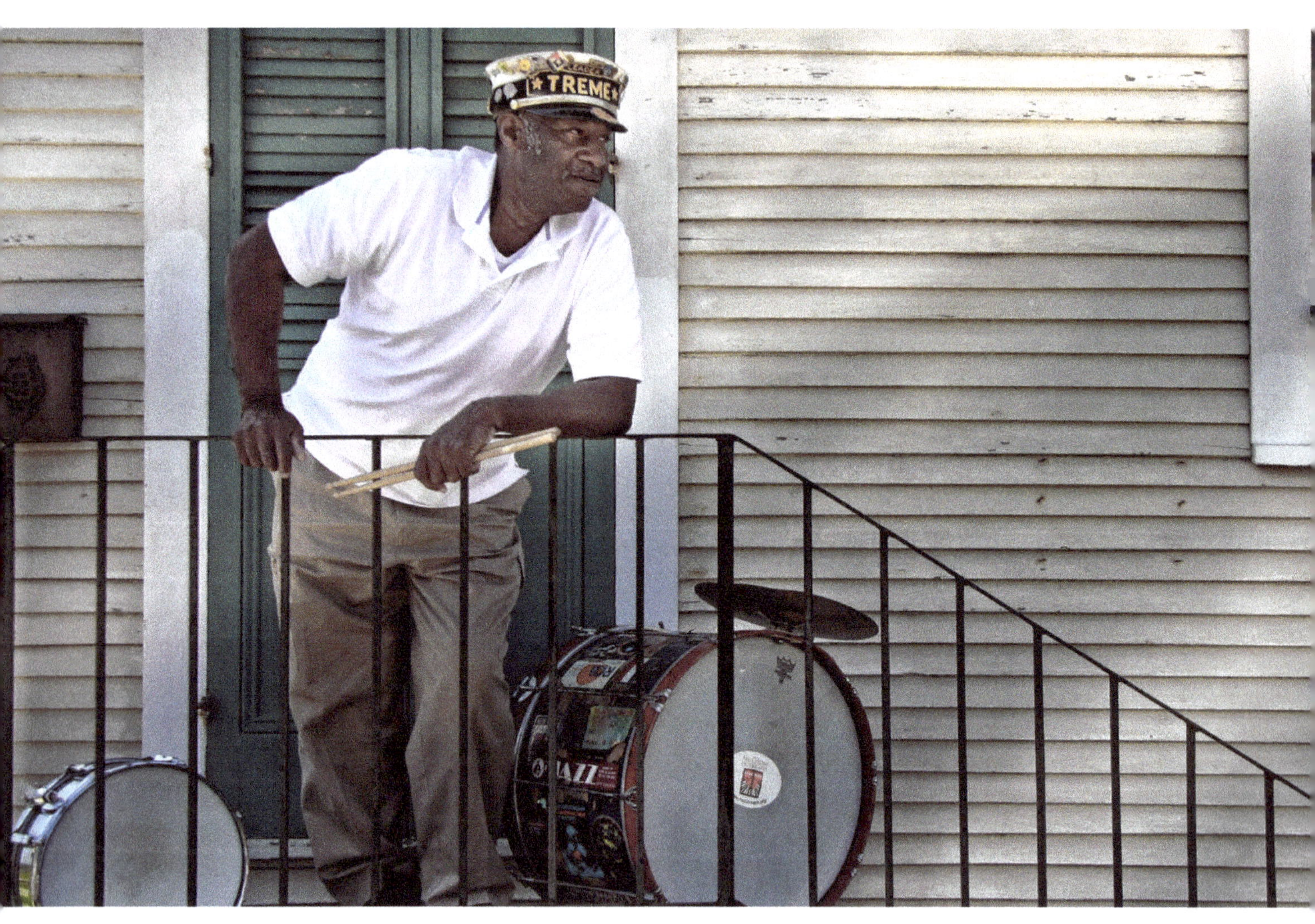

TREME

Bennie Jones

"I come from a musical family. My father was a drummer. My brother, named Eugene Jones, was a drummer. Uncle Lionel is the sister leader of a trivia brass band.

"I have performed with many bands: Olympia Brass Band, Almond Brass Band, Joseph Fuel Brass Band, Tuxedo Brass Band, Michael White Lucy Brass Band... I have performed with some of the old brass bands and some of the young brass bands coming up today. I am the founder of The Dirty Dozen.

"I'm always into music. I travel around the city to different clubs. I listen to music all the time. I listen to the radio at all times. I am very aware of music.

"I love music and that is part of my culture. Wherever I go, I have music in my soul."

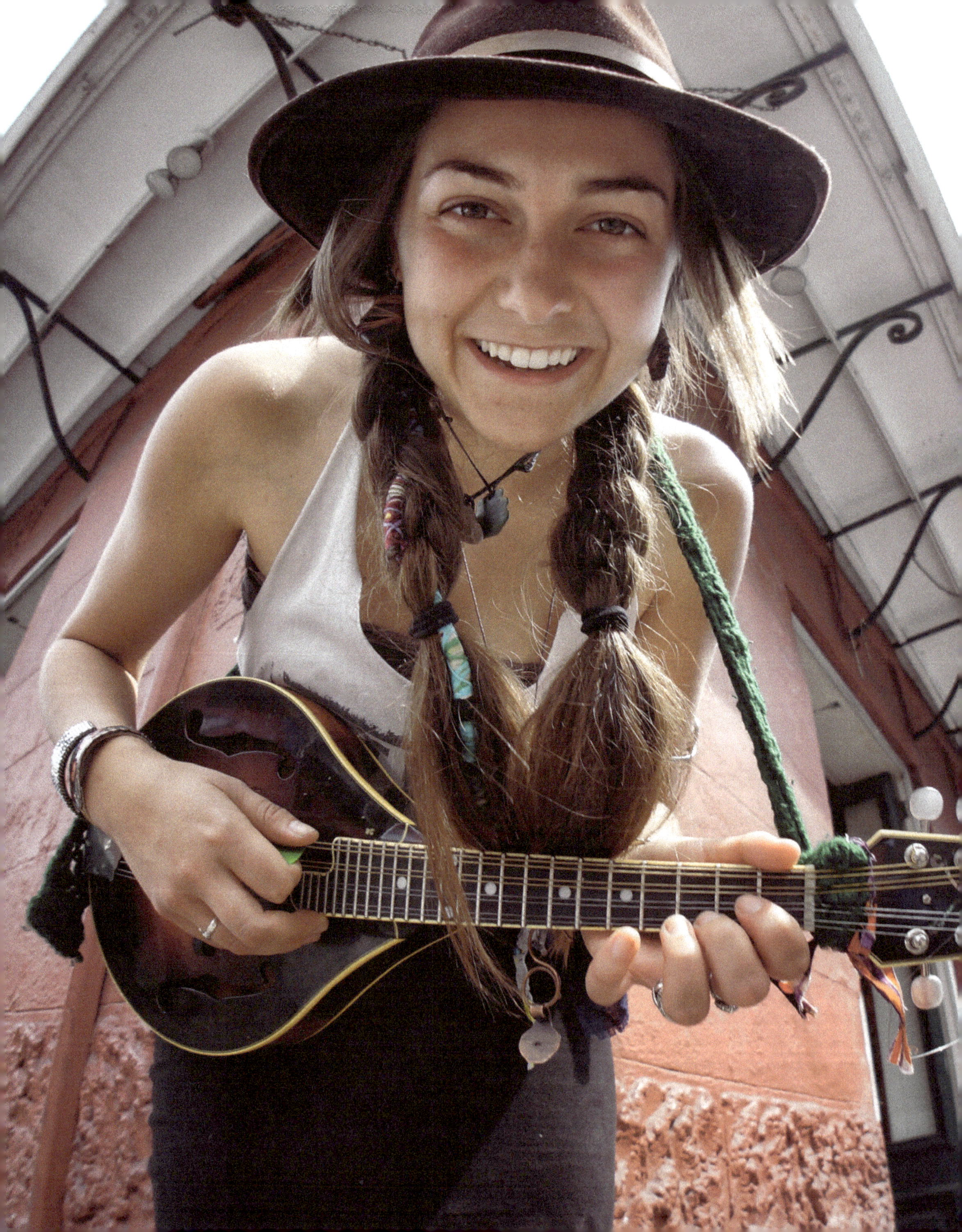

Adrienne Edson

Adrienne grew up in Ann Arbor, Michigan. Her parents both have enjoyed
long careers with Chrysler. Adrienne's father was the lead engineer on the
team that designed the trunk for the PT Cruiser. Her mother works in the
international relations department. Both parents modeled a life devoted
to one company, one career, with the final goal of having a comfortable
retirement all the while providing their family with a comfortable life.

After receiving a degree from Saint Louis University in Music and Theology,
Adrienne ended up going to work at Chrysler. "For 8 to 10 hours a day
I stared at a computer screen, entering 10 digit auto part codes into an
outdated program. Then I had to call up suppliers and ask when the
delinquent parts would be delivered. I am almost grateful for experiencing
that. Now, I cannot imagine doing something I don't care about."

On a whim, Adrienne accepted an offer from a friend and helped drive the
18 hours to New Orleans. After 3 weeks she returned to Michigan. "I left in
the rain, devastated. It had been the best 3 weeks of my life."

"New Orleans lets people be creative and be who they were meant to be—
with a parrot on their shoulder, taking their pet duck (or pig) for a walk."

Adrienne did not want to return home and fall back into a stagnate life. She
kept herself high by sharing stories of Mardi Gras with all of her friends.
Less than a month later she packed up her car, tossed in her mandolin and
headed back to New Orleans. No plan. No career. No retirement package.

A year later, Adrienne describes herself as a busker, an itinerant performer,
(from the Spanish word, Buscar, which means "to seek.") Many of her fellow

buskers call her Bob Dylan Girl. I've never heard Dylan songs played on a mandolin, but to listen to Adrienne play, as she leans back against the corner of a building on Royal Street, her music makes me want to find a nearby bench, close my eyes and drink in every note. Her brown, wide brimmed hat matches her brown eyes. With thick braids and perfect smile, she makes all eight stings on her mandolin come alive.

I asked her if she had ever had any bad experiences in New Orleans.

"One night I was on my bike headed home. My light was out. I got hit. I was okay buy my mandolin broke in half. Sal fixed it for a really good price. Another time I was busking in front of a jewelry store. A lady who owned the shop came out complaining, threatening to call the cops. As she puffed on a cigarette and blew smoke in my face, I played Dylan's, 'I Shall Be Released' as peacefully as I could. Then she flicked her cigarette butt at my feet and left. I walked away feeling really courageous."

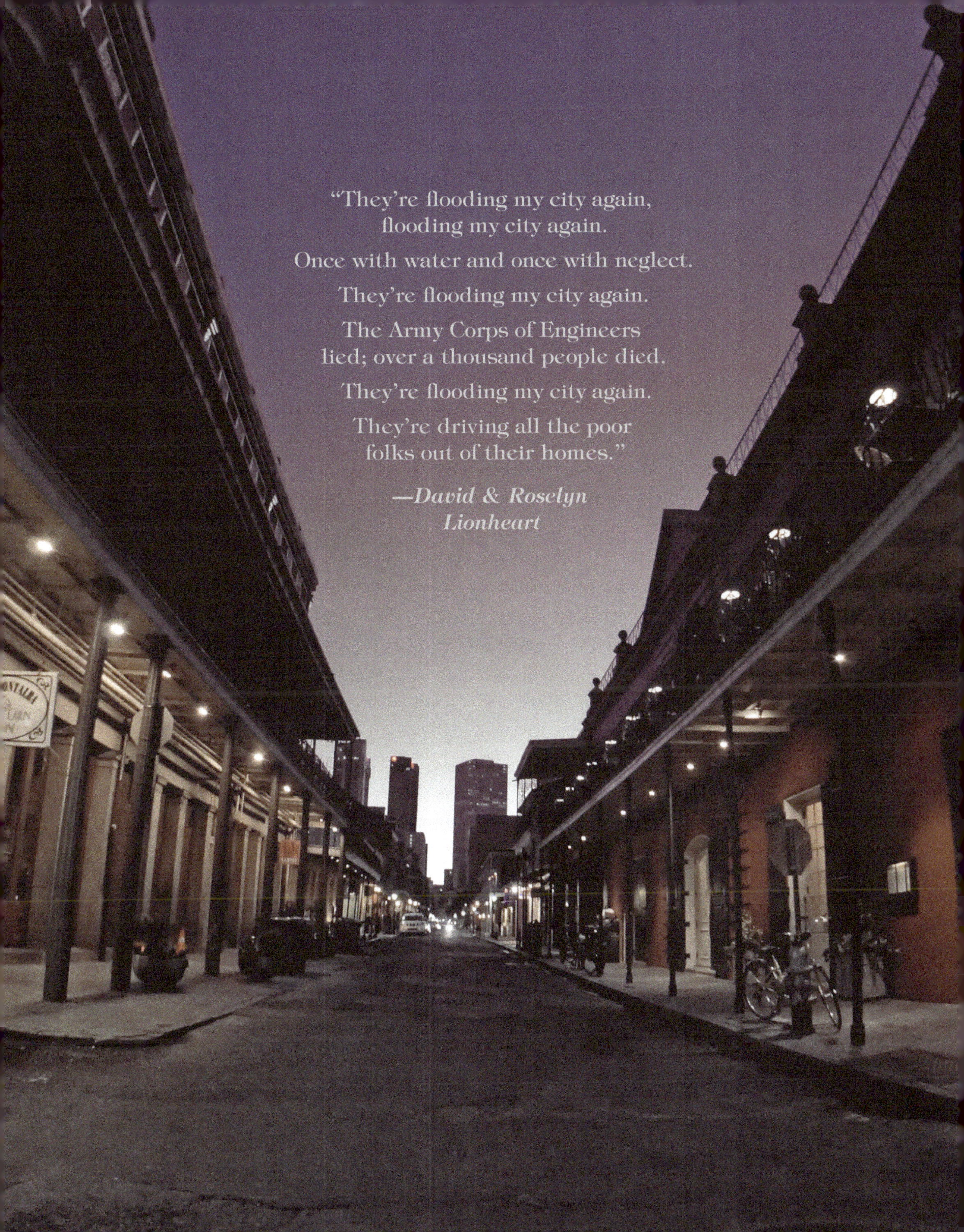

"They're flooding my city again,
flooding my city again.

Once with water and once with neglect.

They're flooding my city again.

The Army Corps of Engineers
lied; over a thousand people died.

They're flooding my city again.

They're driving all the poor
folks out of their homes."

—David & Roselyn
Lionheart

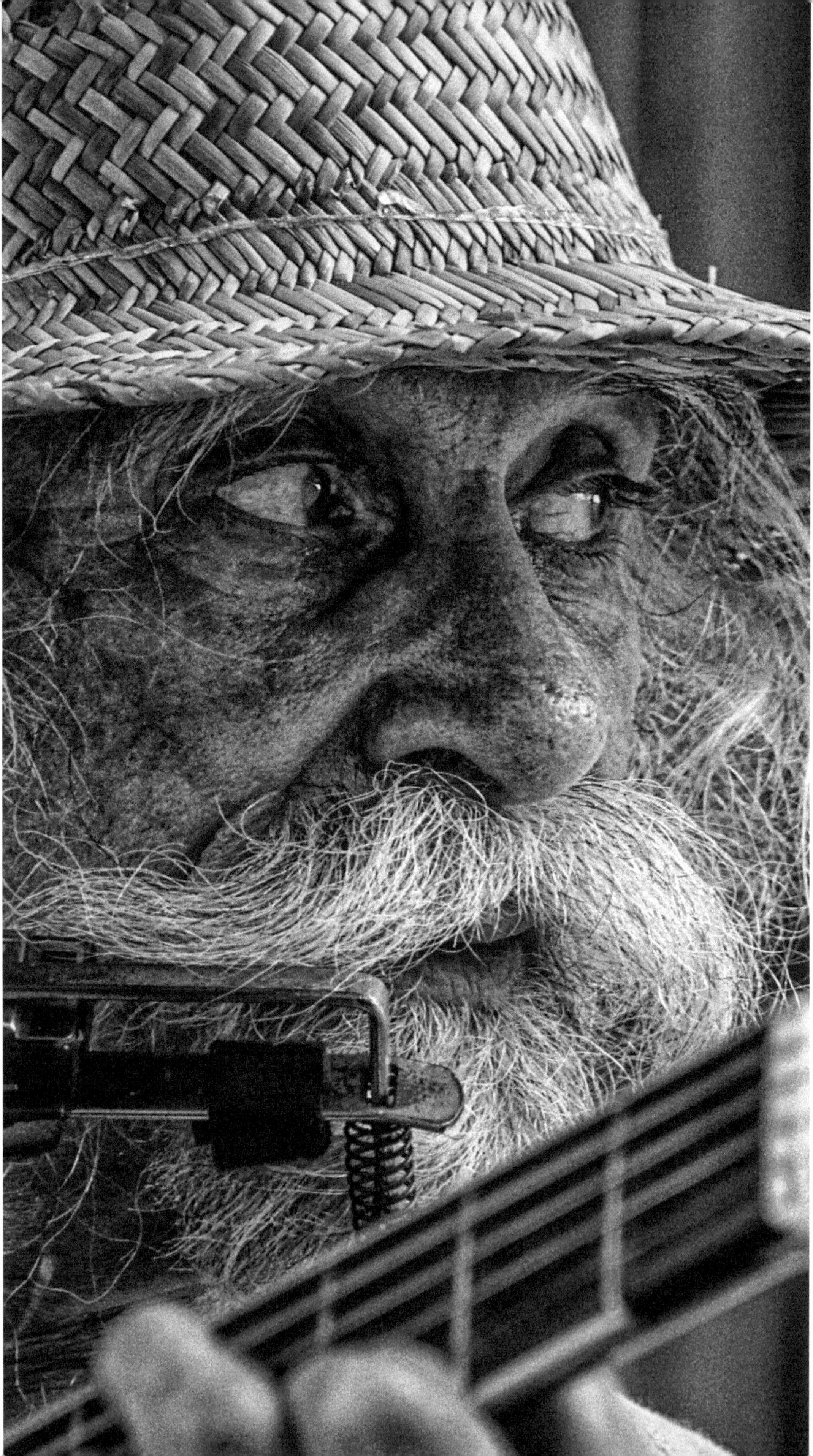

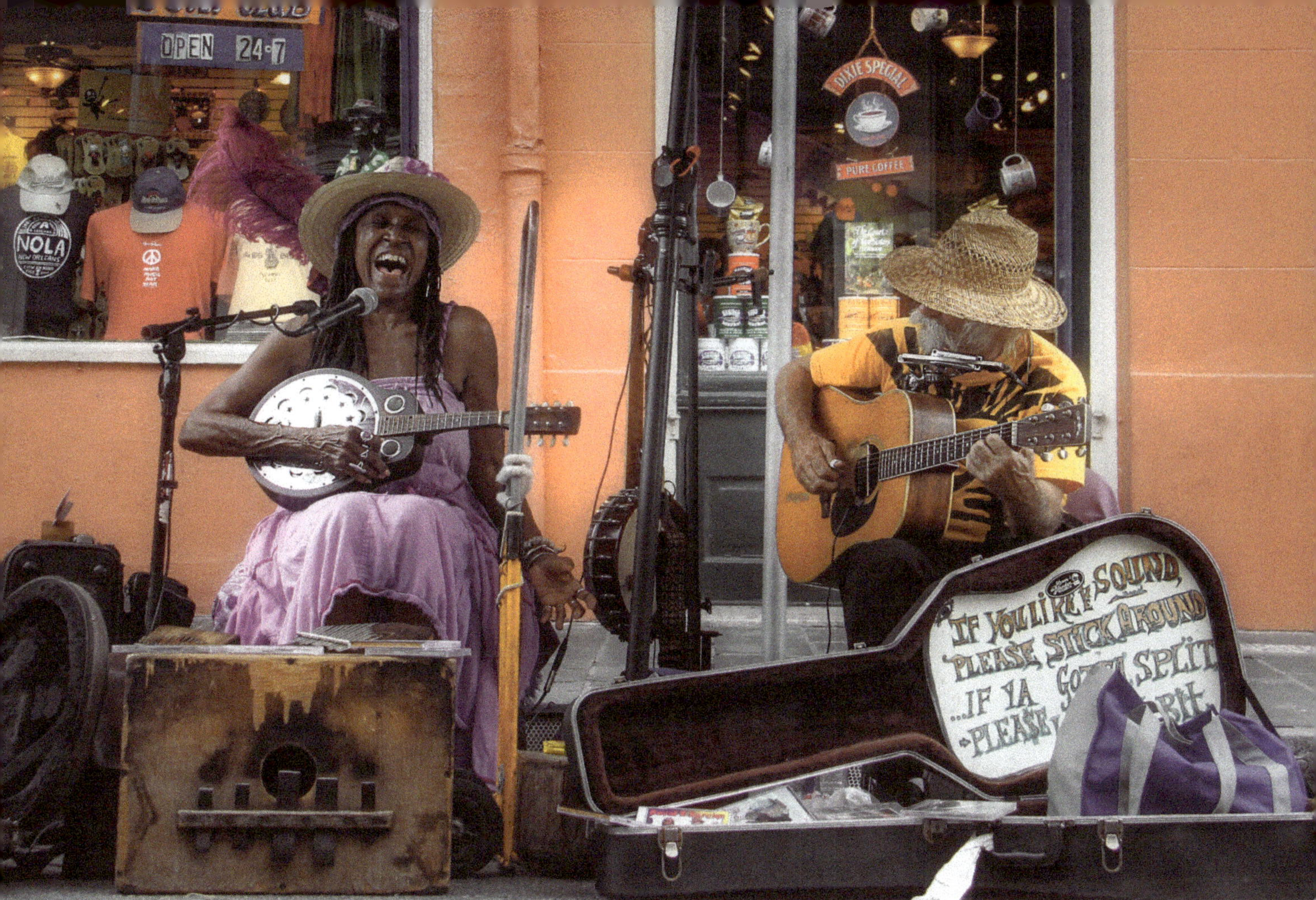

David & Roselyn Lionheart

Since 1975, David and Roselyn Lionheart have found themselves wrapped in the arms of New Orleans street life. They work hard, playing on and off all day long—every day. Their open guitar case fills quickly with cash whenever a crowd gathers. David and Roselyn have played to audiences all over the world, recorded several CDs and have been featured in some documentaries. The couple has raised four children in their Bywater apartment, some of them going on to Yale, UCLA and UC Santa Cruz.

Roselyn Explains New Orleans Music:

"People ask me what kind of music I like and I tell them New Orleans Style. They think they know what I mean. They hear Louis Armstrong trumpets and drums and they are oh so right. And they are oh so wrong. New Orleans style is Creole music. Classical music and jazz and rhythm and blues and rock and roll and gospel and country, Cajun, Zydeco, Creole—mulatto music…mulish music. Mean and low-down and stubborn and light and graceful and airy. Music for and of the survivors."

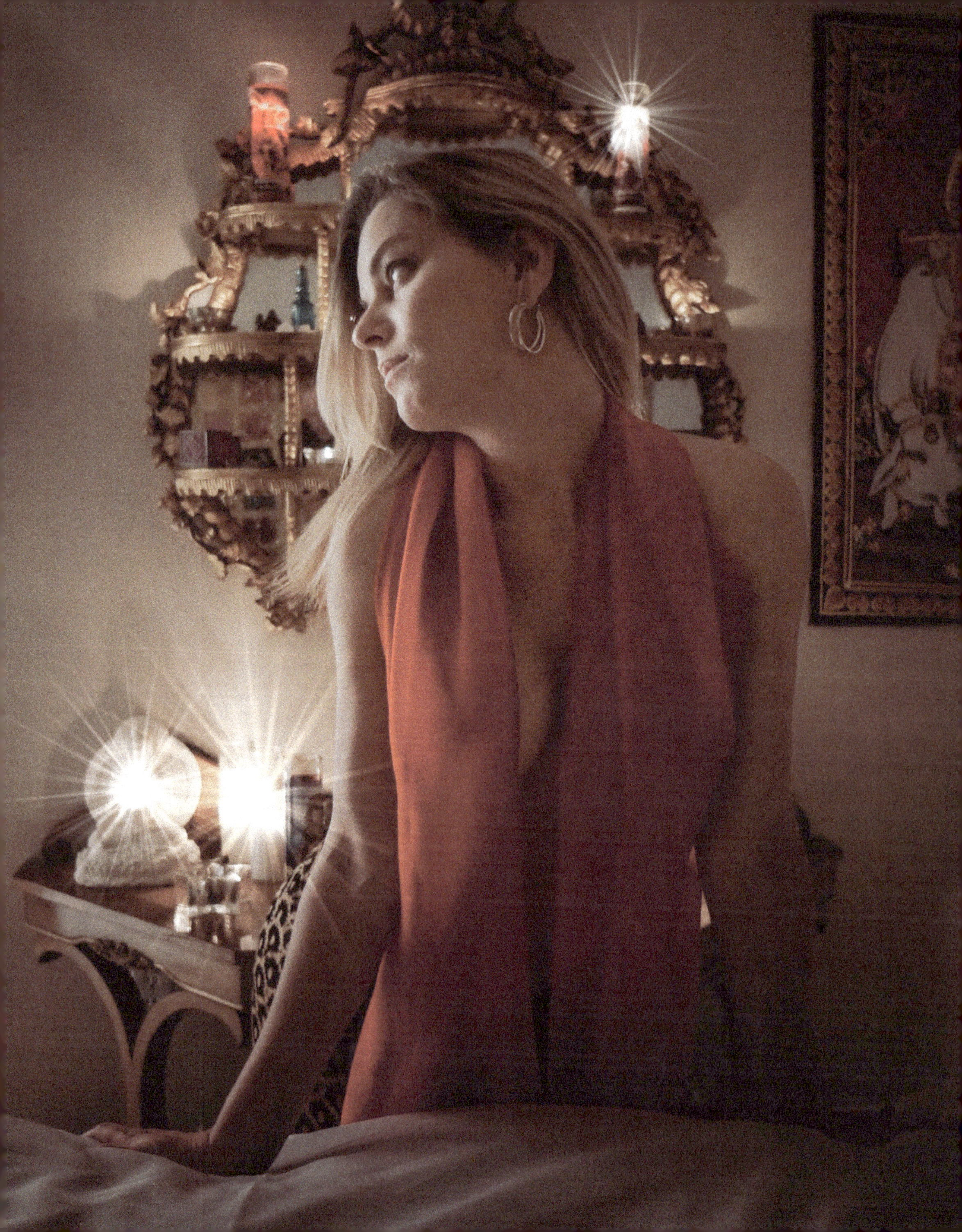

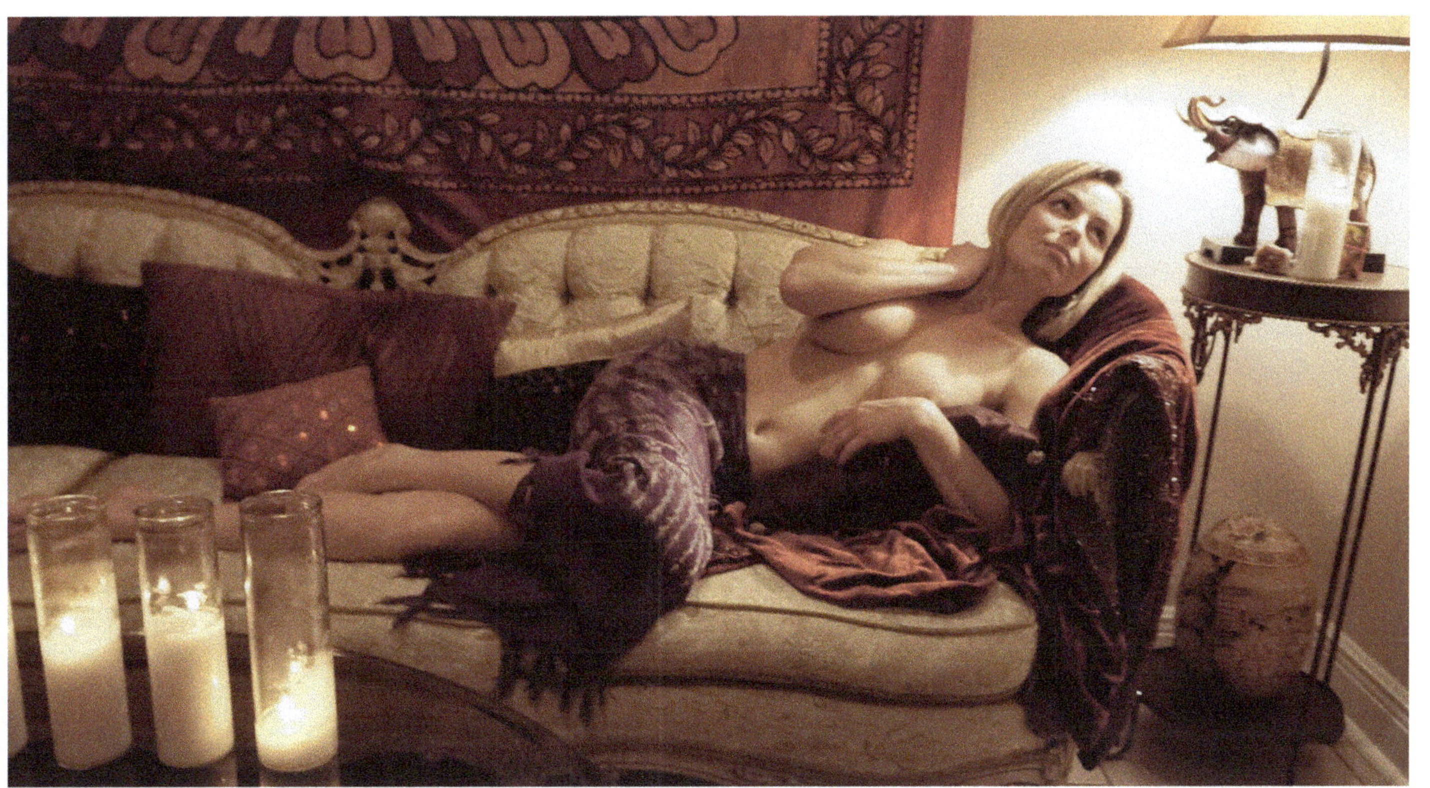

Goddess Celeste:
Healer, Tantrika & Intimacy Coach

"I am Goddess Celeste. Escape the physical world and enter the mystical oasis of my sacred space as you melt into my healing touch.... I tried law school in Vegas, then my husband and I moved to New Orleans but we divorced. I cleaned houses for a while. A client introduced me to Tantra, a 6,000 year old eastern tradition that includes everything from yoga to Taoism. She mentored me and I learned that there is much more to sex then erection, penetration, ejaculation.

"Tantra teaches us about sexual energy. It lifts the veils of the conscious mind so we can align with our original divine self. Many of my clients find me on Backpage and they come to me for various reasons. I've practiced my Tantric art with everyone from surgeons to oil workers. Sessions are like a deep meditation. Clients surrender into the moment. I go to the other side and it's healing for me too."

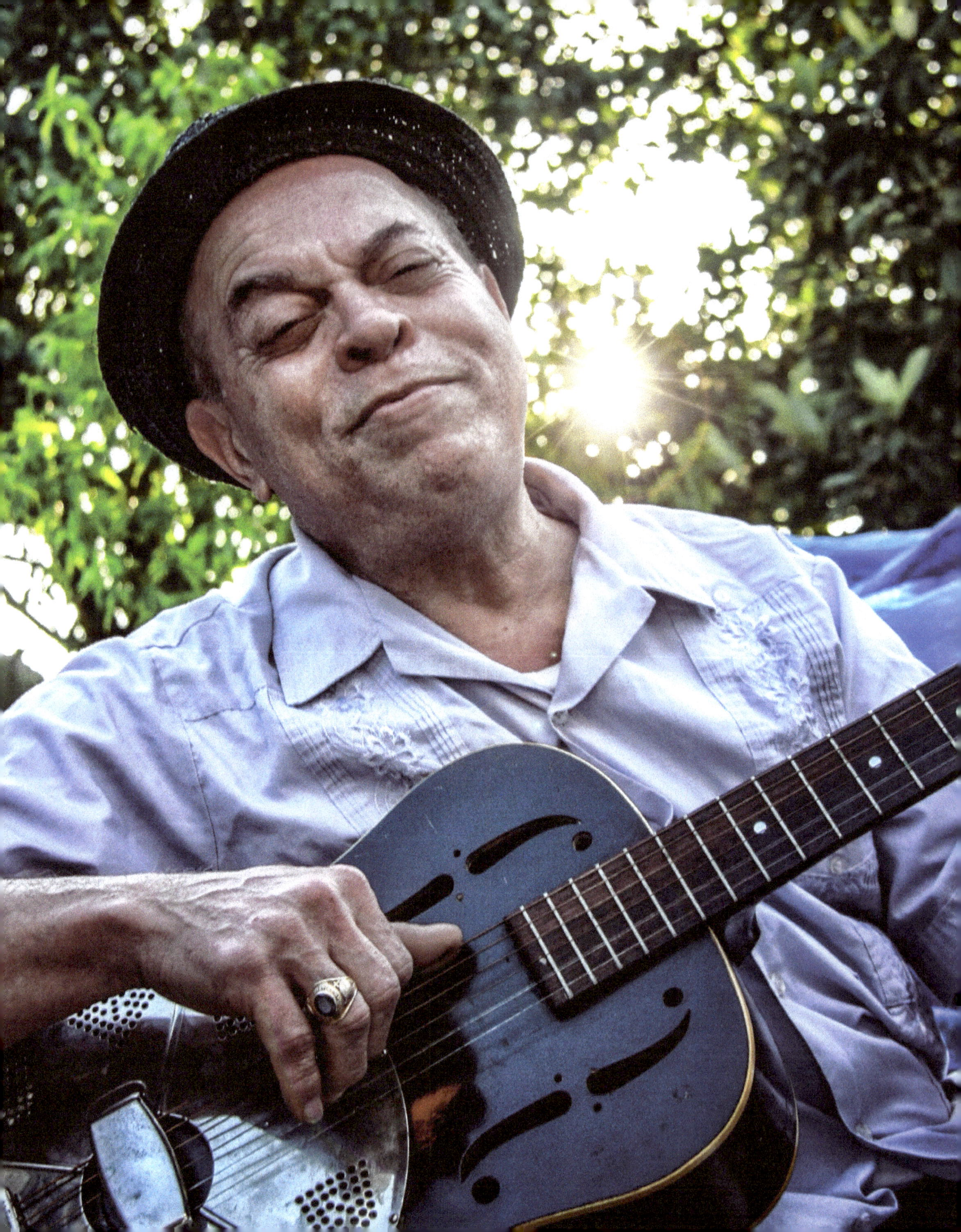

John Edward Moore "Deacon John"

"I am a Voodoo child. I was born on June 23, 1941 on Saint John the Baptist Eve, the first day of the Voodoo Holiday. I am the first African American to be president of the musician's union.

"I was my mother's favorite child. Of her 13 children, I could cry the loudest. She knew right away that I had a singing voice. To solidify her beliefs, she cut my nails under the fig tree. It was an old Creole superstition that if you cut a child's nails under a fig tree he would grow up to be a singer. That is exactly what happened. I never had a day job. I've played music my entire life. I sang in the boys' choirs and in the churches. I picked up the guitar when I was in high school. I am primarily a singer besides being a guitar and banjo player. I do several different styles: Jazz, Blues, Gospel, Rock 'n' Roll. I started playing professionally about 1958 or 1959... for over 50 years, never looking back.

"I have a recording history that goes way back. In the sixties I sang in hundreds of hits like "Tell It Like It Is," "Land of 1000 Dances," "I Like It Like That," Erin Neville's "Waiting at the Station," and huge hit records like "Working in the Coal Mine." I did television commercials, broadcast jingles, even movies. I've had a lot of awards from different magazines and institutions: Lifetime Achievement, Best New Artist, Best R&B Band.

"I get my inspiration from different emotions that come out of the songs. I am a song stylist rather than a writer. They call me The Musical Chameleon; I can go in and out of so many styles. I can draw from all the emotions that come out of songs, sorrow or joy. All different styles: Cab Calloway, Little

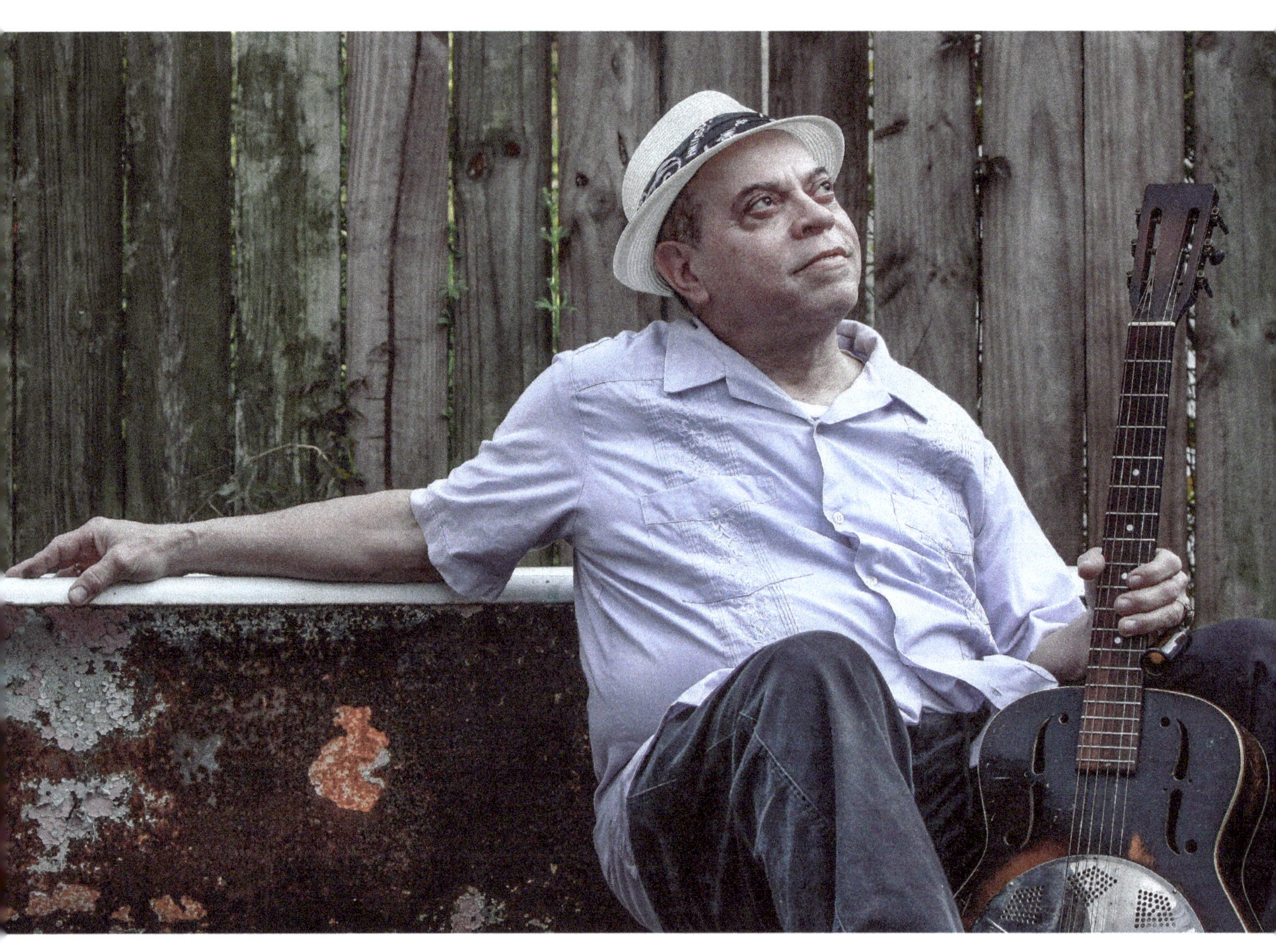

Richard, Count Basie, Curtis Mayfield, James Brown. I can play multiple markets simultaneously. I play debutant balls, graduations, funerals, weddings, corporate events—whatever the occasions call for. I have different sized bands I play with, usually a 10-piece R&B dance band. Two singers, eight musicians. Sometimes we expand to a 16-piece band.

"Jump bands arose out of the Deacon John Project. The Jump Blues Era was the era in music that provided a transition from Big Band Swing to early Rock 'n' Roll. The inspiration came through the dances during the Big Band Era, dances like the Lindy Hop and the Jitterbug. "Jump Children," Louis Jordan, Big Joe Turner, "Shake, Rattle and Roll," all this was early Rhythm and Blues and Rock 'n' Roll in the late forties.

"The demise of the Big Band Era came after the war years. Big Band was displaced by technology. Technology is displacing so many musicians. Technology has taught a generation of children to worship machines rather than play music. They prefer recorded music to live music to the detriment of our musicians. It cheapens the value of music. People give away CDs rather than selling them. People think that music should be free…. Press a button and, boom, out it comes. Now you can steal music. The record stores are all closing. Now the CDs are going away and here are the iPods. Twenty thousand songs in the palm of your hand. We created a monster that's eating us all up.

"Greedy capitalists see another way to make money. We're fighting a bill in Congress, The Performance Right Bill, [which] pays songwriters and publishers but doesn't pay musicians. They are treated like contract laborers. The broadcasters don't want to pay the musicians. Most nations of the world pay their musicians. If we weren't playing all these songs, people wouldn't hear them. Promotional value does not justify the free use of music. All this money is being held up all over the world. It is a complex issue.

"My creative process is helped when I sing gospel. When you're singing about Jesus, it brings out a wealth of emotions 'cause you're singing about God. If I sing "A Change is Going to Come," I'm thinking about Sam Cooke and the civil rights issues or if I am singing about a broken love affair, I may be thinking about B B King singing, "Sweet little angel, I love the way you spread your wings." You have to go into how songs originated to get a history of what you're gonna do on stage to help you deliver these songs. As a singer and a guitar player, you have to draw from your life experiences and emotions. There is an emotional connection between the musician and the audience picking up on the way you're feeling. It is the job of the musician and entertainer to have that spiritual connection between themselves and their audience. Some people are better than others at that. Some people sing for themselves without caring if they make that connection."

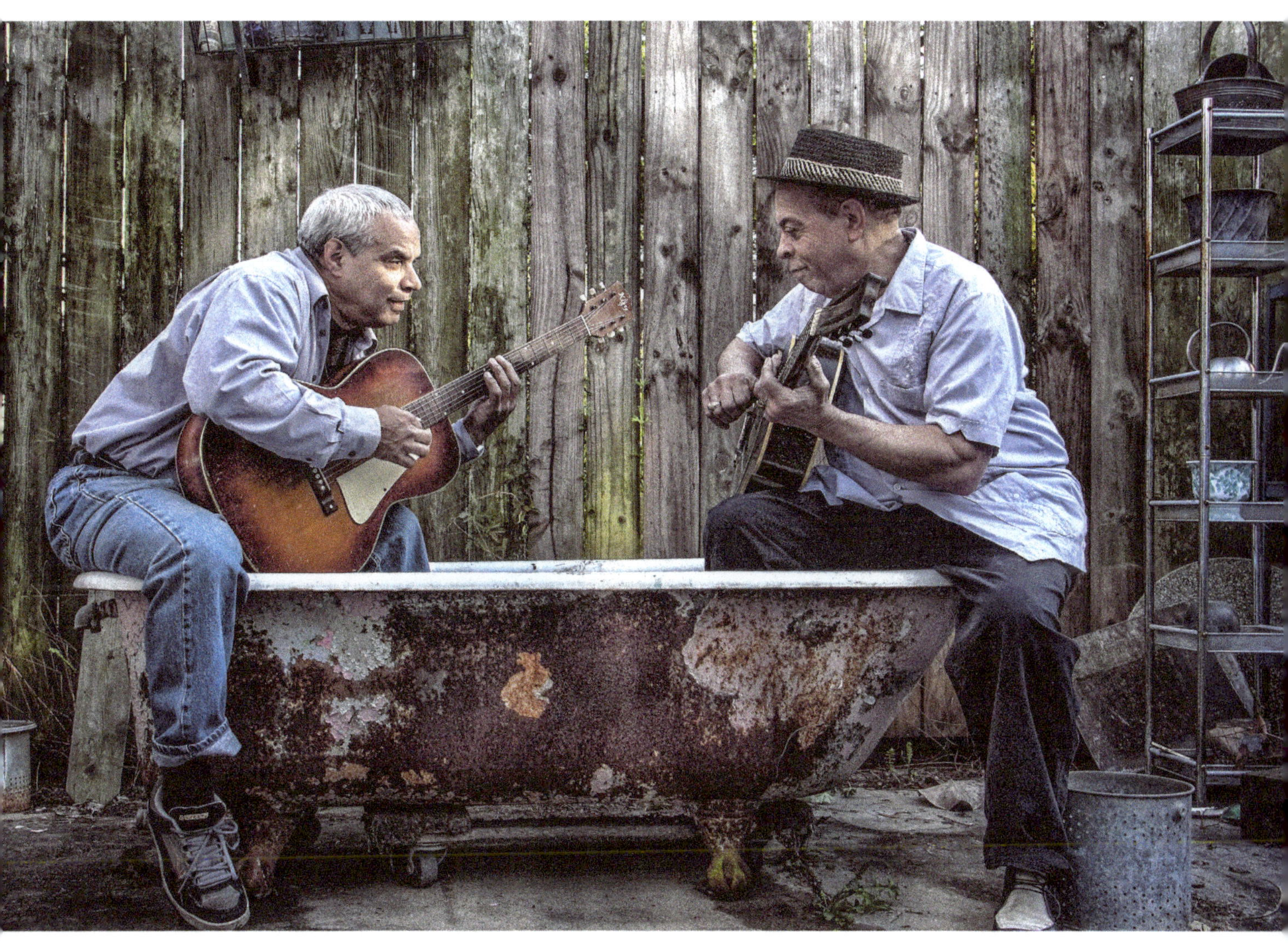

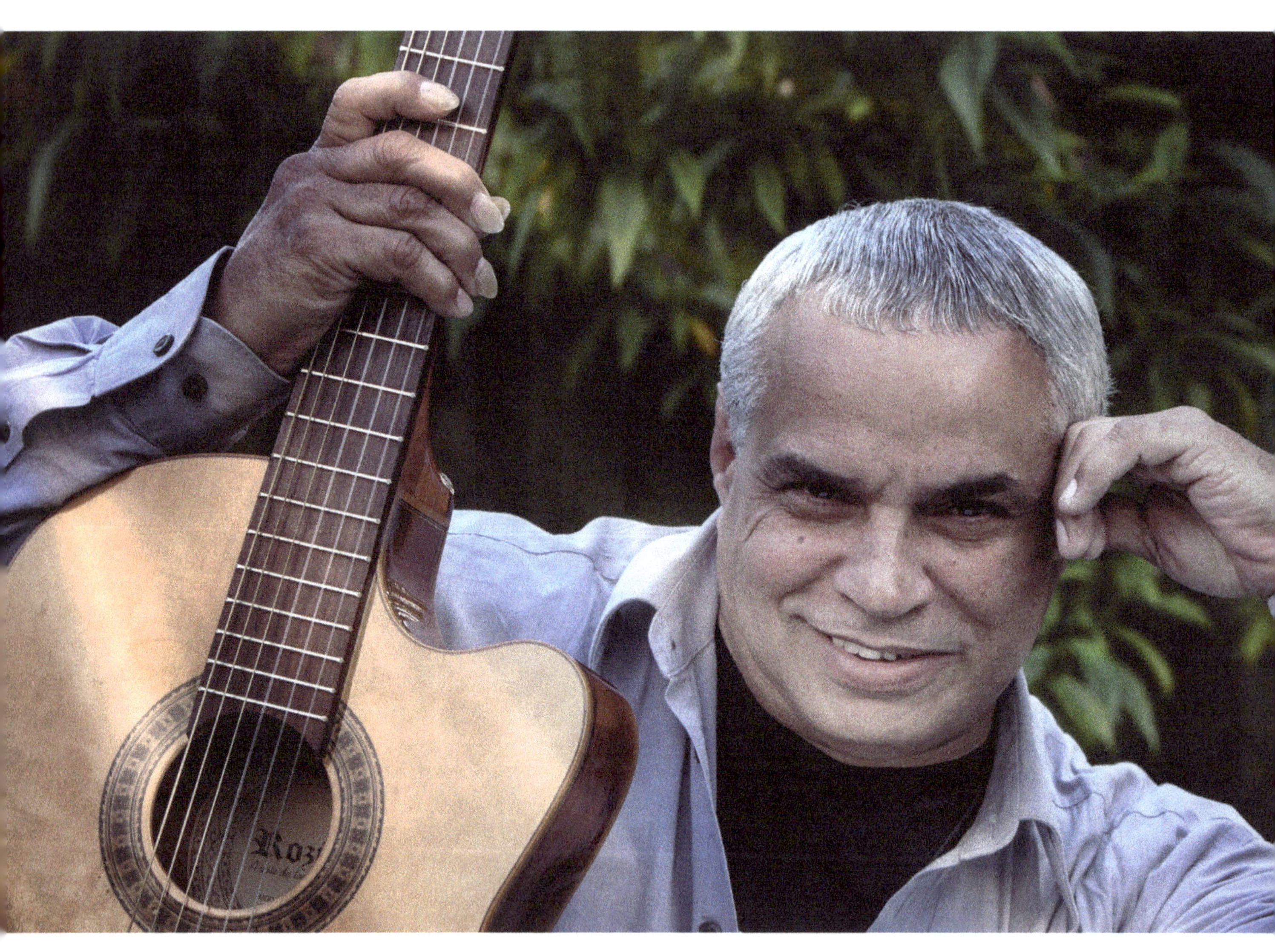

Charles D.S. Moore

"I'm inspired...when I go to movies and listen to the musical theme.
I want to write for movies so I listen to the score. I can pick out
whether it's a minor or major chord and how the movements are
going with the chord changes. After playing bass for 42 years, I
know exactly where the chord changes are proceeding in any
theme. I am more in tune with melodic structure. Some melodic
themes move me because of the emotional content. Right now, I
am interested in Celtic music 'cause they have a rich history that
I am akin to, very sensitive to. Celtic music is different from other
styles of music. My father has Irish blood, so I am prone to it, but
I never grew up with it. Nowadays, I'm drawn to it because of the
emotional content. That's how I am inspired. I've done everything
else—Jazz, Rock, Blues, Reggae—but the real emotional things
come from the symphonic movements.

"I was 11 or 12 when my brother, Raymond, started playing classical
guitar exclusively. He bought all the albums and he would go to the
Warline Musical Company and buy sheet music, come home and
play it. I liked that, so I asked him to teach me. He showed me how
it looked on paper and within a week or so I would learn the piece.
It was just a matter of him showing me what I needed to do with my
fingers. You take two weeks to do this, the finger pattern, then you

take two weeks to do the tremolo and then here's how the piece
goes. [Laughter.] Then you're ready.

"It was an invaluable skill, because I never played with a pick. When
Rock 'n' Roll came along, I started playing Rock 'n' Roll. I dug Jimi
Hendrix, Cream, Ray Charles and all that. I was able to pick them all.

"But my real passion was classical. I played with Little Richard,
Buddy Miles, Carlos Santana in '87. I opened a show with Bob
Morley here in New Orleans at the Warehouse in '77 with a group
called Light Years. I went on the road with Little Richard, and—what
was that other guy's name? Liberace. [Laugher.] I still keep in touch
with Richard.

"I was fortunate during the storm. The water didn't get inside my
house, no mold, no rotting of the floor, just a little roof damage. All
my photo albums, archives, tapes, all were fine. Some folks left and
never came back. They weren't gonna take it anymore. People are
just now getting back to their homes. It's incredible that after five
years there are still people living in trailers."

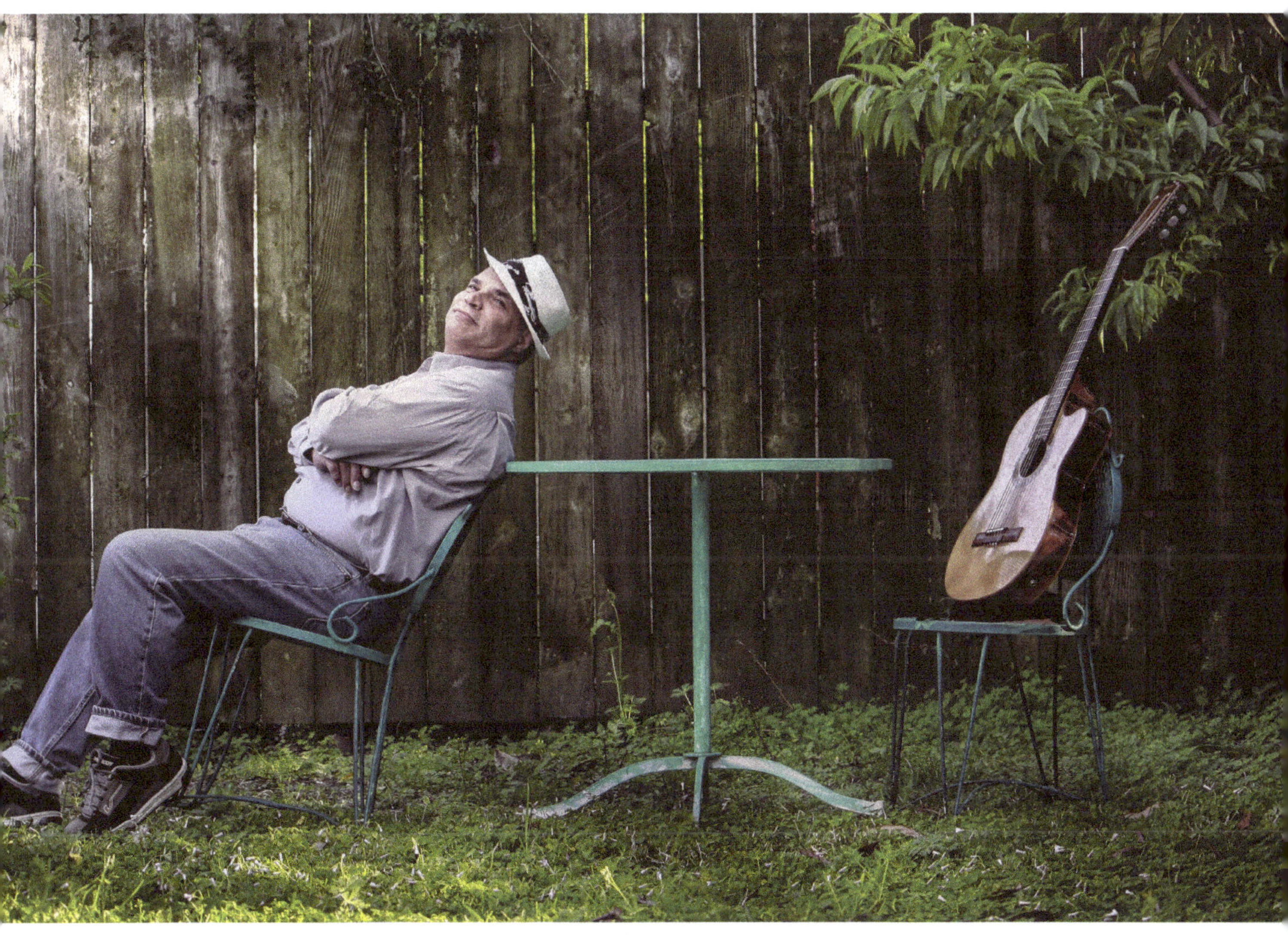

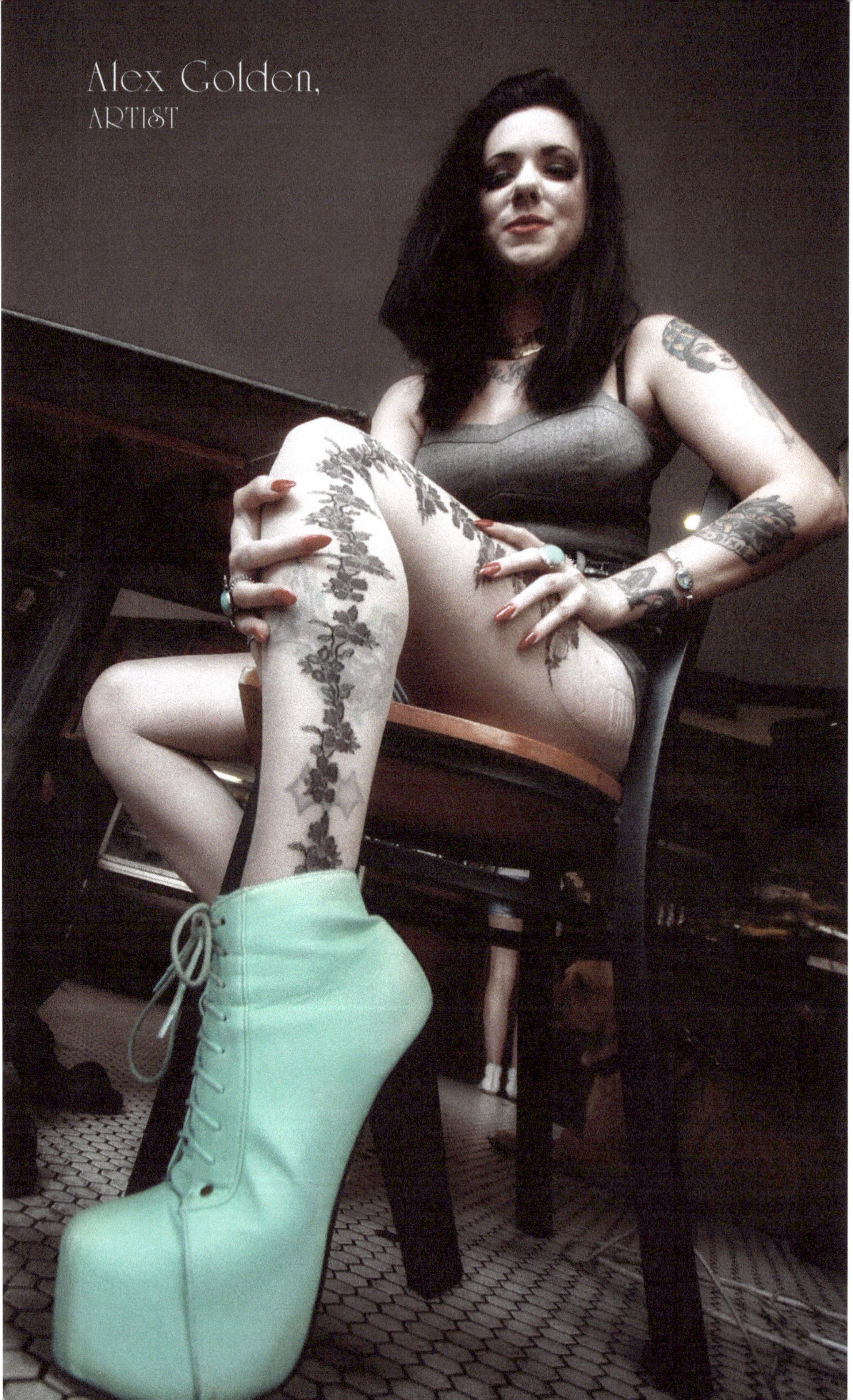
Alex Golden,
ARTIST

Curtis Knapp

You never know who might be sitting next to you at a wobbly sidewalk table, sipping coffee in front of Envie. On any given morning, it could be Curtis Knapp. He has often referred to himself as, "the best know, unknown photographer." While his name may not be instantly recognizable, Knapp is one of the best.

Knapp started out in a career doing children's illustrations, then switched to studio photography in the early 80's, first in Manhattan then Japan. Within just a few months he was working for GQ and *Esquire*, snapping portraits of Stephen King and Perry Ellis. Fast forward a few years and he was able to add to his lineup: Madonna, Andy Warhol, Dennis Hopper, Tina Turner and Tim Leary. "It was much more interesting meeting all of these people than sitting home alone with my watercolors. The money was better, too."

For about 40 years, Knapp has been living his passion, capturing celebrity portraits around the world. A decade ago he settled in New Orleans and lives on Frenchmen Street at Decatu—and sips coffee in front of Envie.

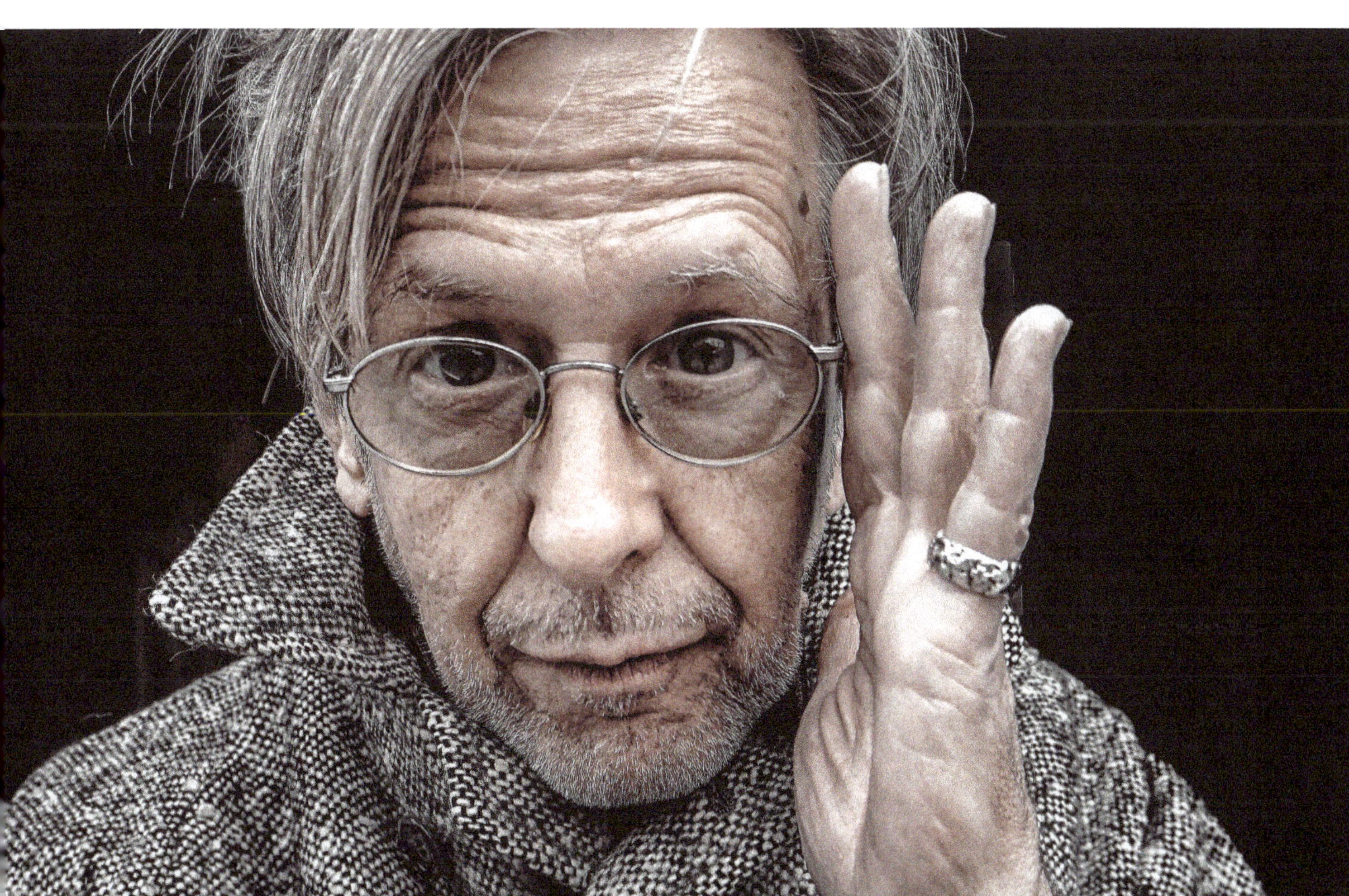

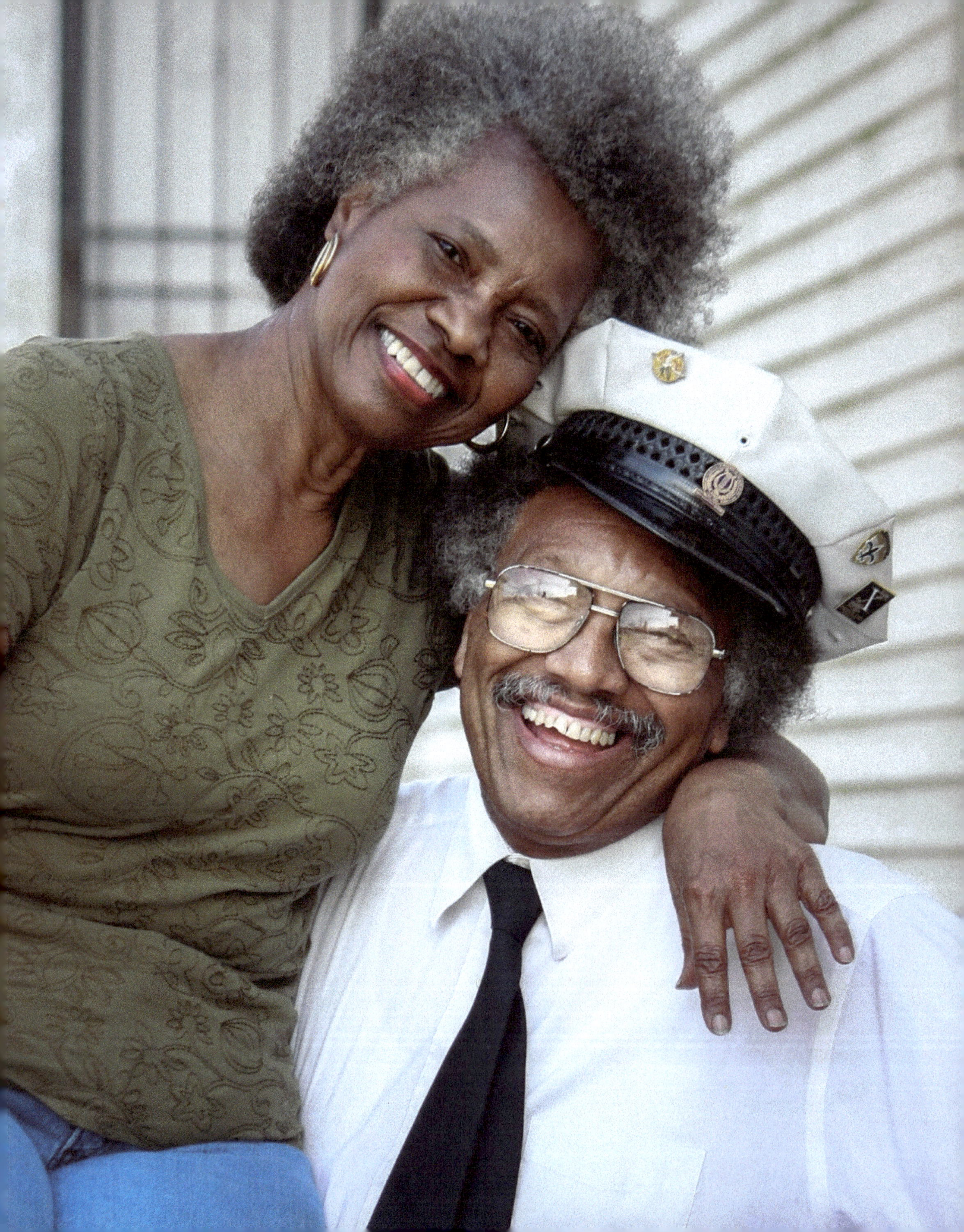

Lawrence & Janice Batiste

Mr. and Mrs. Batiste greet me at the door, warmly with bright smiles. I sit on their couch in a living room barely 10 feet square. I glance down at the new linoleum floors and fresh white wall paint. Homes in this neighborhood are either uninhabitable or newly restored.

Mrs. Batiste brings me a soda. I tell them briefly about the project I am working on. I bring out my wallet and produce the cash I want to pay them with. Lawrence waves it away, saying he doesn't want it. I turn to Janice. "I realize you are in charge here, so please take this," I say. She laughs. I insist and squeeze the money into her hand. I feel so comfortable here I want to stay all day.

I listen to Janice as she tells me about the five children they have raised. One of her daughters is a medical doctor in Texas. Another works for a bank here in town.

Janice and her husband met during the 1940s when he was in the Army. "He had forgotten my name, but somehow remembered my address. When he came over, my momma peeked out the door and said, 'He's kinda cute. We'd better have him in for dinner!'" They both laugh. "During all these years he has been a wonderful husband and a wonderful father."

I wonder if there is any higher compliment a wife can give her husband. Probably not.

Janice talks about their other son, Antoine, 48, who has been developmentally challenged since birth. "He was born feet first. I think that's what did it to him. He's a blessing!" I hear someone stir in the back kitchen. I ask if I can meet him and am led through a small bedroom to the kitchen where he sits. Oprah flickers on a nearby TV set; a program on the latest beauty secrets. Antoine's bright smile, with one front tooth missing, beams up at me. We shake hands. He tries not to let go. Lawrence then leads me through the kitchen to the back porch. Two single beds are squeezed into corners. "This is my son's room. That is my bed over there, but I sleep on the floor. My son has seizures and I have to be nearby."

Our photo session takes place in the shaded driveway. Much of the neighborhood is a wasteland. Lawrence points to the boarded up homes next door and around his property. "The people who lived next door before the storm just never came back. One day I looked over at that one there and saw this guy pulling out all the pipes. I called the cops and they came and arrested him." Then he points to a faint watermark high above my head on the side of his white clapboard house. "That's how high the water came. We left the day before the storm hit. We got out of here just in time."

I open my camera bag and ask Lawrence to sit down on an overturned bucket next to his bass drum. He takes out a pick comb and runs it through his wild, graying hair, looking like he is on his way to impersonate Don King. Dressed in a white shirt, black tie and a matching captain's hat, I can tell he needs some loosening up for this photograph to be successful. All I have to do is ask his wife to talk to him. "Say whatever it takes," I ask. As soon as their eyes meet, the laughter begins. Click, click, click. The task of capturing this happy man, so in love with his wife, is the easiest photo I have ever snapped.

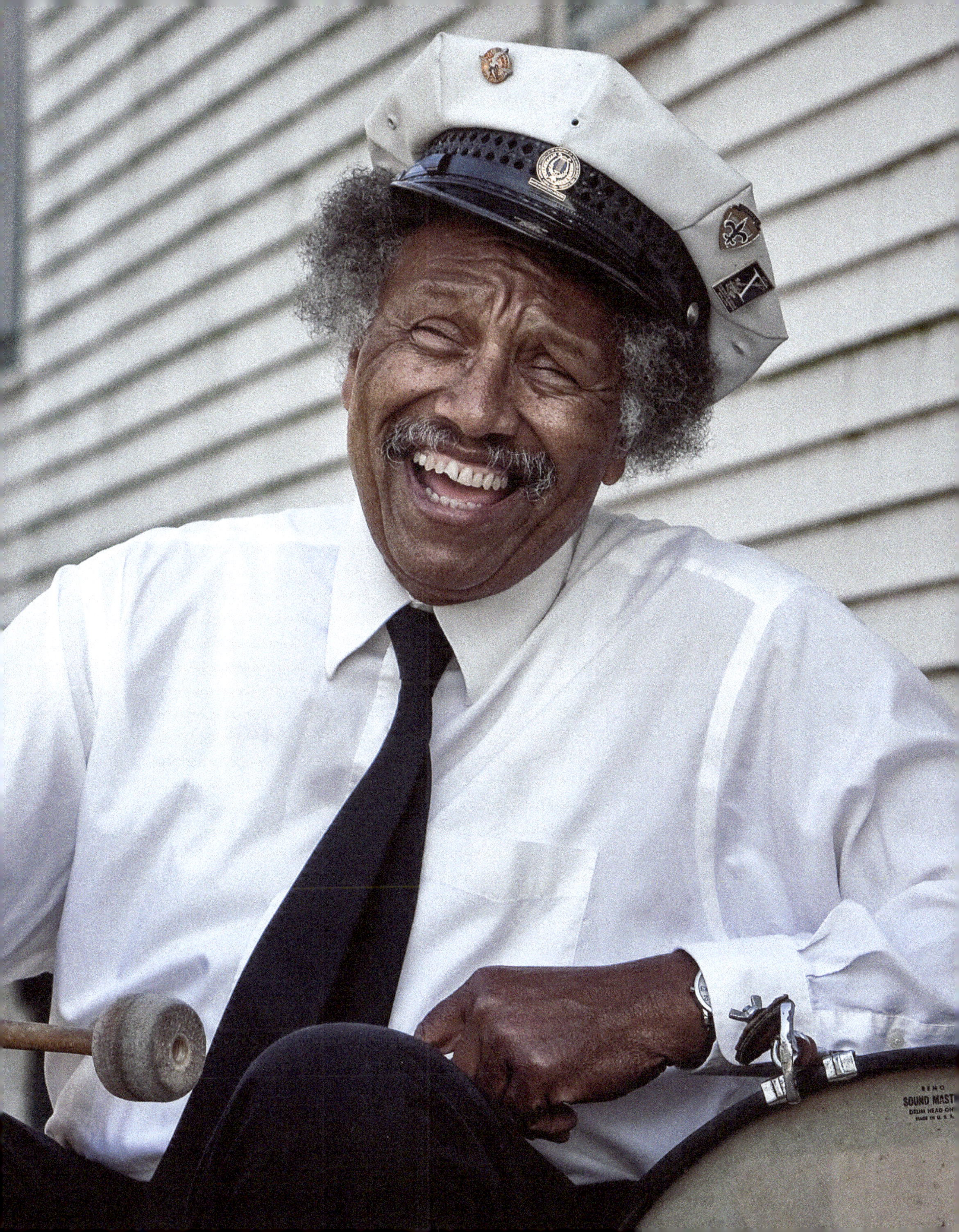

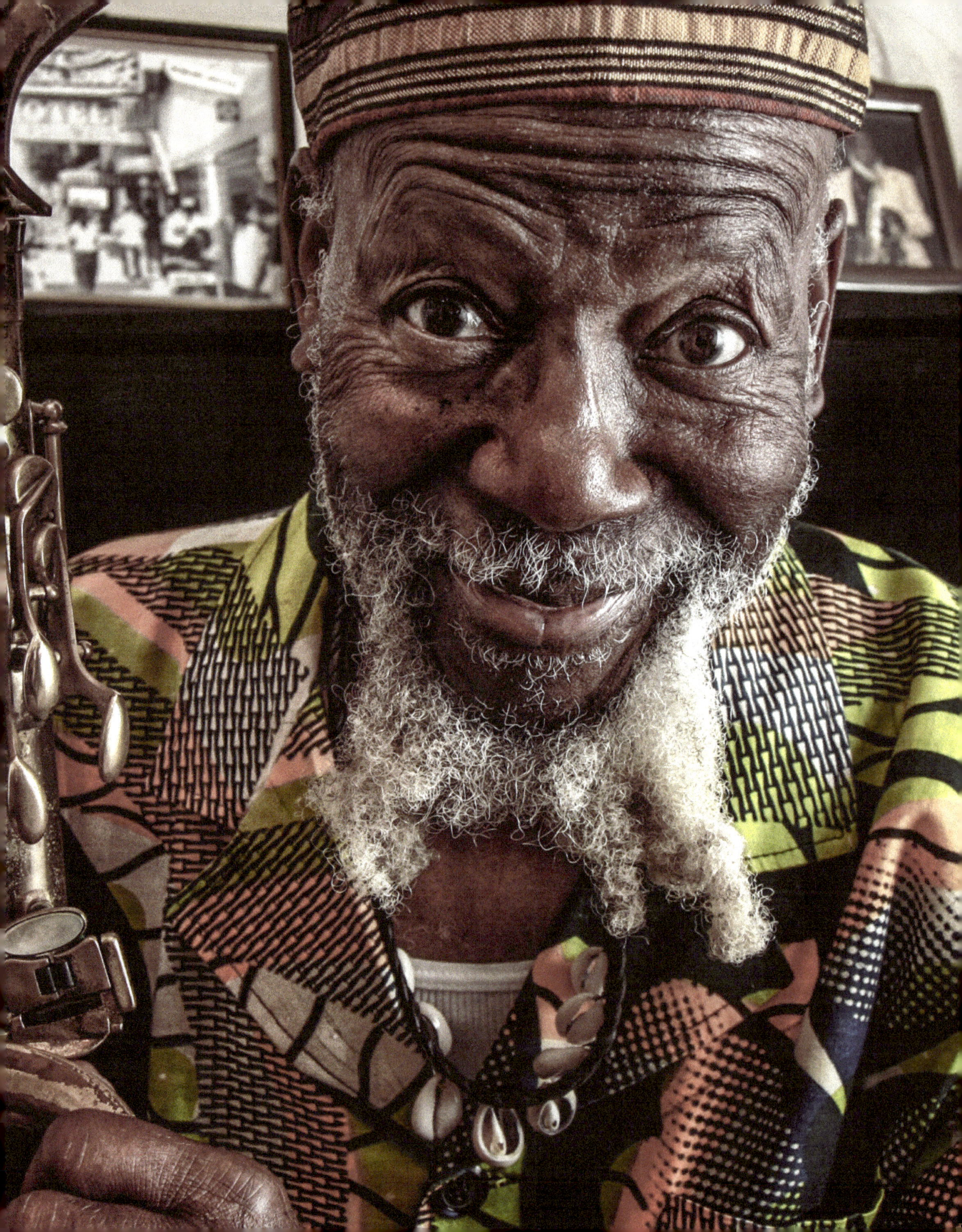

Harold Battiste

"My dad knew how to play music, but he was a tailor.

"You don't know my past, man.... My past is never knowing my value and what I was worth. Sonny Bono did know it.... Couldn't do nothing without me. I didn't go out to L.A. looking for nothin' like Sonny and Cher.... That just happened. Sonny met me while he was still driving a meat truck, hustling songs.... That was before he even knew Cher. Cher was a groupie. She was hanging around the studio with Phil Spector. Cher always wanted to be a singer when Sonny met her. They went out on a date and he saw that she really wanted to be a singer so he came to me and asked if I'd help her. I was working with Sam Cooke at the time.

"I believe that music is a language that all of us can have. You have that. If you can talk, you can sing. The whole idea of writing music like that is secondary. If you can sing and talk, you can play music. It's just a matter of translating what is in you already.

"Like birds, they just sing... It's an expression of how you feel. It is in your heart, what your body feels, like you holler in church. Like, 'Oh wow!' That's music and it tells people who you are.

"The hard thing about music in society is there are so many restrictions. People go crazy when you act just as who you are, because it doesn't conform. That's why people like music that comes out of black people, because it comes out of here [gestures to his heart]. Black people who came off the farm, they used music to escape from what they went through. Black people used music to forget. They had soul.

"White people have it, but it's been restricted. Society here is still trying to lift themselves beyond that. But it is difficult. It's very hard. When you come from a culture that's been fighting for thousands of years, beating up on each other... Might is right. It takes you away from nature; you forget that we are all animals. Intelligence is the answer.

"All intelligence....I don't know, I shouldn't say that. People will think I'm crazy.

"When I look at music, I think of it as a higher form of laughing. I can say things with music that you can't say with words. Words are just confusing. That's what lawyers use and doctors use.

"As a society supposedly progresses, we get further and further from nature. I got students now that go up to New York to listen to music. They don't look at the birds and look at the possums and other animals to see what they're doing.

"When the storm came, the birds, they knew the storm was coming. They were all gone. We had to wait for the weatherman to tell us."

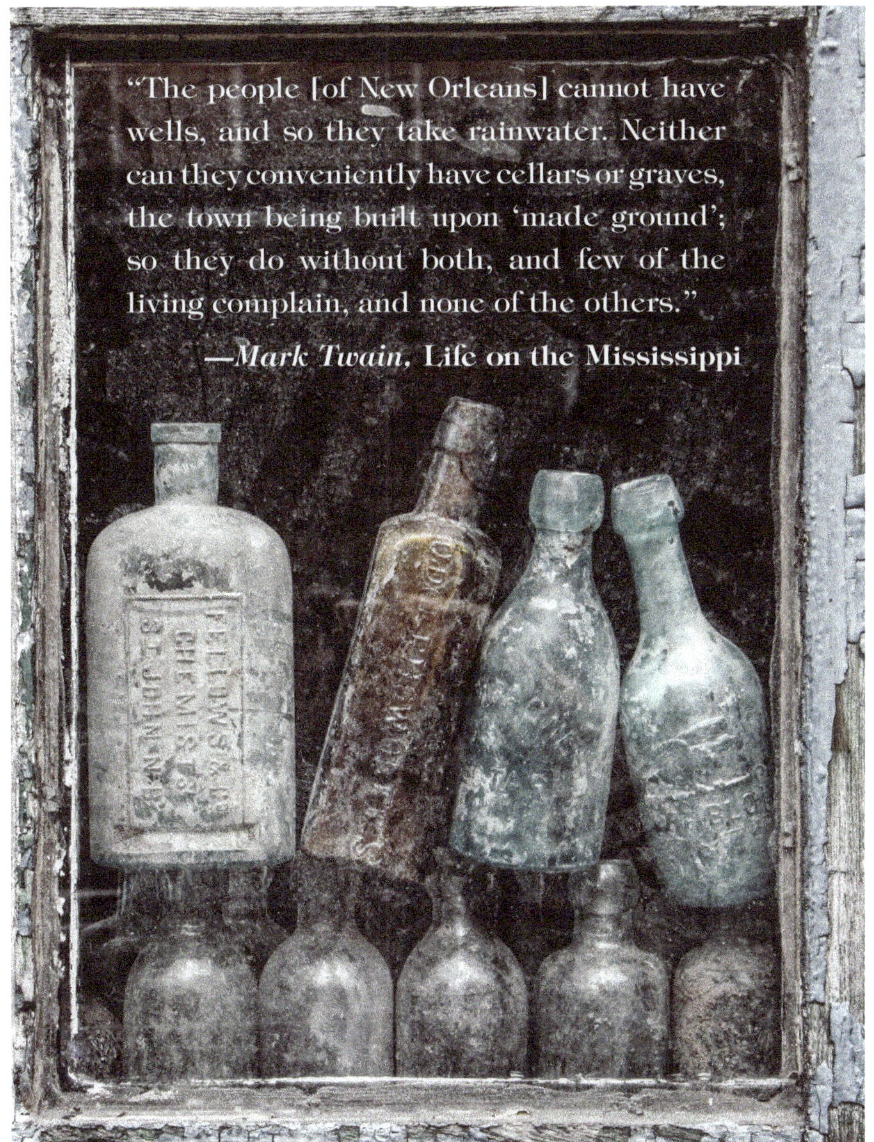

"The people [of New Orleans] cannot have wells, and so they take rainwater. Neither can they conveniently have cellars or graves, the town being built upon 'made ground'; so they do without both, and few of the living complain, and none of the others."
—Mark Twain, Life on the Mississippi

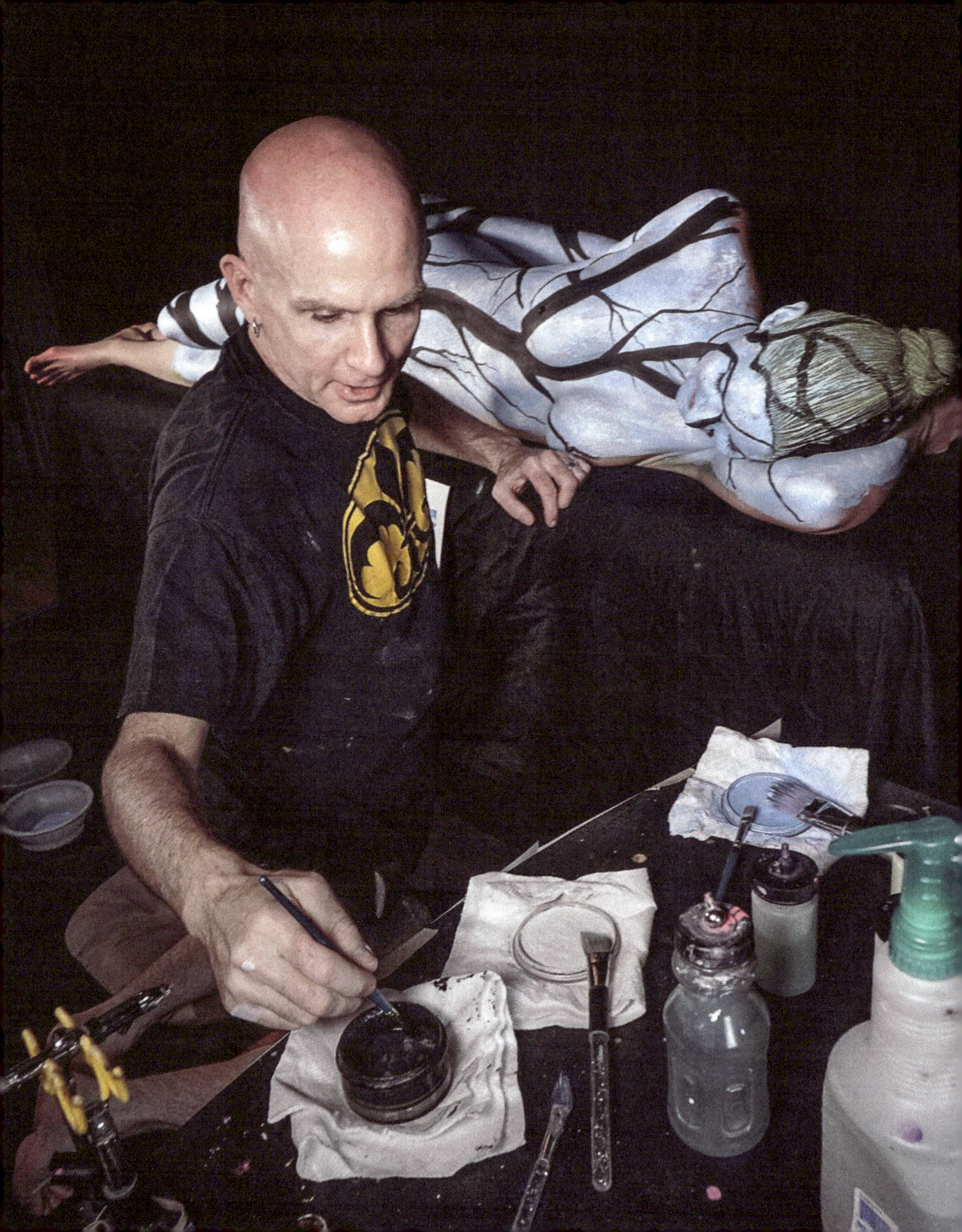

Craig Tracy

Many folks say that Craig Tracy has the best job on the planet: he celebrates the human body as an art form.

If you tour through The Craig Tracy Fine-Art Bodypainting Gallery on Royal Street, it will probably take you a minute or two to realize exactly what you're looking at. You may stare into one of his surreal paintings, enjoying the vibrant colors and grace of a leafy tree, when, slowly, you'll see a sensuous nude revealing herself in the shape of a branch. Suddenly, you can't wait to study the other huge paintings that cover the gallery walls so you can discover and unveil more of Tracy's secrets.

Craig began drawing with pencils and crayons when he was five. By 15, he had saved enough money to buy his first airbrush. "I remember this pivotal moment happened in high school. My guidance counselor looked at my work and asked me if I was going to art school. I told her that my parents couldn't afford it.

"So, she asked, 'If I could get you into art school without your parents having to pay, would you go?' The lights went on; my journey began."

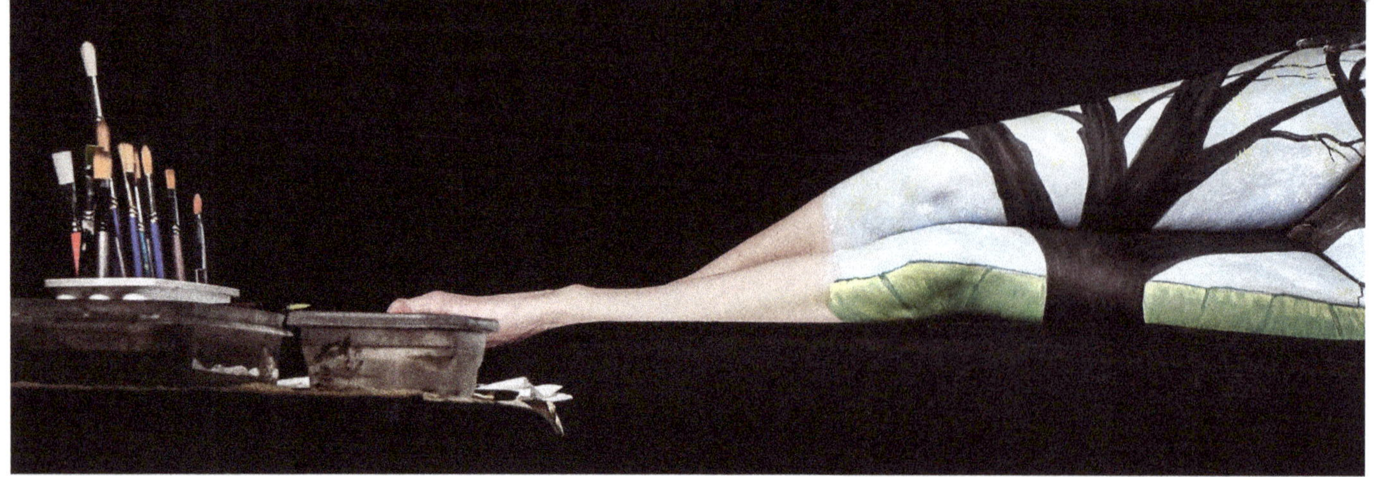

Craig once worked as an illustrator for advertising agencies, a period in his career that he describes as "mind numbingly boring." He began painting on various surfaces, murals, T-shirts, and mannequins. But he had an epiphany when he did some face painting for Mardi Gras.

He remembered an image he saw on the cover of *Vanity Fair* of a naked Demi Moore in full body paint. He began painting bodies. Today, Craig is internationally renowned and frequently serves on the judges' panel for a reality show with body painters called *Skin Wars*.

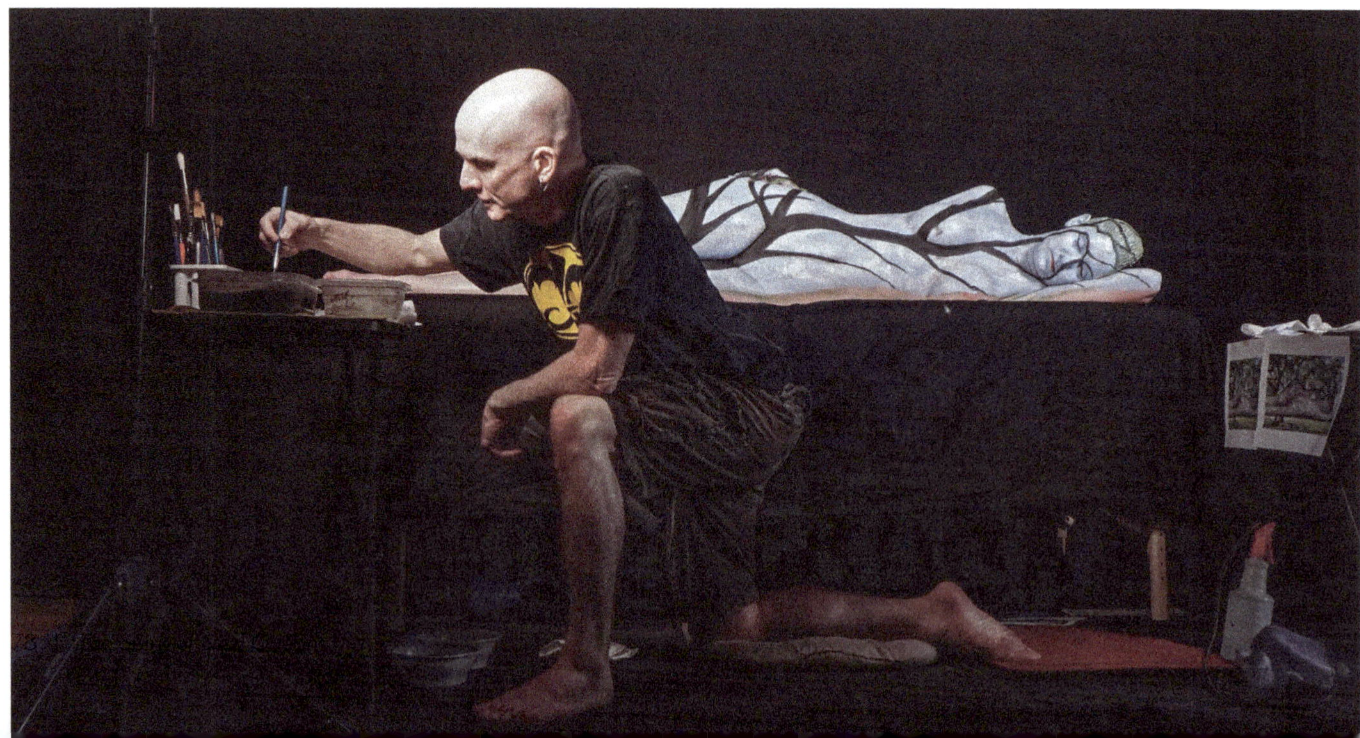

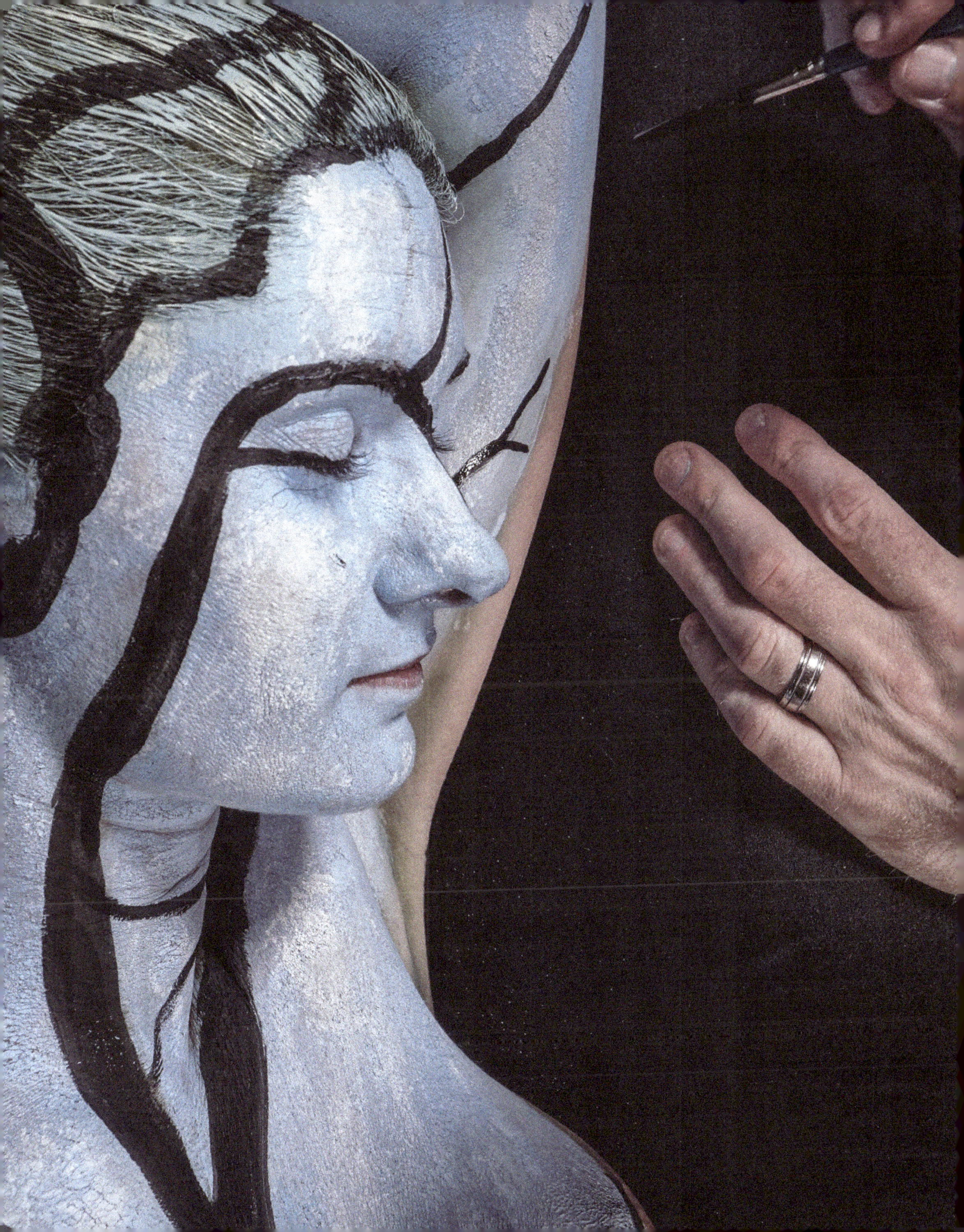

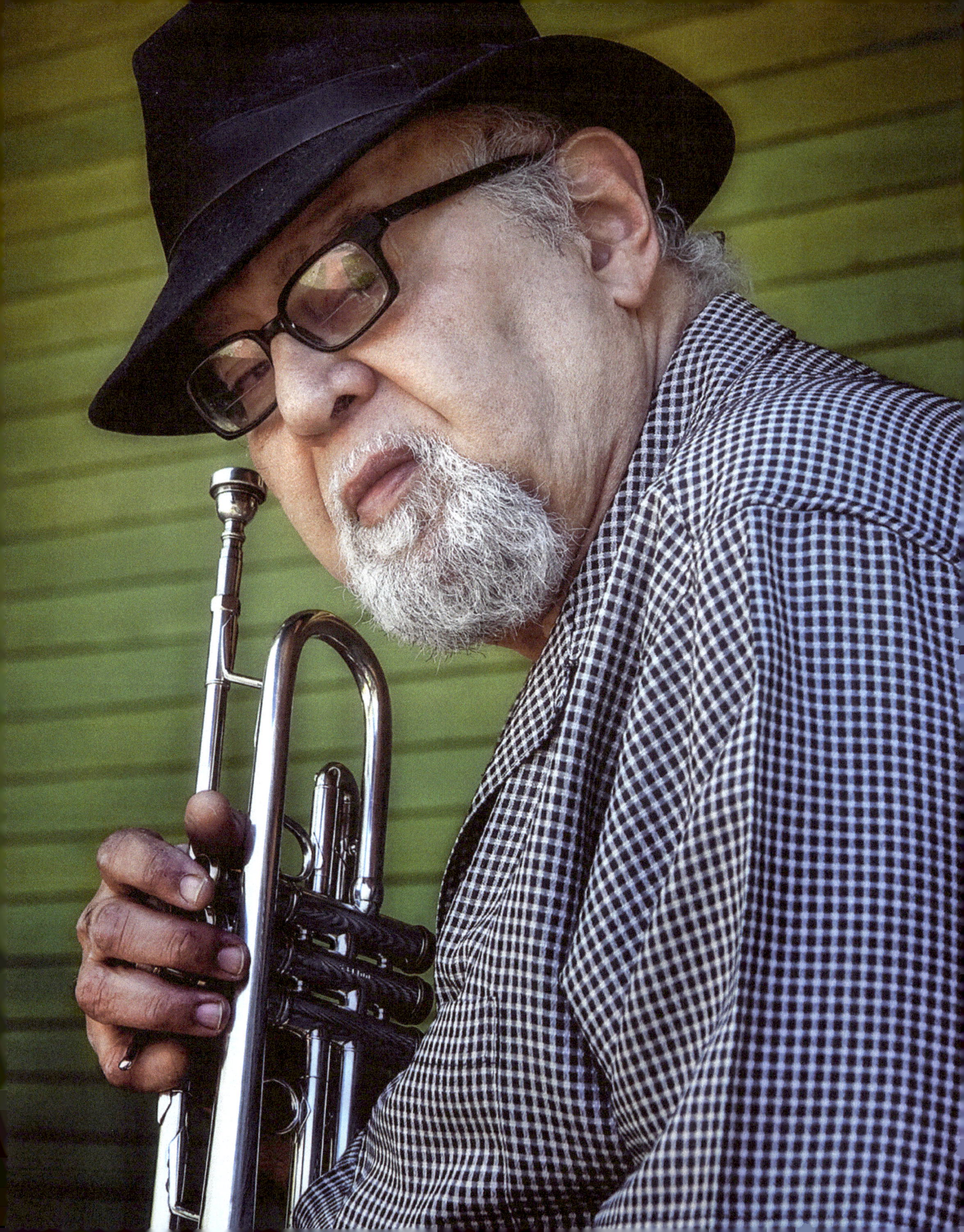

Clyde R. Kerr, Jr.

"At age nine, I got my first trumpet. I began experimenting with it and started making different sounds other than what the trumpet sounded like.

"My father would arrange music compositions. He was a scientist, too, and made machines that made all kinds of weird sounds, so I tried to do that on my trumpet. When I went to high school, that is when I started getting into it a little bit more, but I hadn't committed myself. Then when I got a scholarship for music, that is when I started to deal with it on a more serious basis.

"I thought I was going to be a visual artist. I used to like to draw. I tried to incorporate [into my music] what I would see. My CD cover of 1980 with the Neville Brothers is one of my drawings. I come to find out Miles Davis was a painter. I could see the lines that he was creating and the music and the sounds and colors…. It's all the same.

"I see lines…. Straight lines, curved lines and dots, arpeggio. Curved lines are like scales, dots are like intervals and you bring them all together.

"Everything comes from the vanishing point. Everything starts like a blank sheet of paper and when you play that first note that is when the picture starts. Sometimes it's real good, sometimes it's not, but that is what it is when you take a chance like that.

"Chance is the creative part. Chance is the best part—that's when the good things happen. Like Beethoven…..You write 100 symphonies, maybe two or three are great. Most musicians play what they know…they aren't risk takers. I like to practice things, so maybe I won't play that, but I'll play something off of that. Just like language, if you have a command of the language then whatever comes up, you can react to it. That's what I like!"

"I was planning The Escape from my husband when Hurricane Katrina
hit. After we were evacuated, it took me another year to slip away
from him. Sometimes I feel like I'm swimming upstream and don't know
if I have the energy. My body is only going to let me do this for so long.

"I've taught dance most of my life. When I started here, there were
only a couple of shows a week and a few private corporate events.
Now the market is saturated and there is always a younger dancer
coming up, with more money and better costumes. I'm tired.

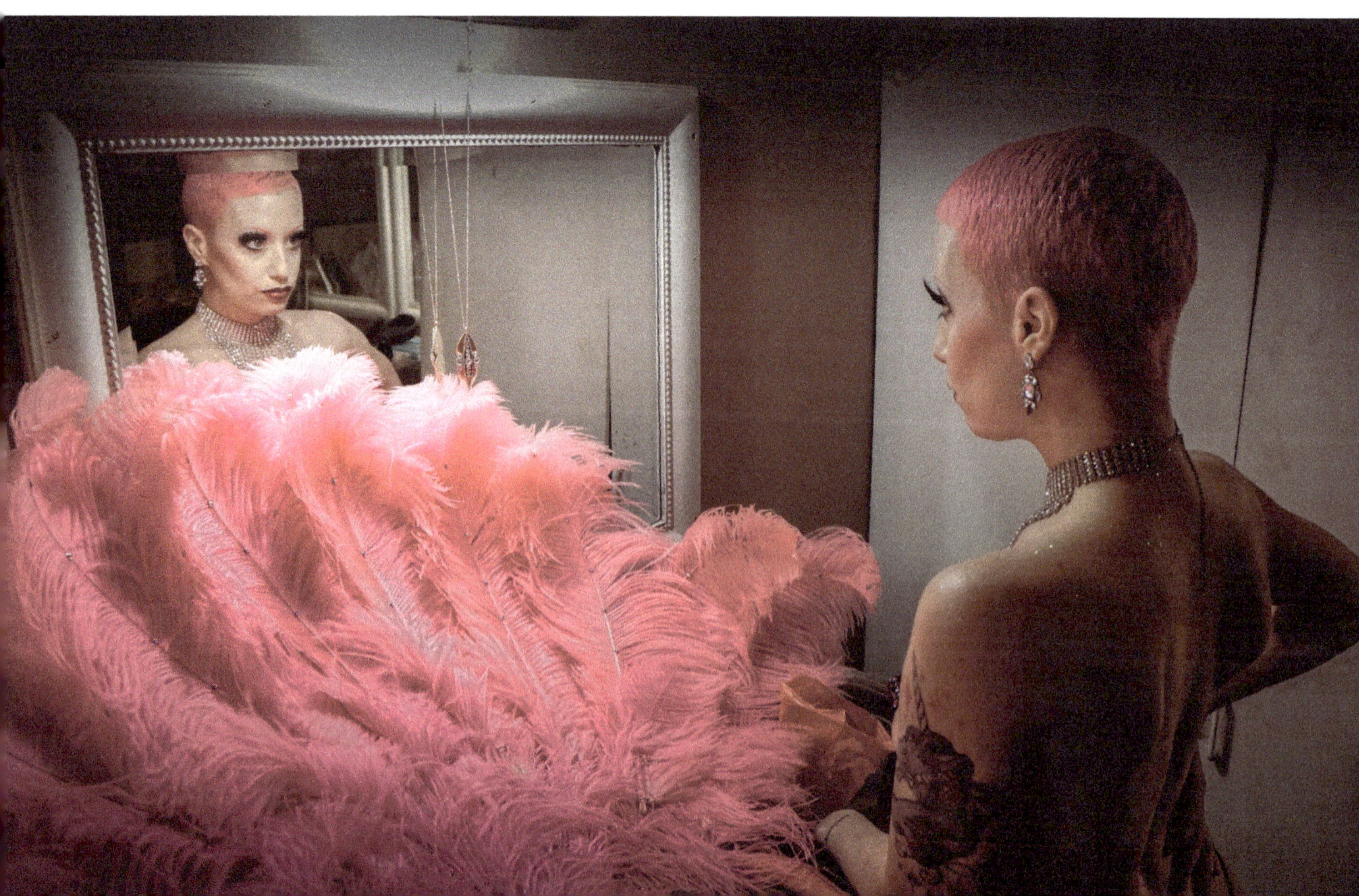

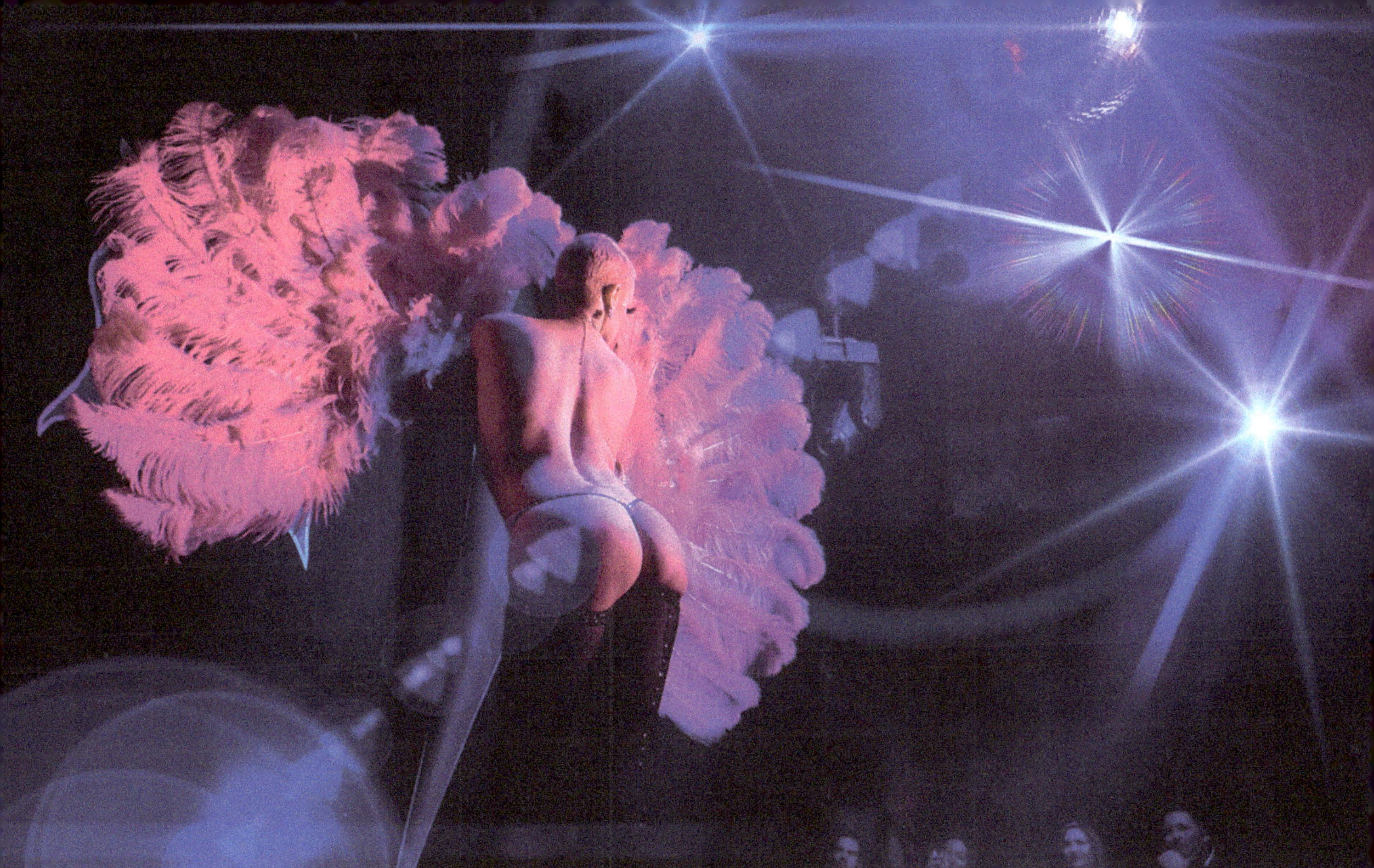

"Everybody remembers their first time in New Orleans. It's an honor to be a part of their memory forever. I make eye contact with everyone in the room, often seeing faces from around the world. The Fan Dance is my favorite. It forces me to rely on nothing more than the fans, with little else to distract my audience.

"I didn't know what a rich history and roots burlesque had in New Orleans. I like to teach a bride and all her bridesmaids at bachelorette parties. They don't think they can move and be sexy. I build their self-confidence and help them be fully in their bodies. That's what burlesque can do."

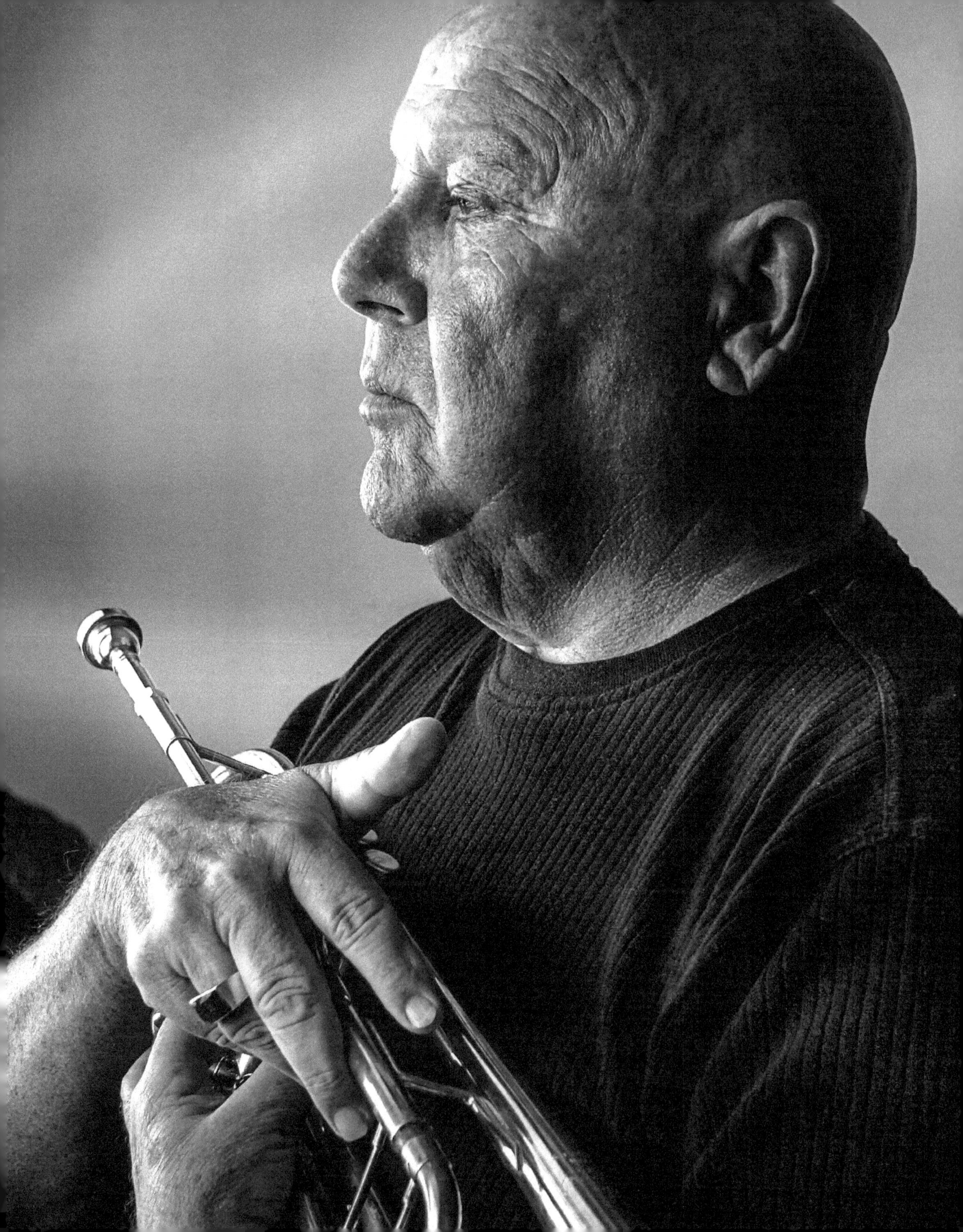

John Simmons

"A lot of the musicians I learned from are dead now.

"The old musicians are from right out of the turn of the century. I tried to learn the best I could from their style. I would try to perpetuate the older style of playing, which has disappeared almost. I used to play with brass bands... the old-type brass bands, not the 'funkified' new brass bands. The music has gone in a different direction. They still call it traditional Jazz, but with a more modern flair and more modern influences. Musicians now are better schooled than the old-time musicians. The old-time musicians played from the heart. They learned music by listening, not from the radio or TV, but from live music. They learned from each other.

"I played at the White House in '76. Jimmy Carter was there then. That was the 25th anniversary of the Newport Jazz Festival and they brought a lot of the musicians in like Dizzy Gillespie, a lot of the 'modern' musicians and the band I was in, The Young Tuxedo Cross Band.

"I have been semi-professional all my life, since about 1986. For twenty-some years, it has just been music. I used to work for the telephone company as a telephone repairman. When AT&T split up they laid me off, and I said, 'I may as well go do music.' But I always played even then.

"My initial visit to New Orleans was in 1964. I met the old-time musicians. I knew I had to come back. Unfortunately, many of the old-time musicians are gone; even the old buildings are gone. The French Quarter used to be like a village.... Everybody knew everybody. But then they built the skyscrapers on Canal Street and it lost its charm. New Orleans is always 10 years behind the rest of the country."

"During the storm, my wife's parents came up from the Ninth District with two sisters and a brother-in-law. They lost everything. We watched the water come up higher and higher.

"The horns started blowin' and the lights started flashin'. Beep, beep, beep, the horns were all beepin' as the water shorted out the electricity in all the cars.

"A rescue boat came. Someone yelled, 'You get in!' Now the water was even higher. I told them, 'I have two 90-year-olds with me and I know they don't want to walk through the water and I damn sure don't want to walk through it myself!'

"I had planned to stay in our apartment alone, but when the security lady said she was leaving I decided I better leave too. The helicopter eventually picked us up on the roof, about four o'clock Friday morning. They took my father-in-law by himself. Later, we found him sitting by the bridge watching the helicopter trying to find somebody else. We were put on the bus to the airport and we stood in line there for 12 hours. Our next stop was San Antonio. They were going to put us in an airbase under lock down. Weeks later, we came home. Somebody stole our safe box. Passports, birth certificate, marriage certificate…. All this stuff is no good to anybody."

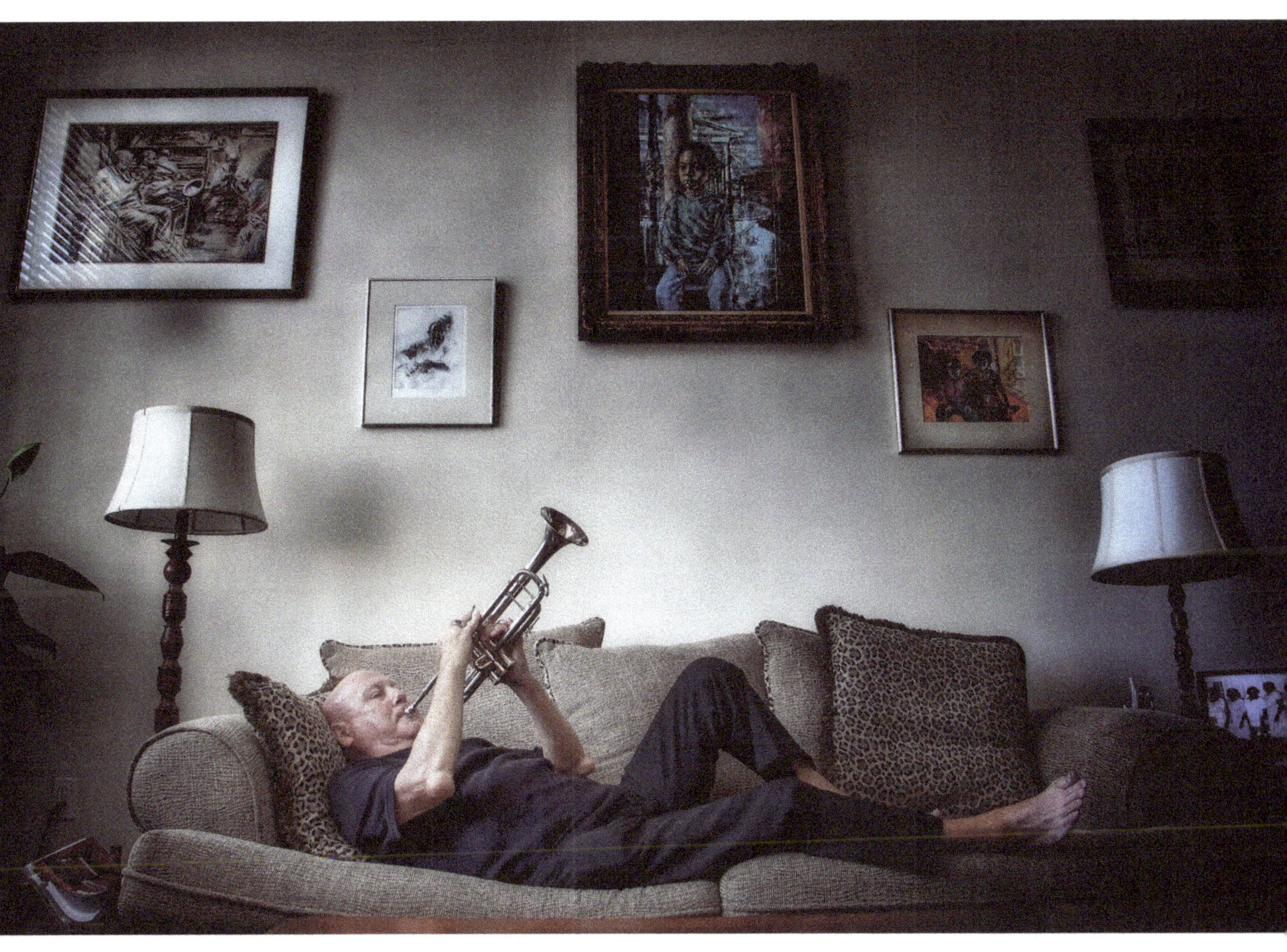

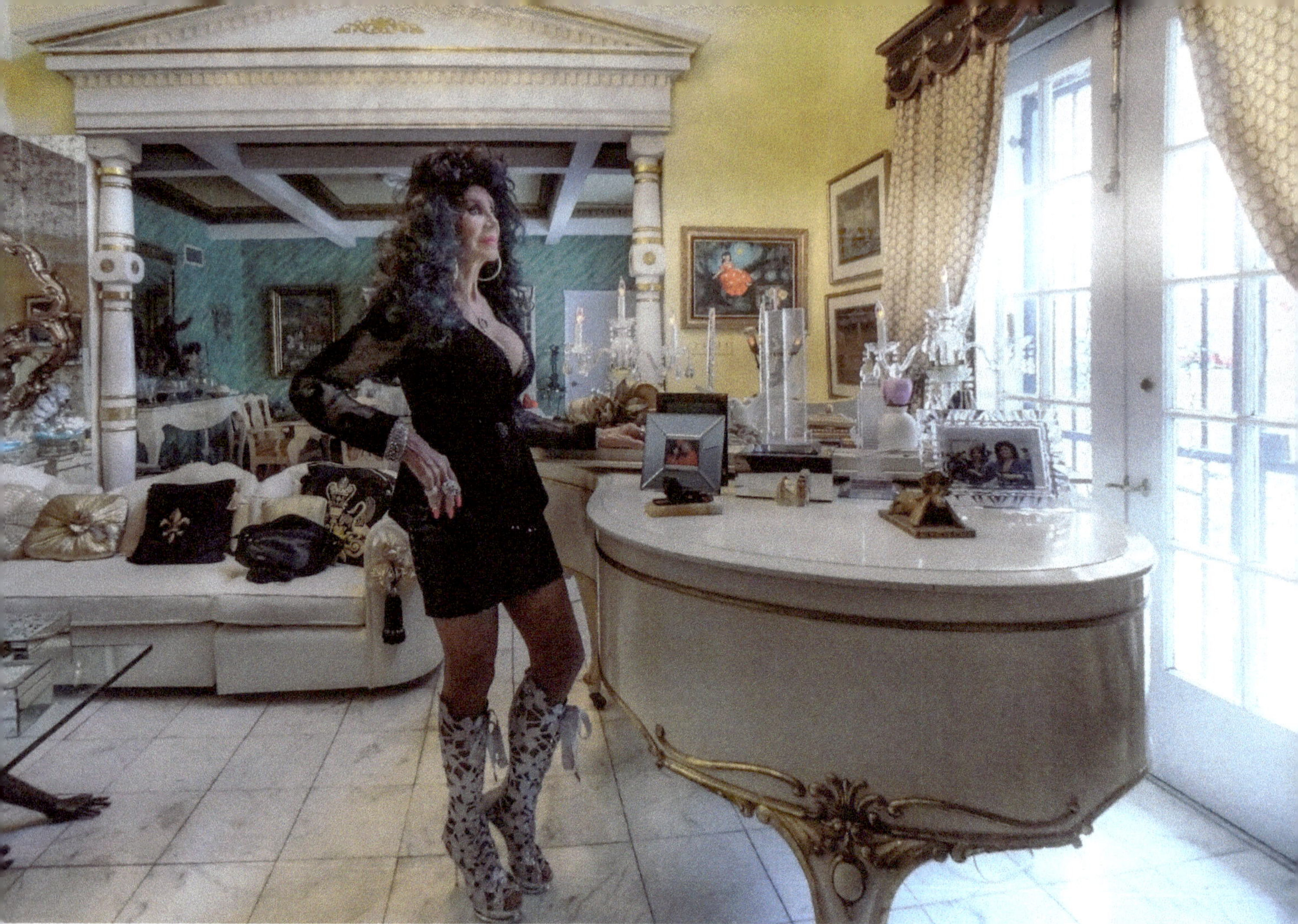

Chris Owens, Queen of Bourbon Street

A 1956 *Times-Picayune* columnist wrote, "Chris Owens is a regal, vivid and sensuous-looking brunette of undeniable beauty and grace... (with) a dynamic quality which, translated into the torrid Latin rhythms, suggests the throbbing power of a DC-6 warming up for the takeoff."

In 2006, Chris was inducted into the New Orleans Musical Legends Park with a statue created in her likeness positioned next to musical greats Fats Domino, Pete Fountain, and Al Hirt.

Today, her club is still one of the most famous landmarks on Bourbon Street and she continues to perform at age 85.

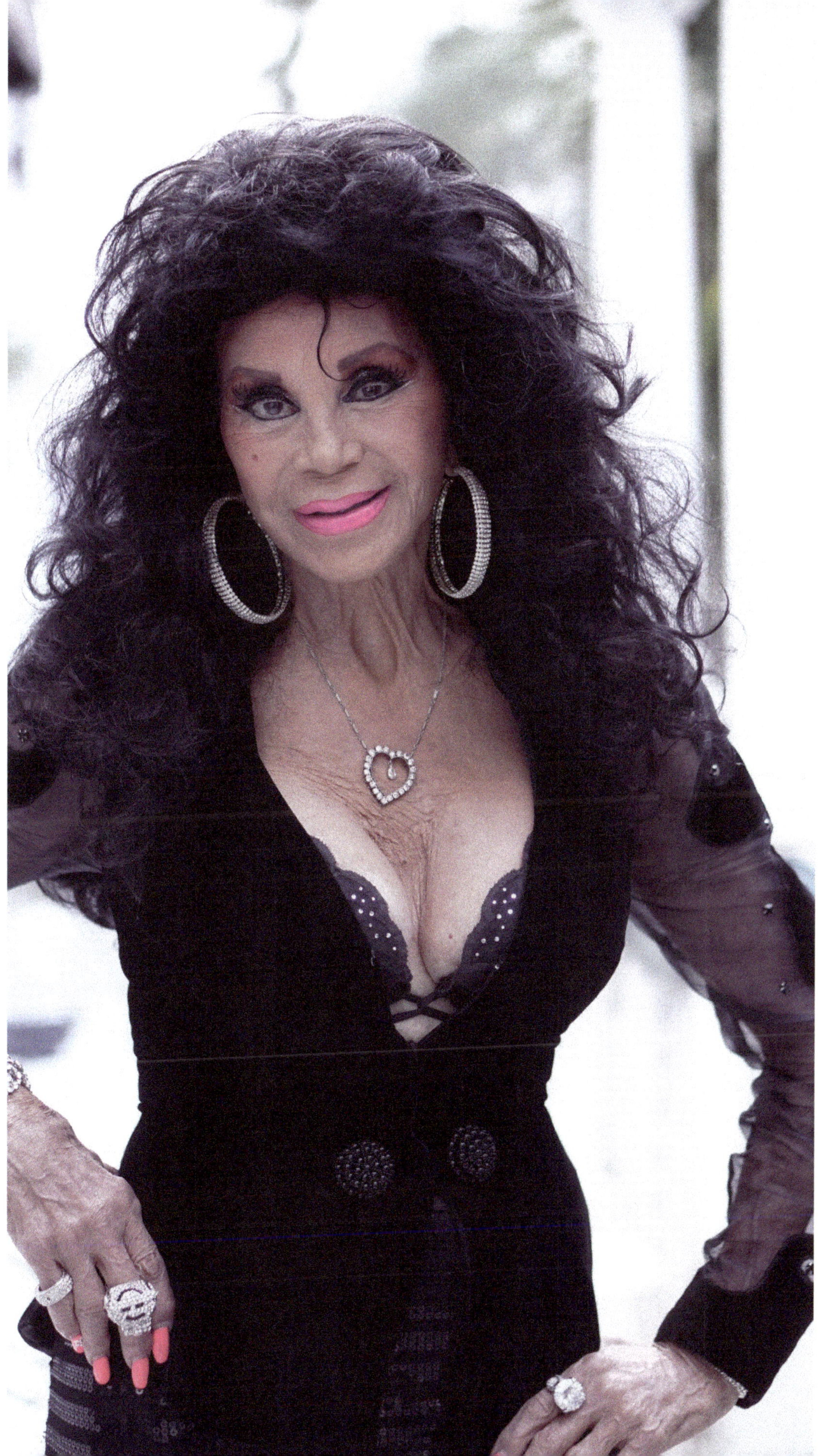

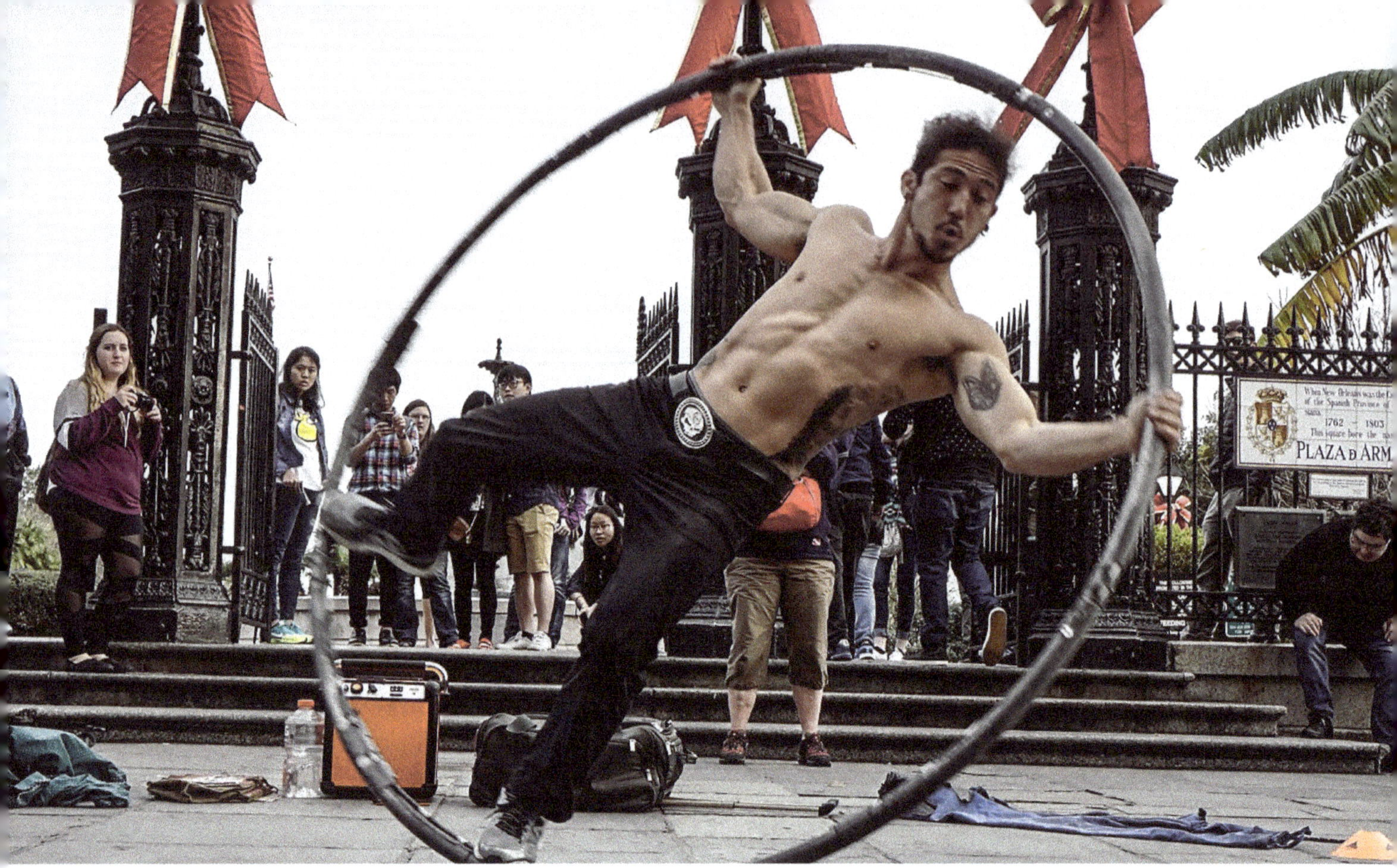

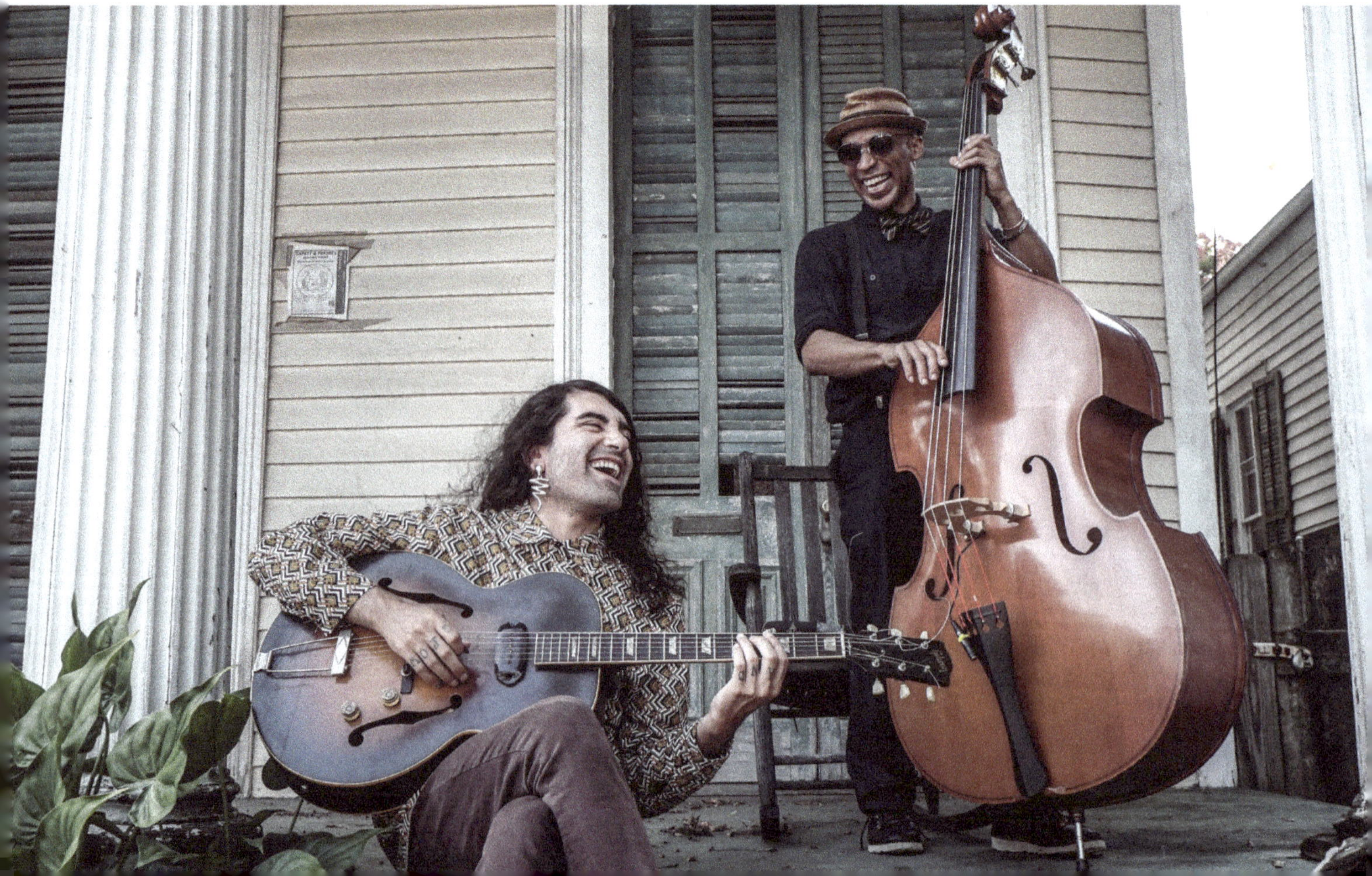

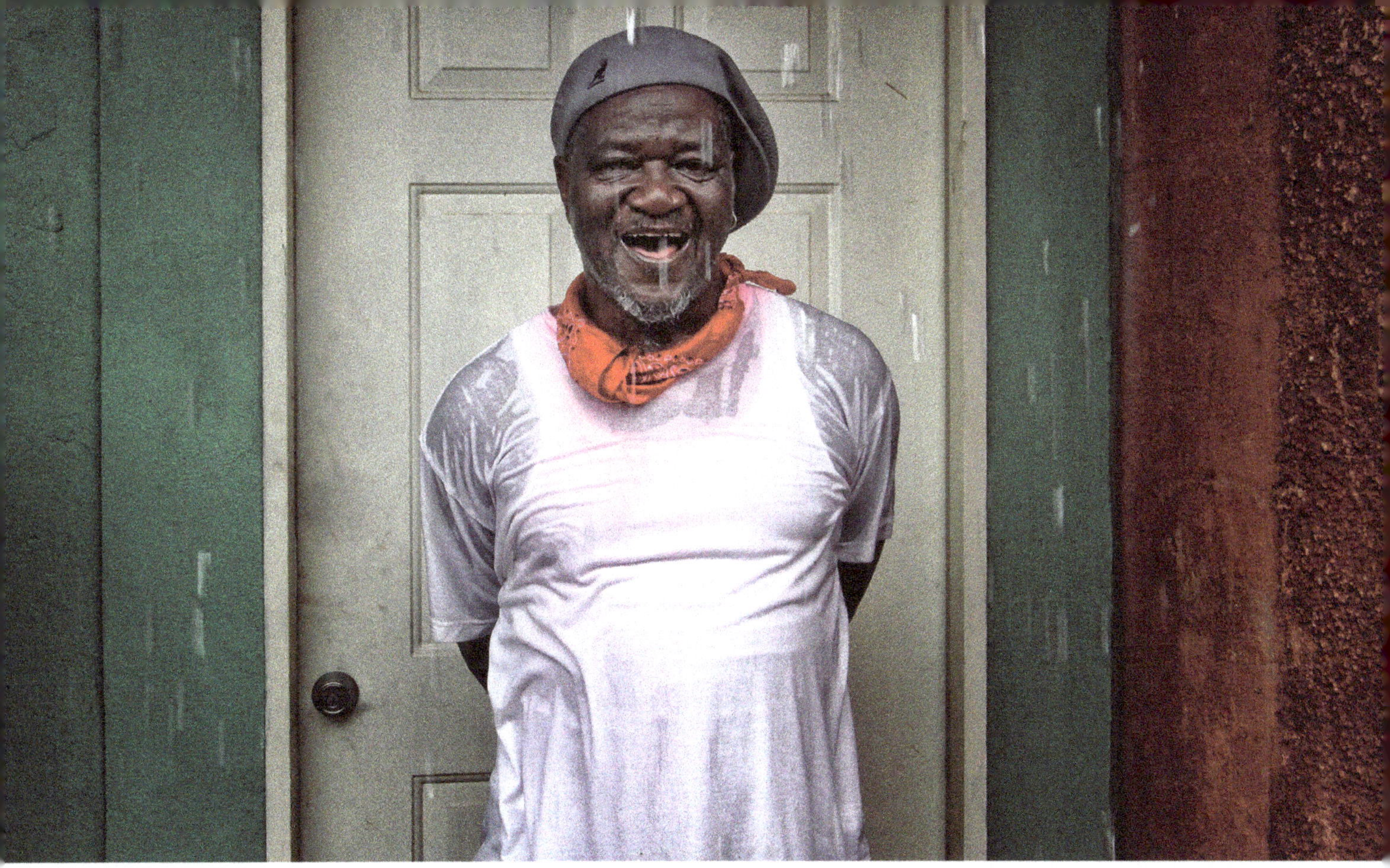

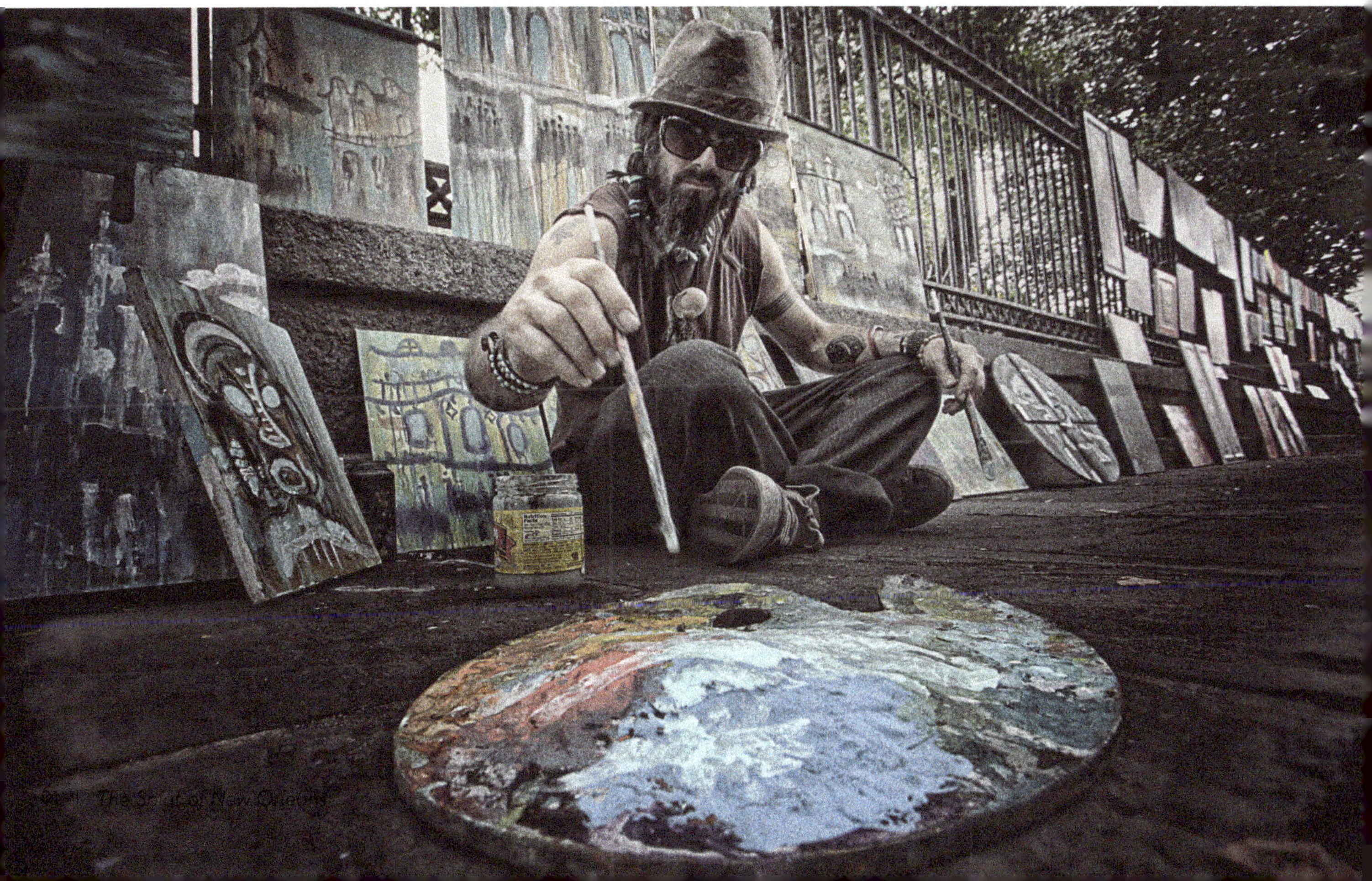

The Soul of New Orleans

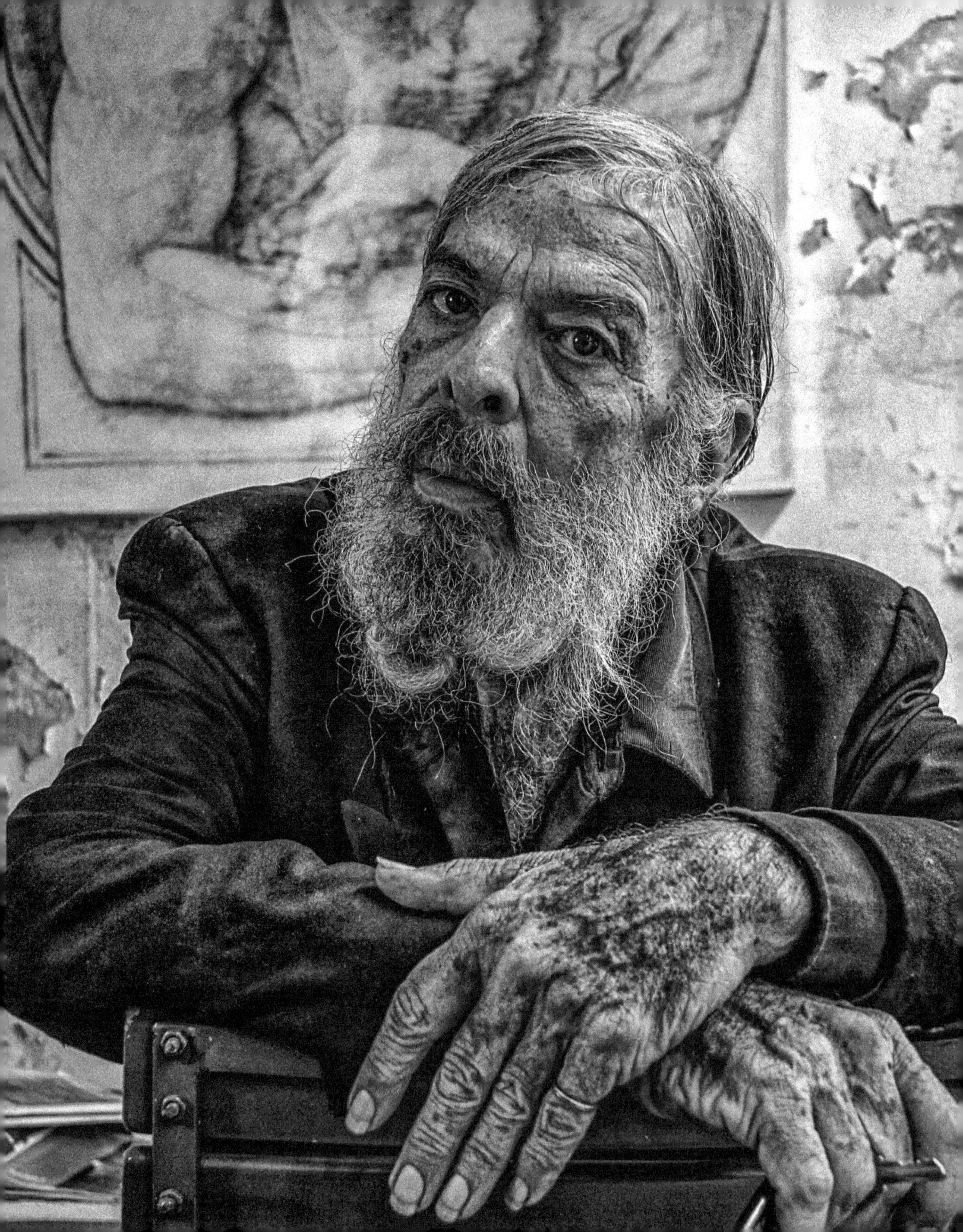

George Dureau

I walk with Amzie down Bourbon Street, past open bars, on a sidewalk that always smells like beer. George pulls up to the curb on a rusty bike, looking more like a homeless man than an eighty-one-year-old famous artist. Amzie greets him like an old friend, but George doesn't say much. He sits on his bike and then suddenly howls at the sky, clearly disturbed. I instinctively bring up my camera and steal a few snaps. George's eyes widen and he roars directly into my lens, shouting, "What do you want?!" Then he pedals off, weaving around tourists who aren't sure how to react.

Amzie tells me a bit about the man who is now in the ruthless throes of Alzheimer's. "Dureau grew up here. His art has been exhibited everywhere. He and Mapplethorpe used to be buddies in the seventies. Mapplethorpe totally ripped off George's style, even his compositions, and made them his own."

LATER, WHILE WALKING in the French Quarter, Amzie shows me George's studio on Bienville Street. With perfect timing, George wheels up again. He gestures for us to come in, all the while ranting. I glance around his dirty-white foyer and realize I probably have only a few minutes to make a portrait of George. The window light is ideal, grazing across an unfinished cracked wall, with paint peeling around one of George's charcoal canvas drawings. I pull up the only chair I can find, muttering to Amzie to keep talking to him. George straddles the chair, still holding onto his front door key. He sticks his tongue out at me, before launching into another tirade. "What do you want?! What do you want?!" he yells, all the while flicking his cap at my crotch. I open my camera bag and hand him the first draft of my photography book, *Bathtub Blues*. Suddenly, a calm comes over him as he carefully turns the pages. Looking up at me, his mind seems to clear. He announces, "Okay, I'm ready."

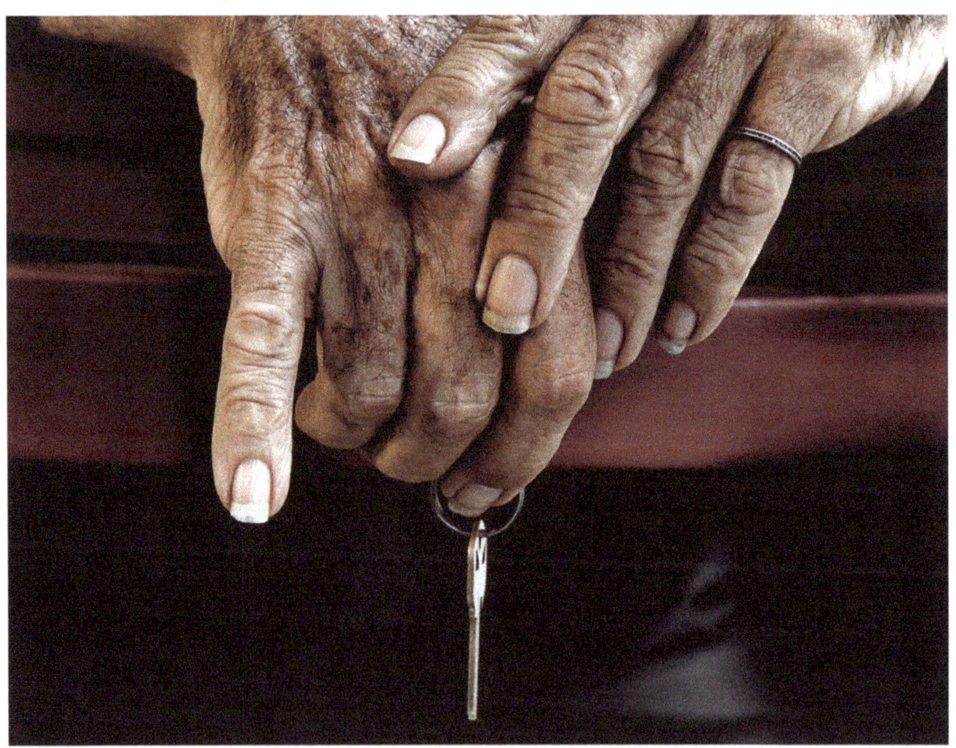

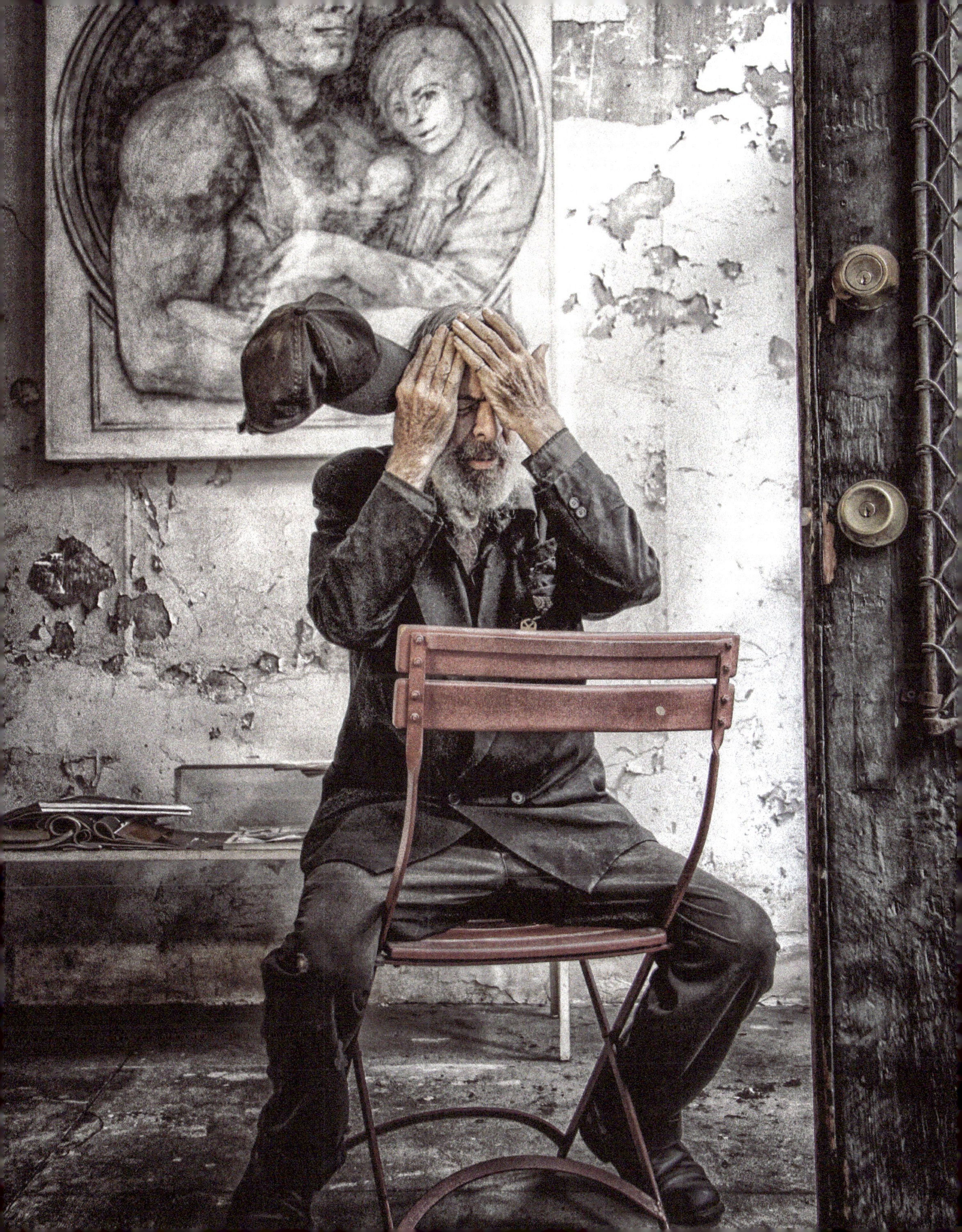

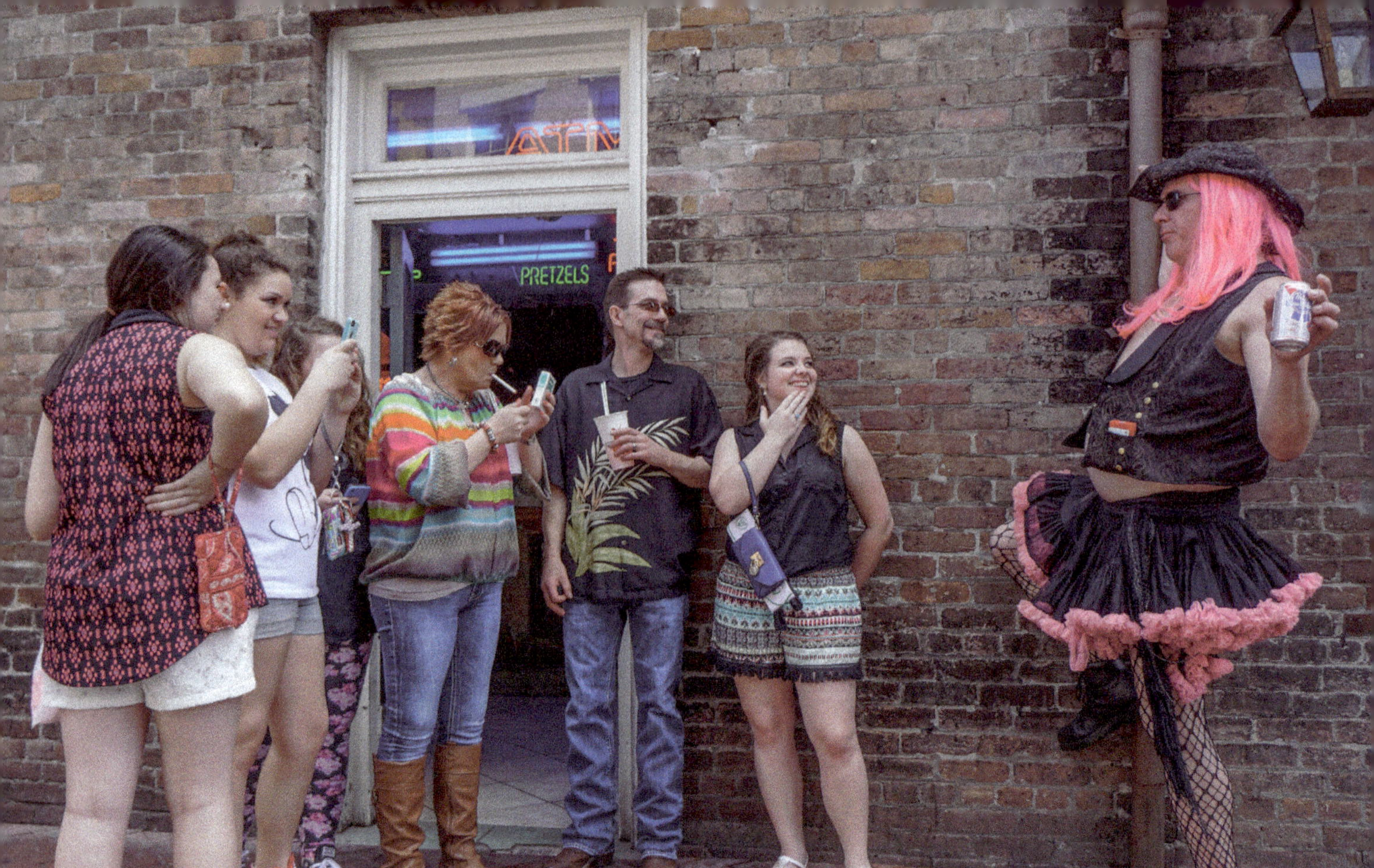

Jason Beckhouse, AKA, "Big Sexy"

"It was 2002. I was 22, living in Excelsior, Minnesota, working in a McDonalds, which I hated. One day, I threw my headset at the manager and walked out. I had $60 in my pocket, which I spent in a bar getting drunk. That night, the TV weatherman said it would be warm the next day. Good for travel, I thought. So I started hitching rides and two weeks later I arrived in New Orleans.

"People treat me like shit on a regular basis. They snap my photo and run, laughing. That hurts my feelings. I know that they just want to show their friends back home how freaky we are here. Besides posing for photos with tourists (hoping they tip and not run), I'm also a door-guy at a bar. But I don't like being called a bouncer because every time I throw some drunk out they don't bounce, they skid."

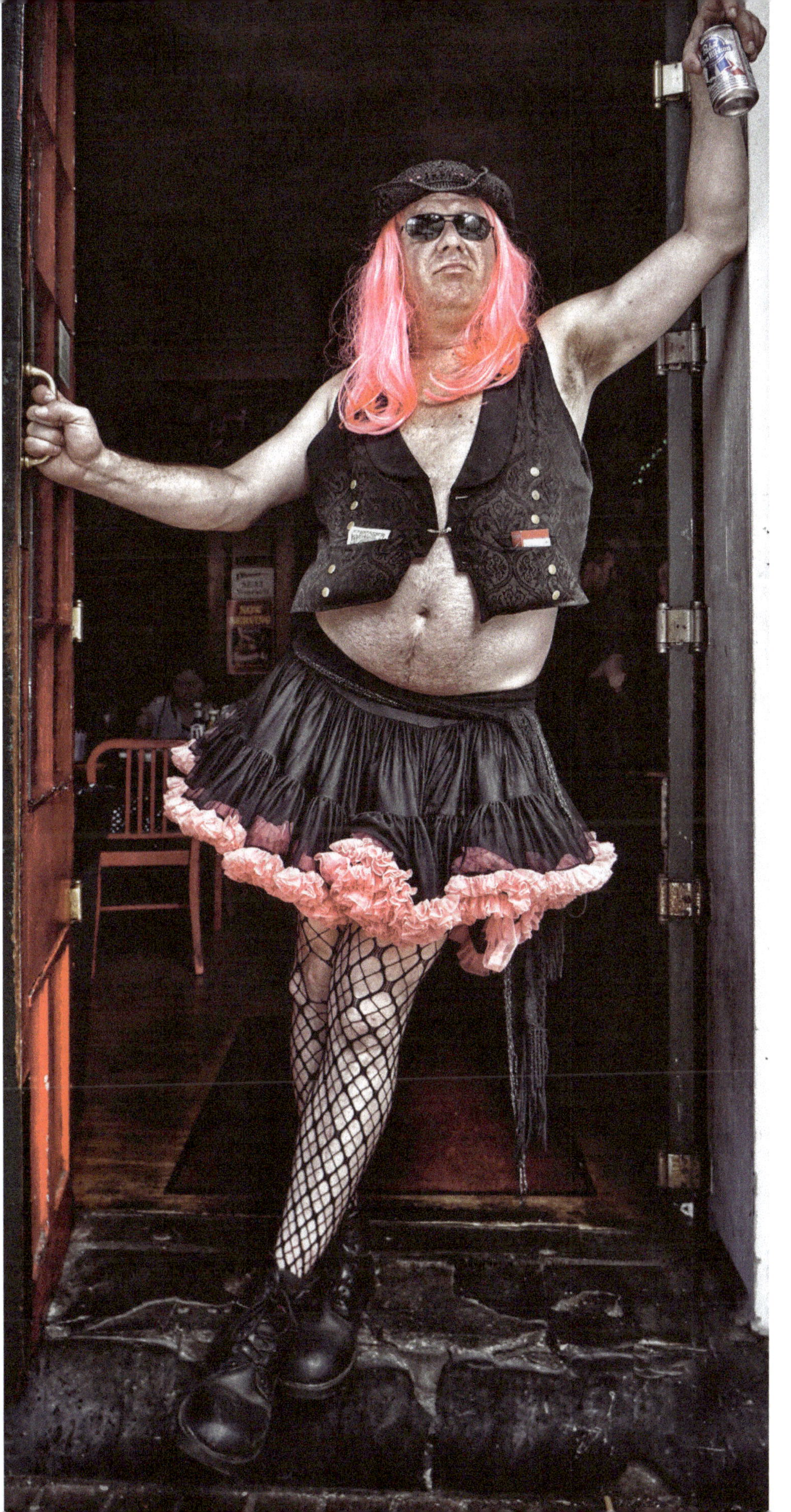

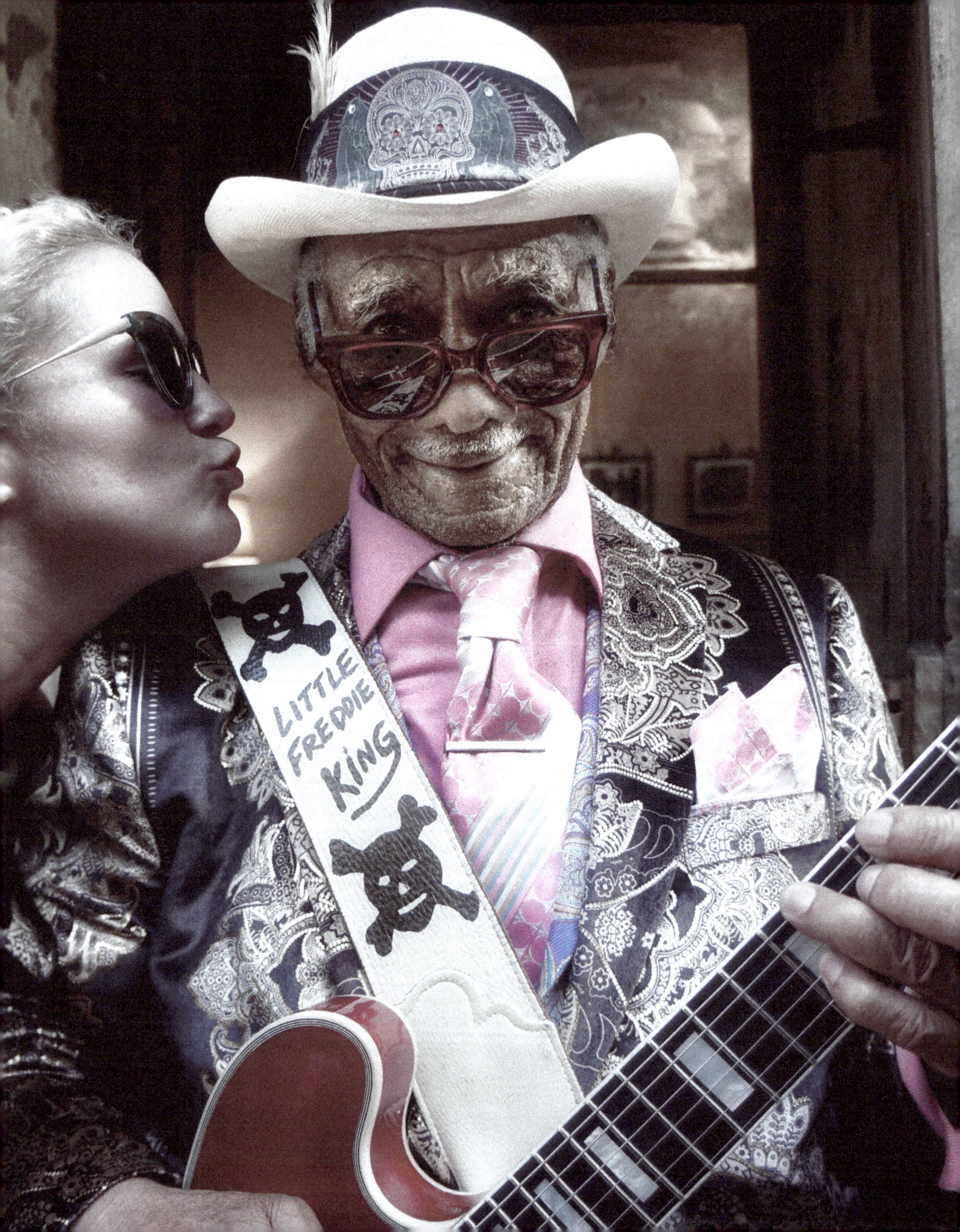

LITTLE
FREDDIE
KING

Little Freddie King

I'm in the middle of the 9th Ward, looking for a house that was partially submerged during Hurricane Katrina. Amzie Adams is driving. His funky car feels as though it was dragged out of the flood. It's alternator is fried. Last night we had to drive with flickering headlights that were no brighter than dim cell phones. I'm not complaining. If it weren't for Amzie, I'd be isolated in some white-bread hotel, off the French Quarter, disconnected from the very soul of New Orleans.

Bluesman, Little Freddie King, unlocks his screen door and invites us into his tiny living room. The walls are covered with photos, paintings and posters celebrating Freddie's decades as a music icon. I'm there to photograph him for my book, The Spirit of New Orleans. I feel as though I'm in the presence of royalty and sit cross-legged on the floor. Freddie plugs his guitar into a little amp and starts to jam, sitting on the edge of his couch. Amzie plugs in too, his electric dulcimer across his lap. I feel as though I might need a seatbelt as Little Freddie's Gut-Bucket, down-and-dirty blues pin-balls around the room. By the time Freddie starts to sing in his gritty, lived-in voice, I have goosebumps.

At 74 years old there's a soft warmth and humility about this man. Freddie's strut may have slowed a bit, but his soul still brims with a Mississippi talent that grew from seeds planted when he was a kid, sitting on the front steps of juke joints, listening to his daddy play the blues inside—singing tales of woe and mischief.

He made this first guitar-like instrument from a cigar box. Freddie took wood from his family's picket fence for a guitar neck and tuning pegs and used wire to make frets. He didn't have any black paint so he mixed his own creation from fireplace soot and pine resin. He didn't

have any strings either, but then Freddie noticed the swooshing
sound made by his daddy's horse's tail. Snip, snip. He had strings.
When he was 14, King hopped a train and rode the rails to New
Orleans. After a job at a gas station he was able to buy his first real
guitar, an acoustic Silvertone from Sears, Roebuck and Co.

Years later he played on stages along side John Lee Hooker and Bo
Diddly and toured the world.

It's dark and Amzie's car dies quietly a block from his pad. Little
Freddie is kind enough to leave us a pass at the front door of The
DBA club on Frenchman Street. The place is packed. It takes some
careful maneuvering for me to get to the foot of the stage. Little
Freddie, wearing a red vest, as electric as the songs he plays, is rock'n
the house. His white brimmed hat shades his trademark sun glasses.
The drummer, "Wacko" Wade, drives the beat. Also on stage, Robert
Louis DiTullio, Jr. blow'n hard, hands flap around his harmonica—
tethered to an electric-orange amp cord. He leans into Freddie,
keeping a close eye on King's left hand as it glides over the frets.

>   *I don't want you to be no slave / I don't want you to work all day*
>   *I don't want your money, too / I just want to make love to you.*

Photographing bands on stage is always a challenge—the constantly
changing colored lights, keeping the focus sharp, anticipating a classic
stage gyration—praying that it will all come together in my camera
the same way my mind is seeing it, with the same feeling that my ears
are hearing it. At times I'm so close to one of the stage amps that my
camera vibrates to the bass. I wonder what damage is occurring to my

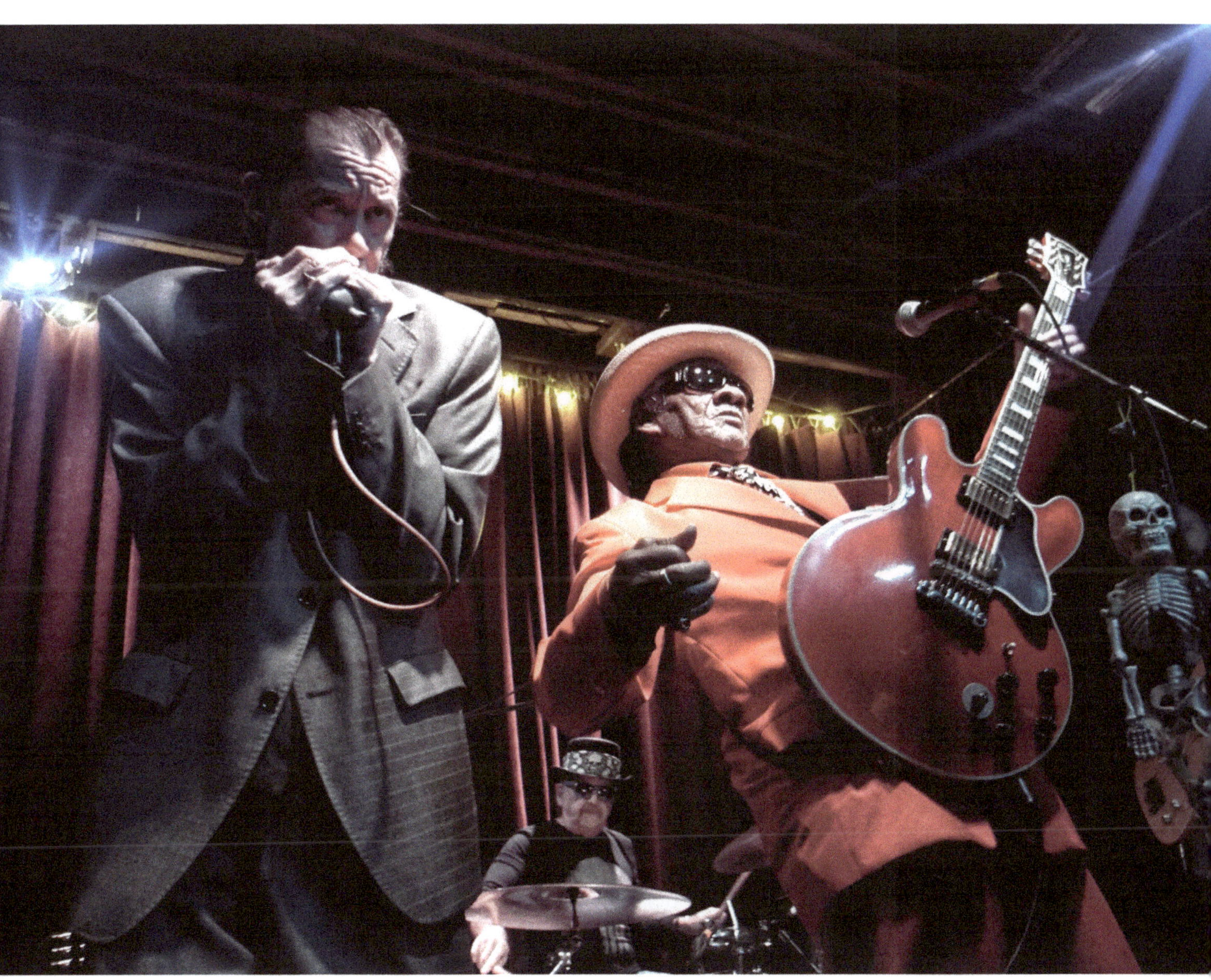

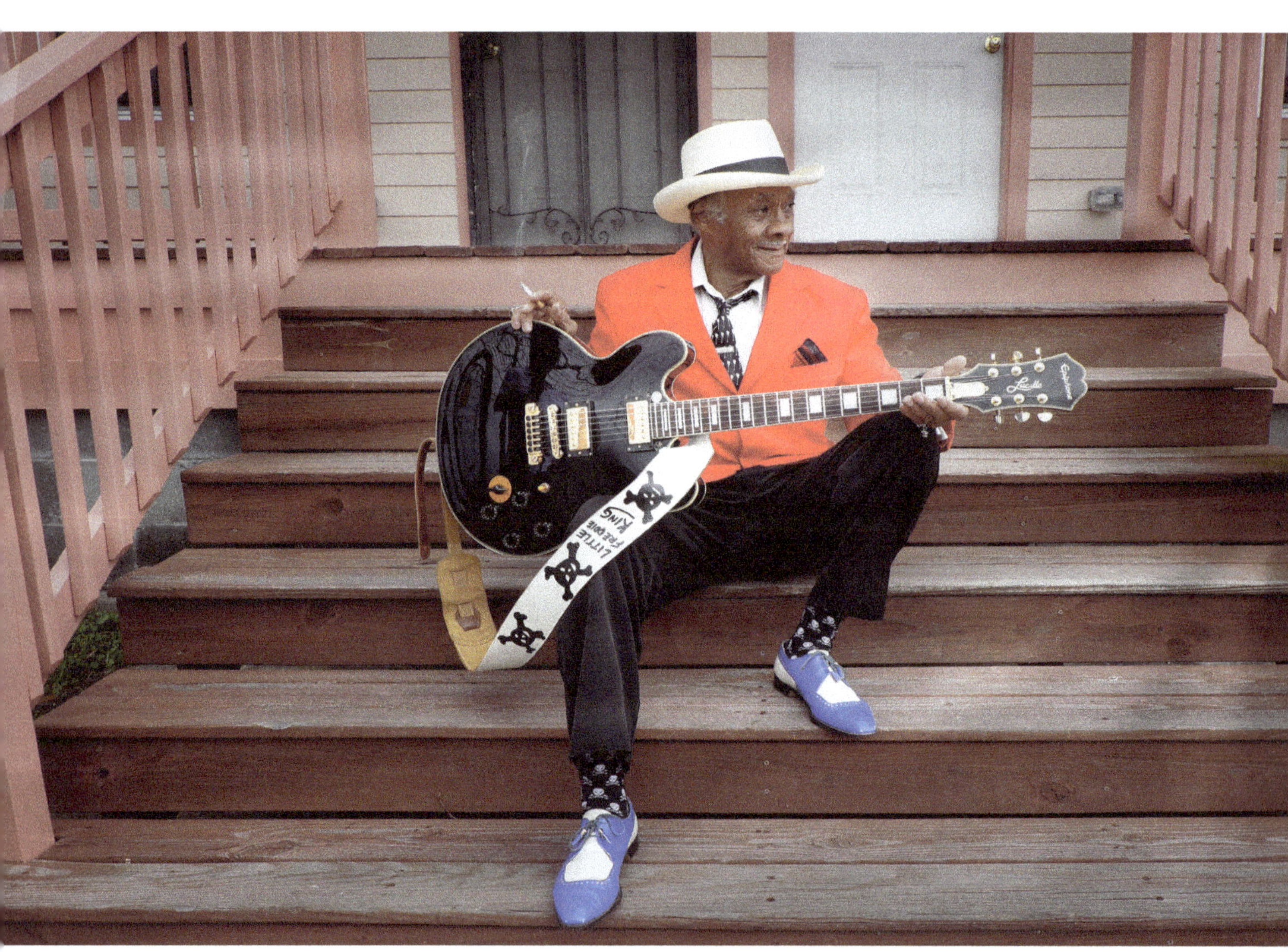

LITTLE
FREDDIE
KING

ear drums. I'm concerned about getting in too close to Freddie—being too obtrusive—and at the same time I turn around to apologize to the much smaller woman I'm standing in front of. My brain is fast-forwarding to a time later that night, when I will be at my computer editing the work, probably wishing that I'd shot more and moved in even closer, elbowing the barriers of politeness a bit further to get better shots.

I lean in and press the shutter release—hold it down—hoping to capture its own crisp tone.

Little Freddie plays deep into the night. I finally relax the grip on my camera and lower it to my side. The music is powerful. I need to let it all in and accept that I have shot enough. I realize that my payoff is beyond a few good photographs. I want to enjoy this icon who rules the stage and crowd with a heartbeat-passion - his universal language—that cannot be taught in any classroom. The adoring crowd is clapping, hollering, dancing—always wanting more. I stand still, in awe, watching the joy Freddie brings to so many, knowing that Little Freddie, is Da King.

Crime in New Orleans

The first time I visited the French Quarter, a local resident warned me against walking on the sidewalk after the sun went down. "The bad guys hide between parked cars," she said, "so, walk down the center of the street."

Crime is a problem that never goes away here. In 1994, the city was officially named the "Murder Capital of America," with 424 homicides that year. In 2017, New Orleans had the highest rate of gun violence in the U.S., surpassing even Chicago and Detroit. No wonder that barely half of respondents recently reported they felt safe walking home alone at night.

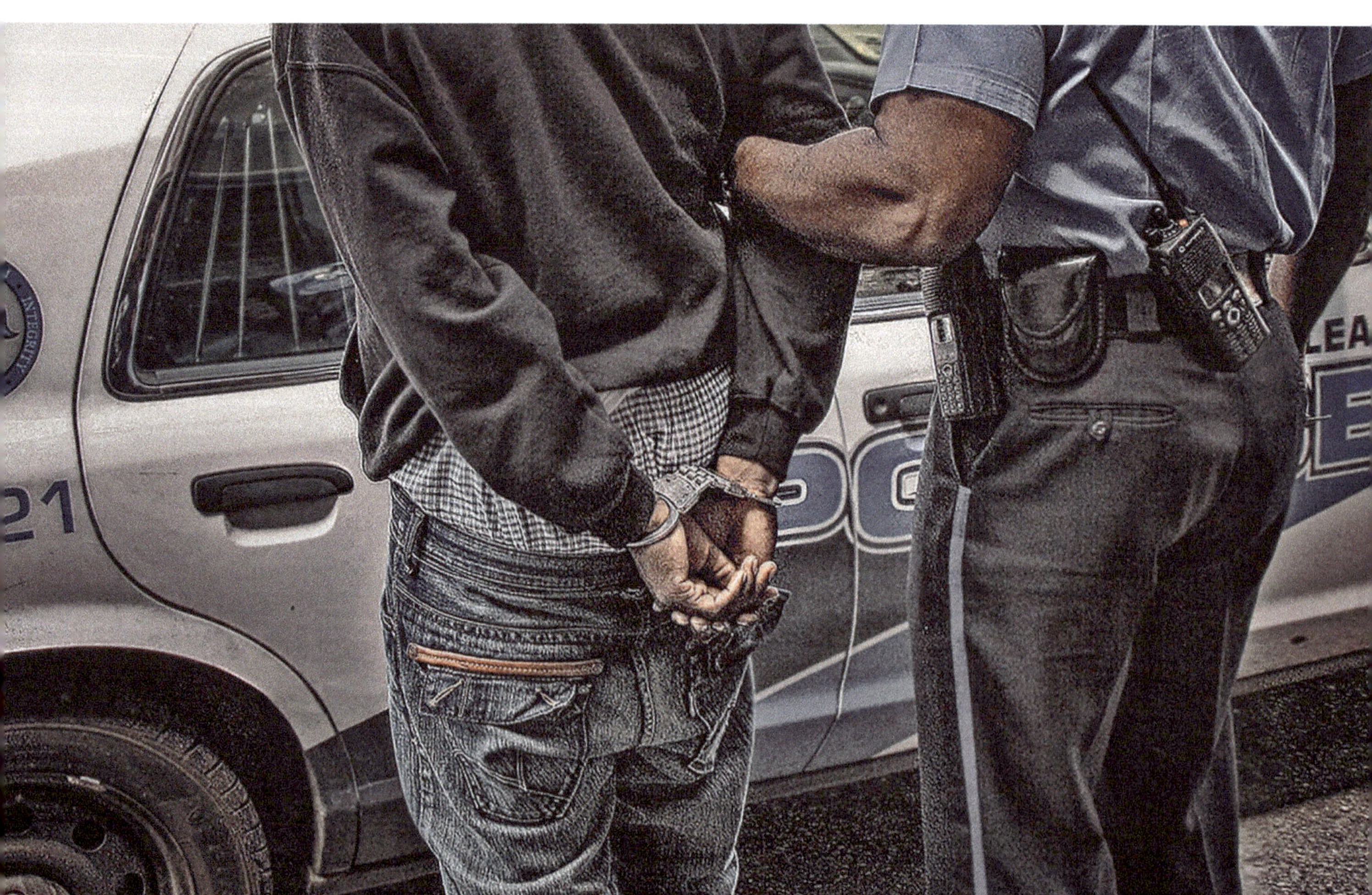

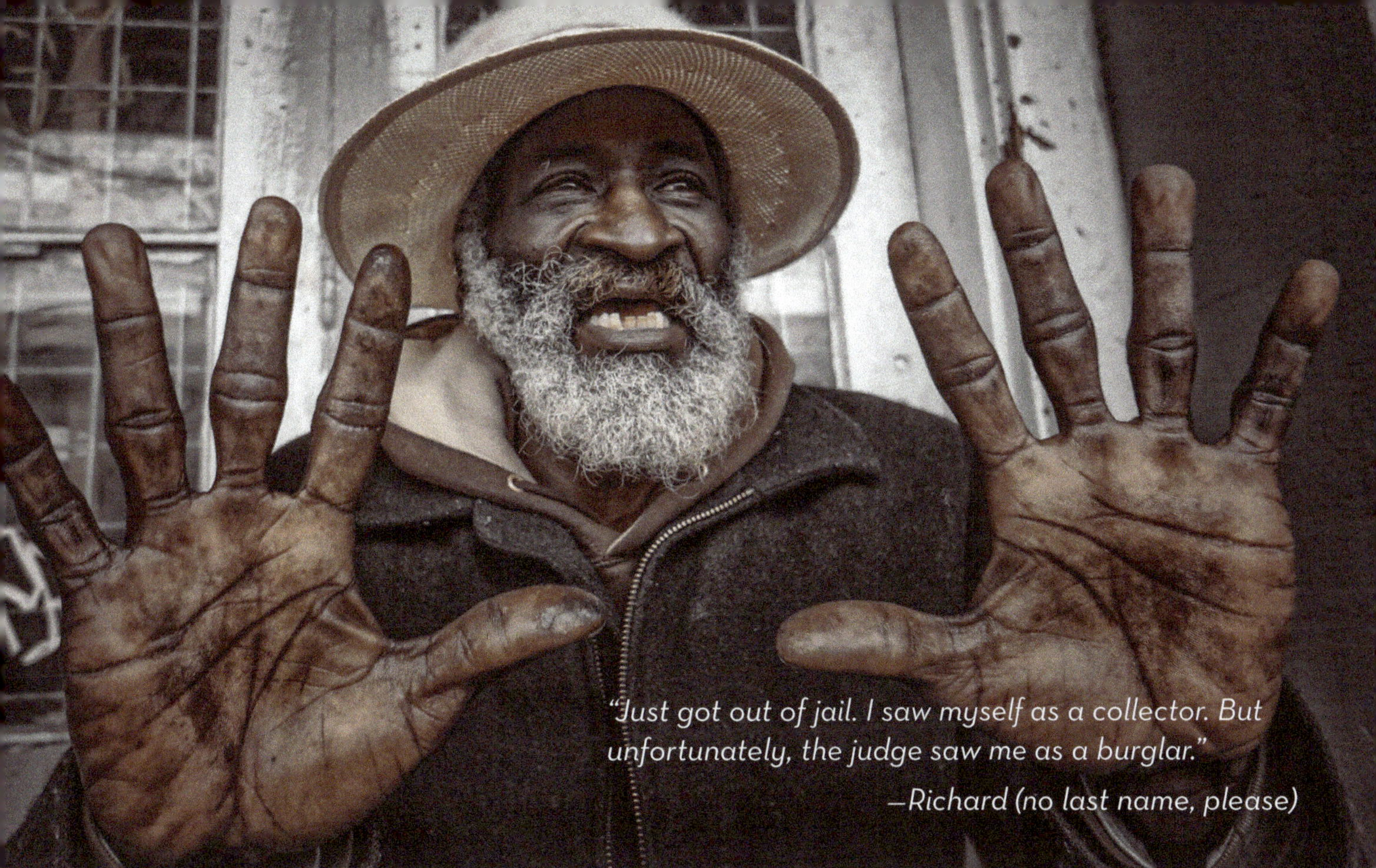

Local entrepreneur Sidney Torres decided to help. When he'd been frustrated with ineffective cleanup efforts after Katrina, he'd created his own fleet of garbage trucks. After his home was burglarized, he developed the French Quarter Task Force, with several armed officers zigzagging the neighborhood at all hours in militarized golf carts, blue lights flashing. City police might take forever to respond to a 911 call—which residents deem a lost cause—but Torres's team is always present and reachable via the free crime watch app he created that enables anonymous reporting.

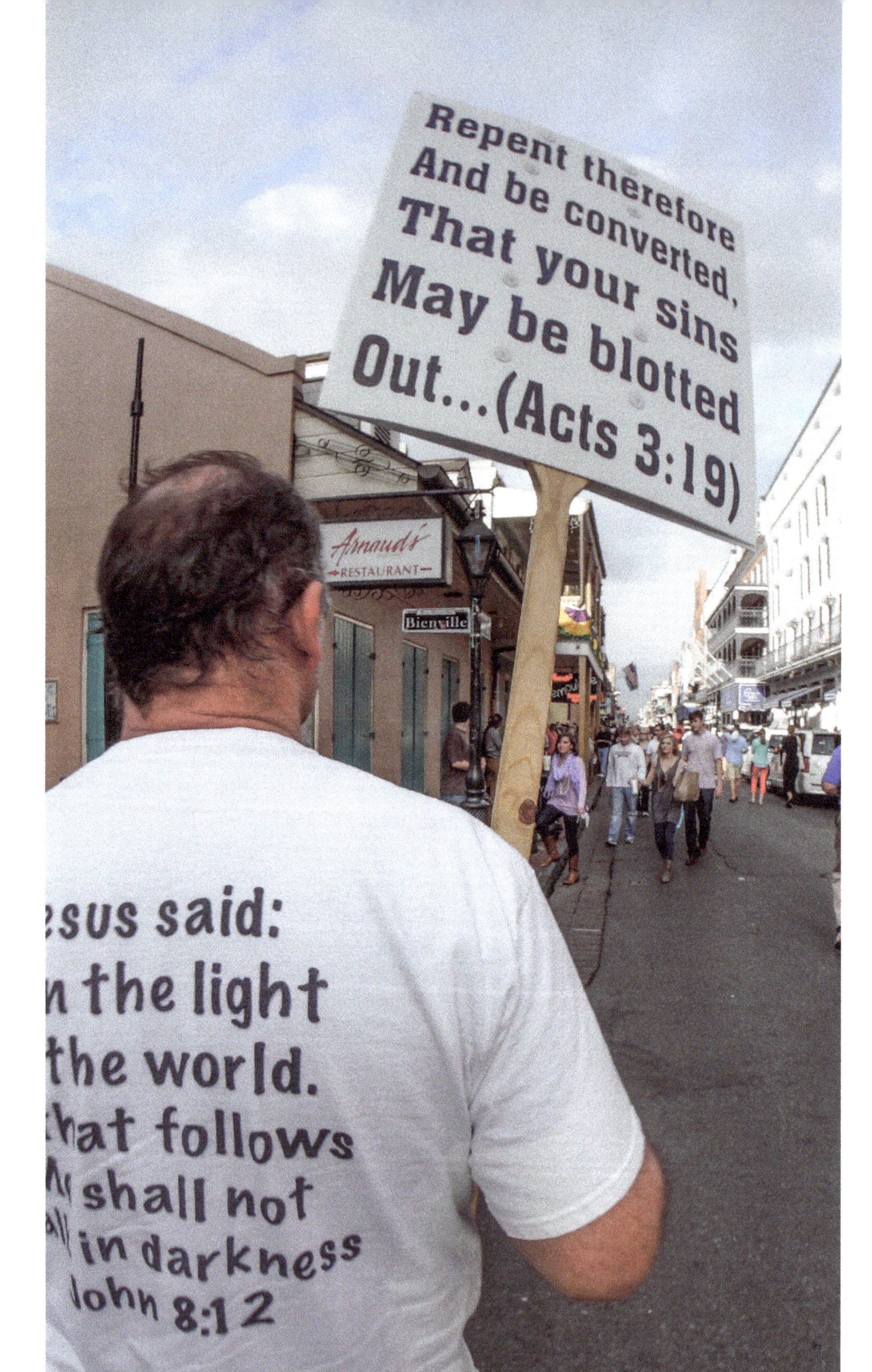

Repent therefore
And be converted,
That your sins
May be blotted
Out...(Acts 3:19)

Arnaud's
RESTAURANT

Bienville

esus said:
n the light
the world.
hat follows
shall not
in darkness
John 8:1 2

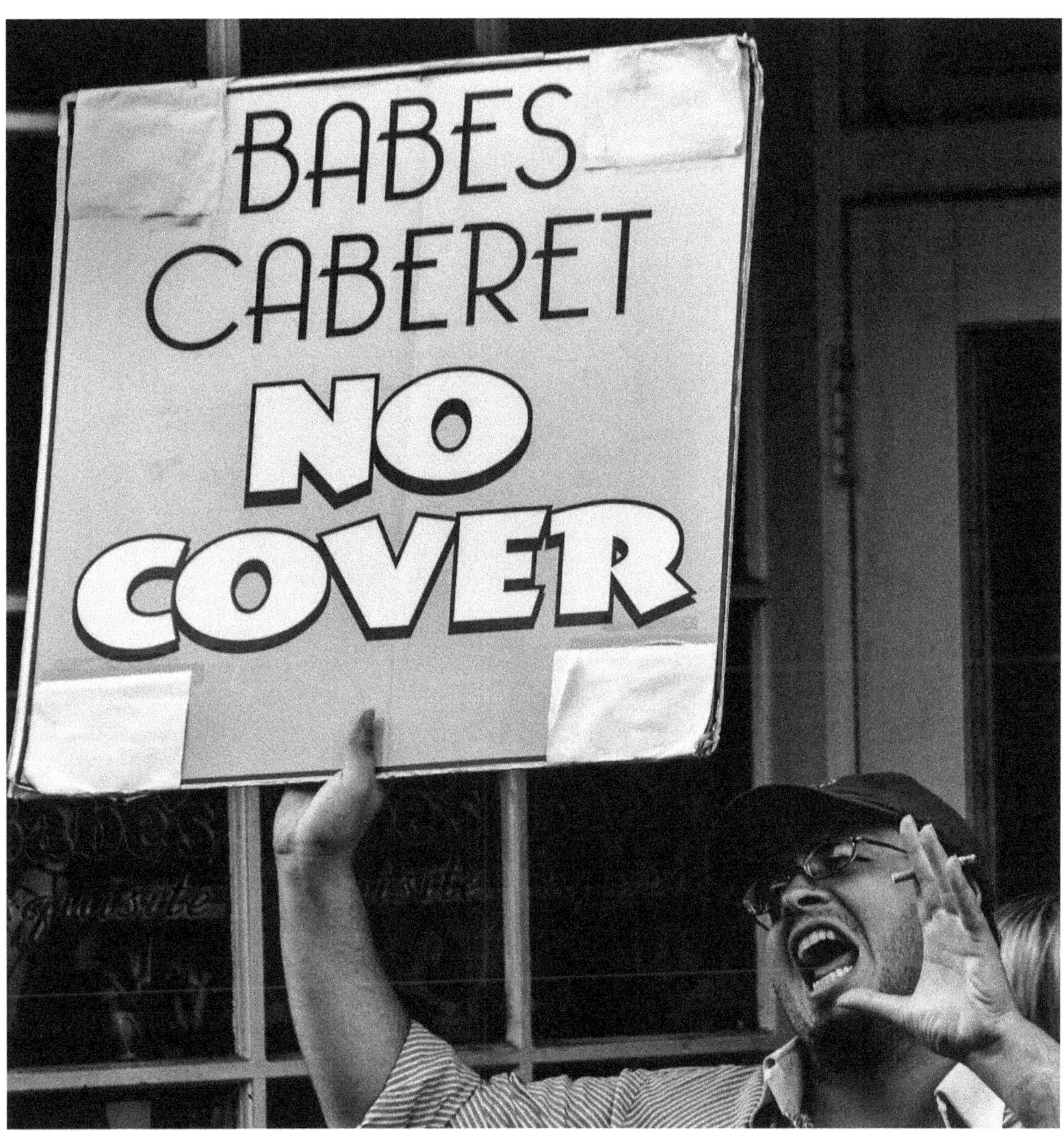

BABES
CABERET
NO
COVER

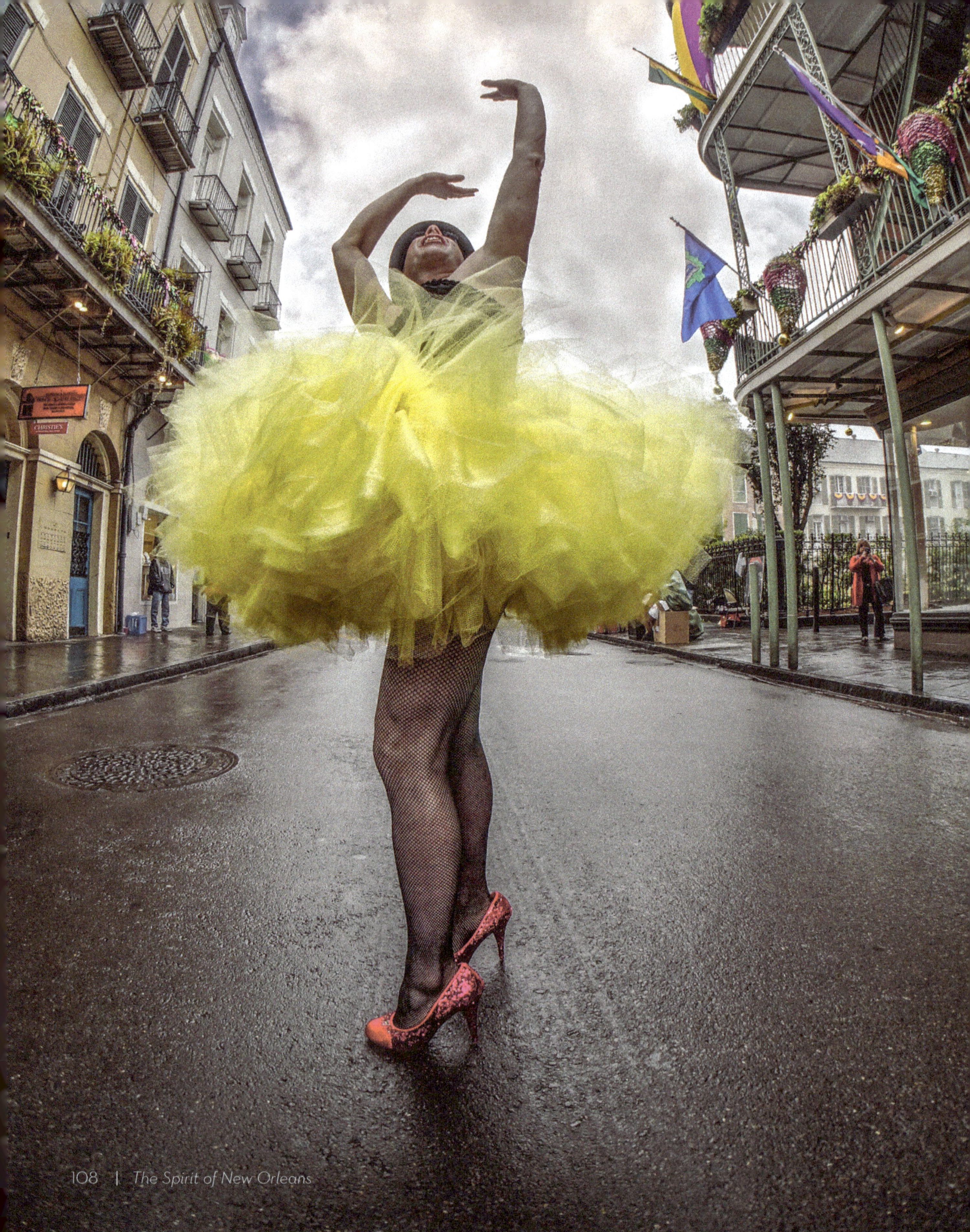

Curtis Quate, aka, Tutu Lulu

"The moment I was pushed out of my mama, I felt out of place and alone. It wasn't until I first visited New Orleans as a 13-year-old kid from the Indiana cornfields that I felt like I belonged, instead of being a cast-out.

"I remember the foggy morning when I first spotted Ruthie, aka The Duck Lady, crossing Royal Street on roller-skates, wearing a wedding gown. Her ducks were following behind, waddling all the way down to the river for a swim. I instantly knew that I wanted to be just like her. She was always her authentic self and never let anything bother her. She had a joyous life without worrying about tomorrow or next week.

"With her inspiration, the idea of Lulu was born. At first, I dressed as Lulu to deliver sandwiches on my bike. Over time, Lulu evolved to a beer wench in a doorway and then into a classy lady.

"I love to dance, but certain heels work and others don't. I hand sew my performance costumes. Now, I can offend a Democrat as well as a Republican, but I prefer to see them all smile and hear them all laugh. Ruthie love Lulu; I wish she was still alive.

"When my Mama was on her deathbed, I asked her for two things: send me a nice guy and, if it's at all possible, let me be the actress I always wanted to be. Thanks Mama, I made it."

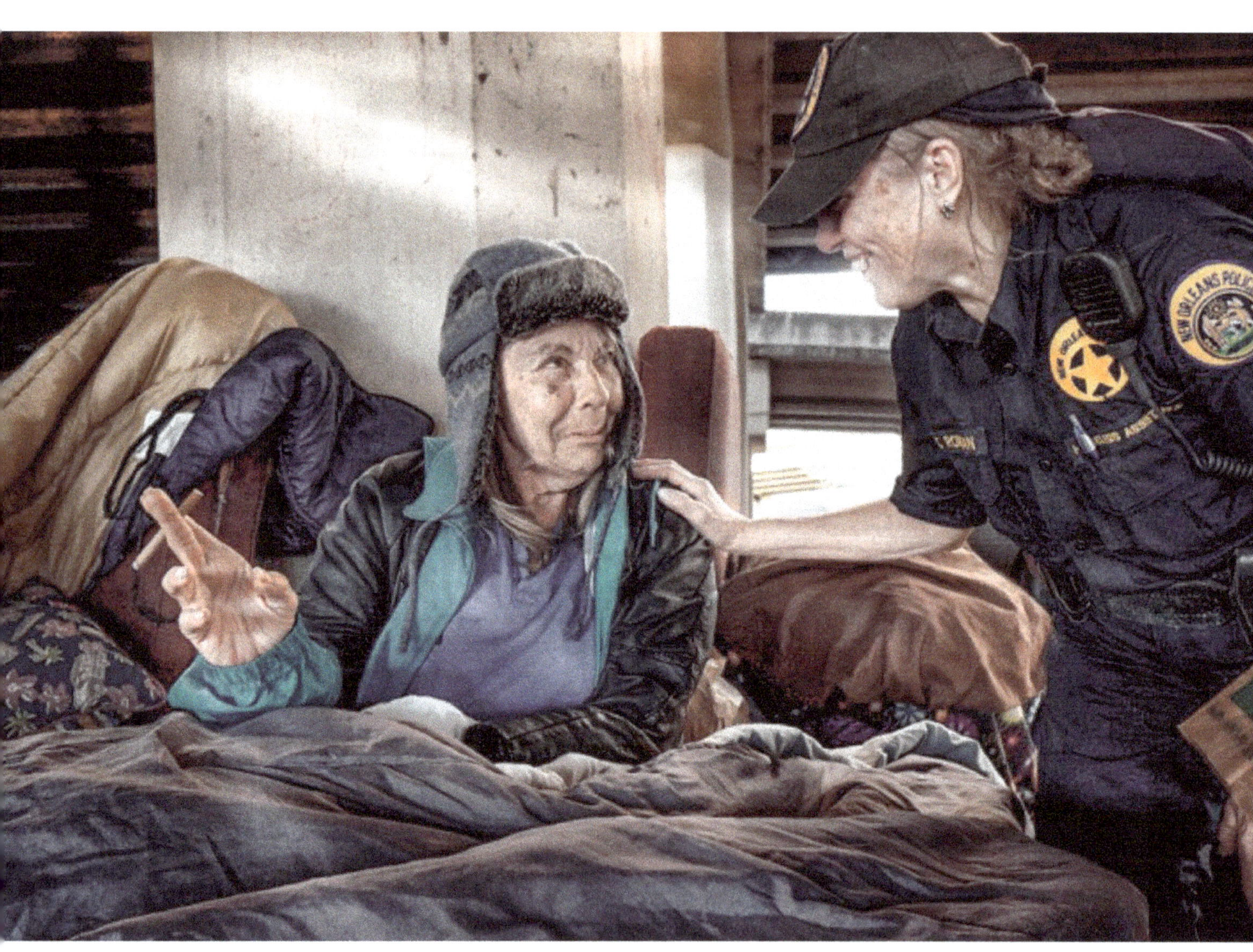

BB St. Roman

II found divine inspiration under a freeway overpass in New Orleans. It wasn't a holy setting, but these things never are. Police tech B B St. Roman is doing her thing, mingling with a group of homeless folk, laid out across the asphalt in their sleeping bags, eating cold macaroni.

B B, an eleven year police veteran, is rarely behind her desk on the second floor of the historic 1826 Bank of Louisiana building. She prefers to be out here, working with the +- 1,500 homeless people making do with what little options they have. She looks confident in her blue uniform. Many might miss the nearly 3 feet of dreads neatly tucked into a net behind her police cap. But they won't overlook her rock-solid black combat boots. "I feel very protected with my uniform on," B B proudly tells me. She does not carry a gun. "My smile is my weapon," she says.

In fact, B B once knew Mother Teresa. Before becoming the Homeless Assistance Director for New Orleans Police Department, B B worked with documentary film crews as a sound recordist, lugging around a shotgun mic through 30 countries. In 1983, she was in Beirut, working on a documentary about Mother Teresa. When the bombs started to drop, B B and her film crew had to be evacuated by helicopter.

She met the Dalai Lama, too.

LATER, B B WAS DR. JOHN'S road manager. When she introduced me to the six-time Grammy award winner, he pointed to the heavens and told me, "B B was sent to me from up there."

"I was Dr. John's road manager 24/7 for 10 years—organizing band members, music charts, stage gear, hotels, transportation—I put it all together," B B says. "I love organizing and being efficient. Dr. John showed me a lot of respect, letting me do the job in my own way."

On her infrequent days off, BB likes to ride her flat black Honda Shadow motorcycle. With only a turquoise bandana to cover her head, her dreads fall past her belt. Most weekday mornings, back in uniform, B B pedals her bicycle to work through the quaint streets of the French Quarter. Many times she is surprised to see someone chasing her. "Wait! B B, wait!" Instead of pedaling faster, B B puts her boot to the curb as a homeless man, out-of-breath, runs up to her. "I just want you to know how much I love you, Miss B B !" With tears in his eyes, he goes on, "You are in my heart."

This kind of scene, in which B B plays a central role, repeats itself almost daily with different characters, all with their own stories, all of them unique, yet many the same.

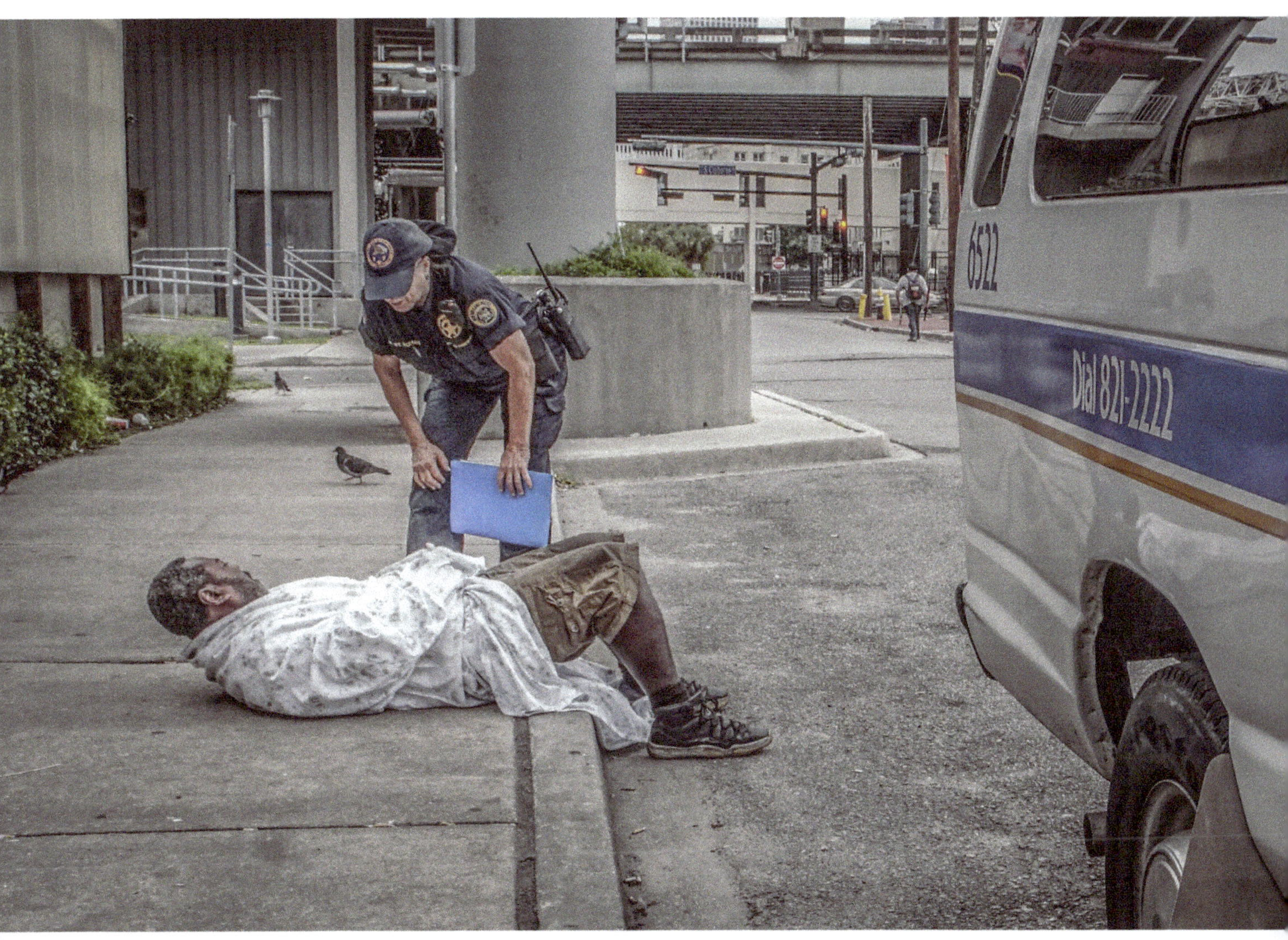

6522
Dial 821-2222

B B explains with compassion, "These people are disconnected. That's why they're homeless. They are stuck. Some are smart and some are not so smart. There is so much loneliness and depression. They feel invisible. The public looks the other way."

To quote Mother Teresa, "One of the greatest diseases is to be nobody to somebody."

B B's strategy for offering help can sometimes be surprisingly simple: "Plenty of times they need nothing more complicated than help getting a state I.D. Without that, they can't stay in a shelter, get a post office box, cash a check or have any hope of getting a job. Any program, any service they need, requires a state I.D. That's a big part of my job. I am constantly working to get them the services they need."

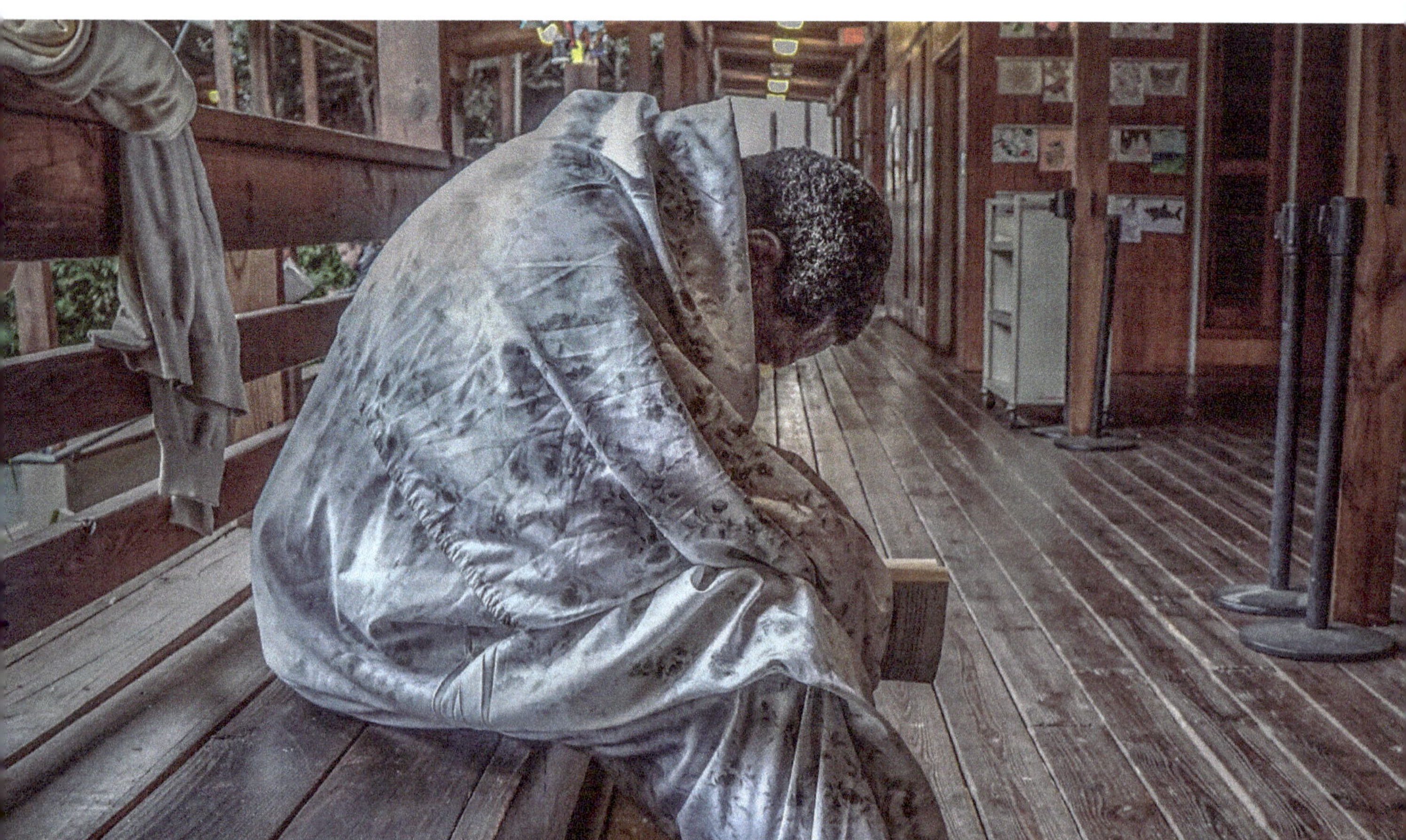

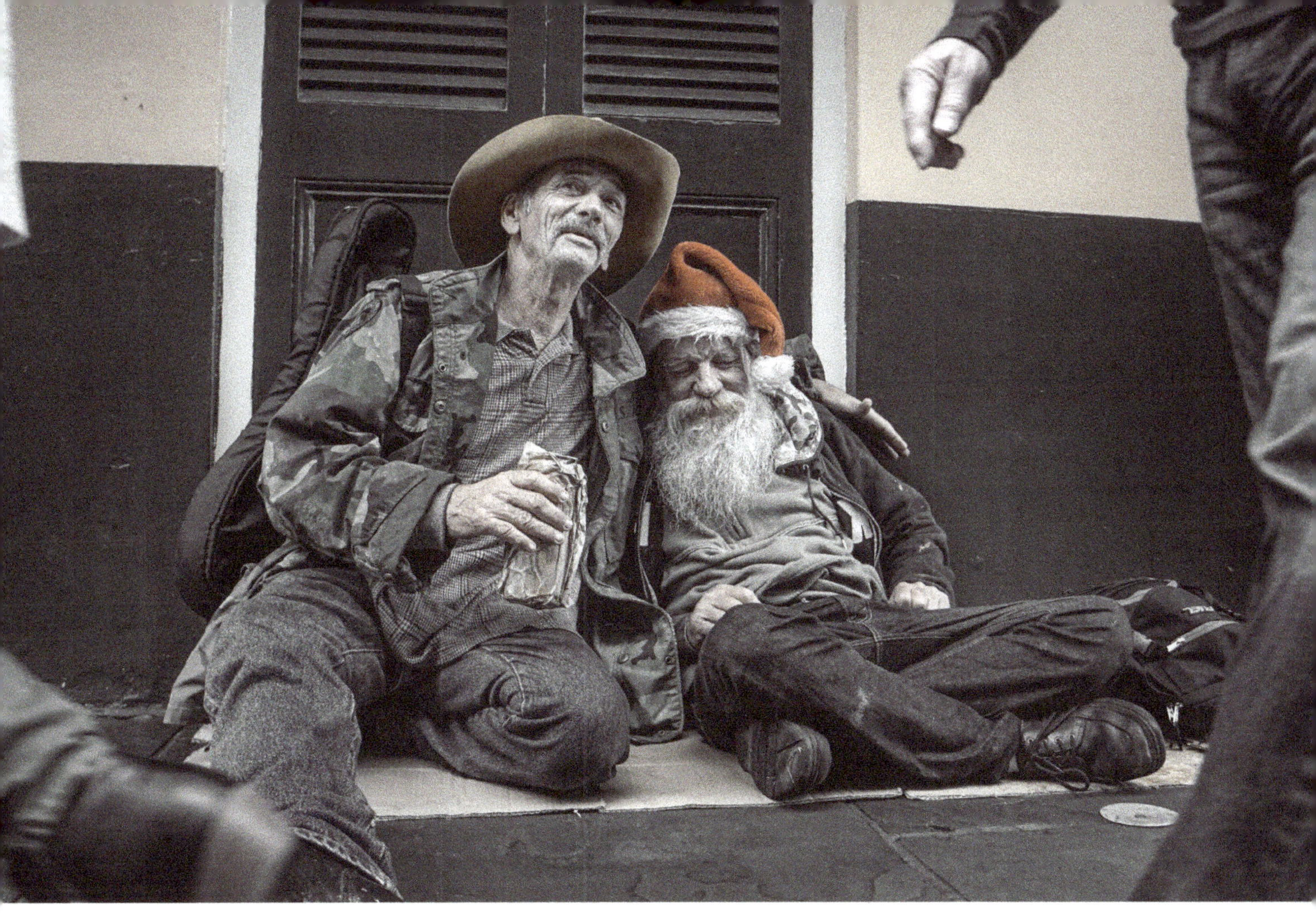

*"One of the greatest diseases is
to be nobody to somebody."
—Mother Teresa*

THERE ARE NO FUNDS AVAILABLE to pay B B for the umpteen extra hours she works. Most of her time—including many nights unto 2 a.m—is spent working for the homeless. To B B, there is no "overtime." Her work is her passion, her life. Her real paycheck arrives with every hug and every tear of gratitude. That is what drives B B.

New Orleans continues to have one of the highest murder rates in the country. In 2013, 155 people were killed in the city. I asked B B what was the worst thing that has happened to her during the 10 years she's worked for the police department. I expected to hear the kind of scary stories I'd already heard from friends in town. She looked away and thought before responding. "The worst times? Those are the times in my police van when I've got a homeless person sitting in the back seat who needs my help and there is no service available for what they need. I have to put them back on the street."

B B looks into my eyes and smiles. "But most of the time, I find some way to help. Miracles show up every day in my job."

Not all heroes wear capes. This one wears a mean pair of black combat boots.

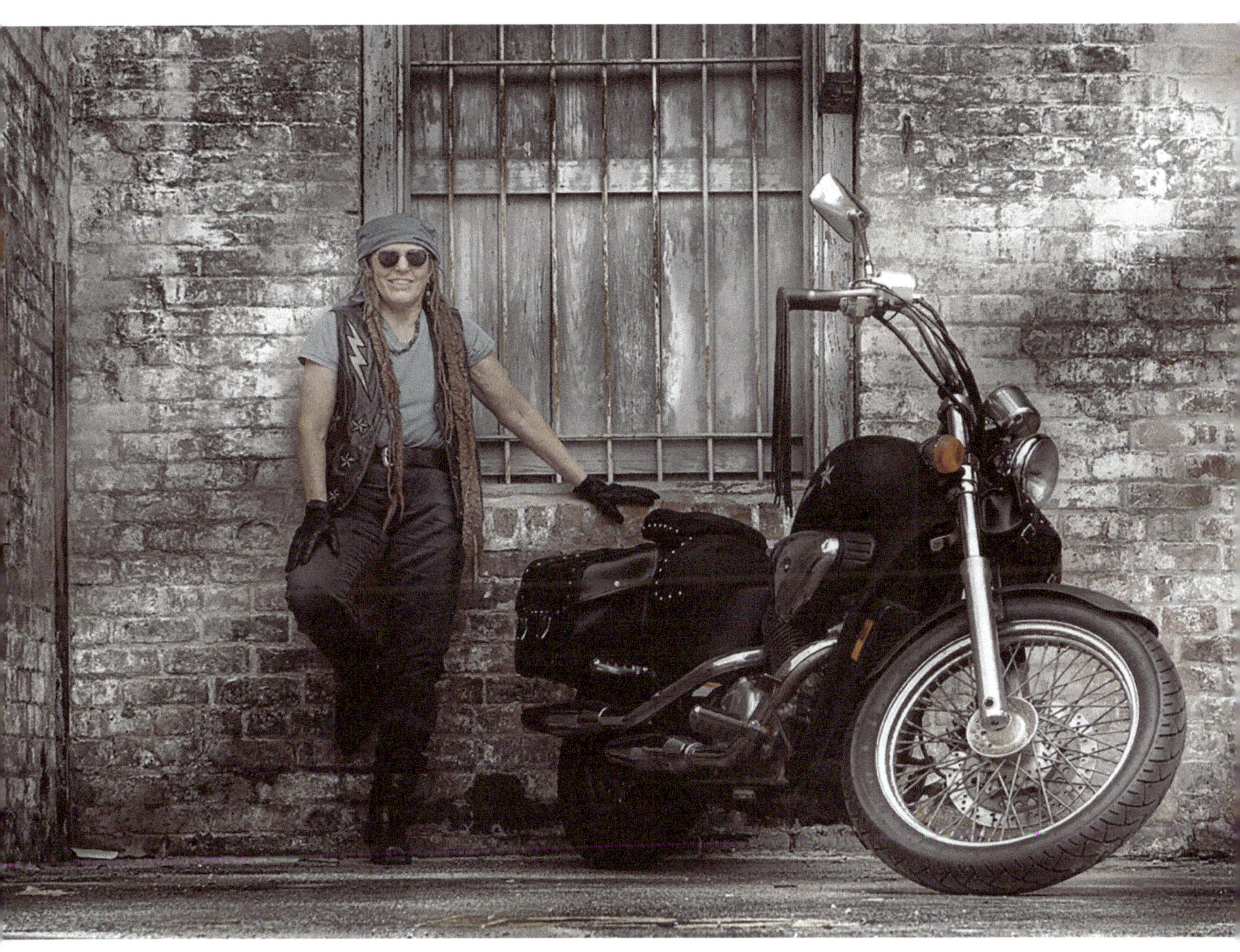

"If home is where the heart is,
New Orleans is where the soul is."
—four-time Grammy winner, Dr. John

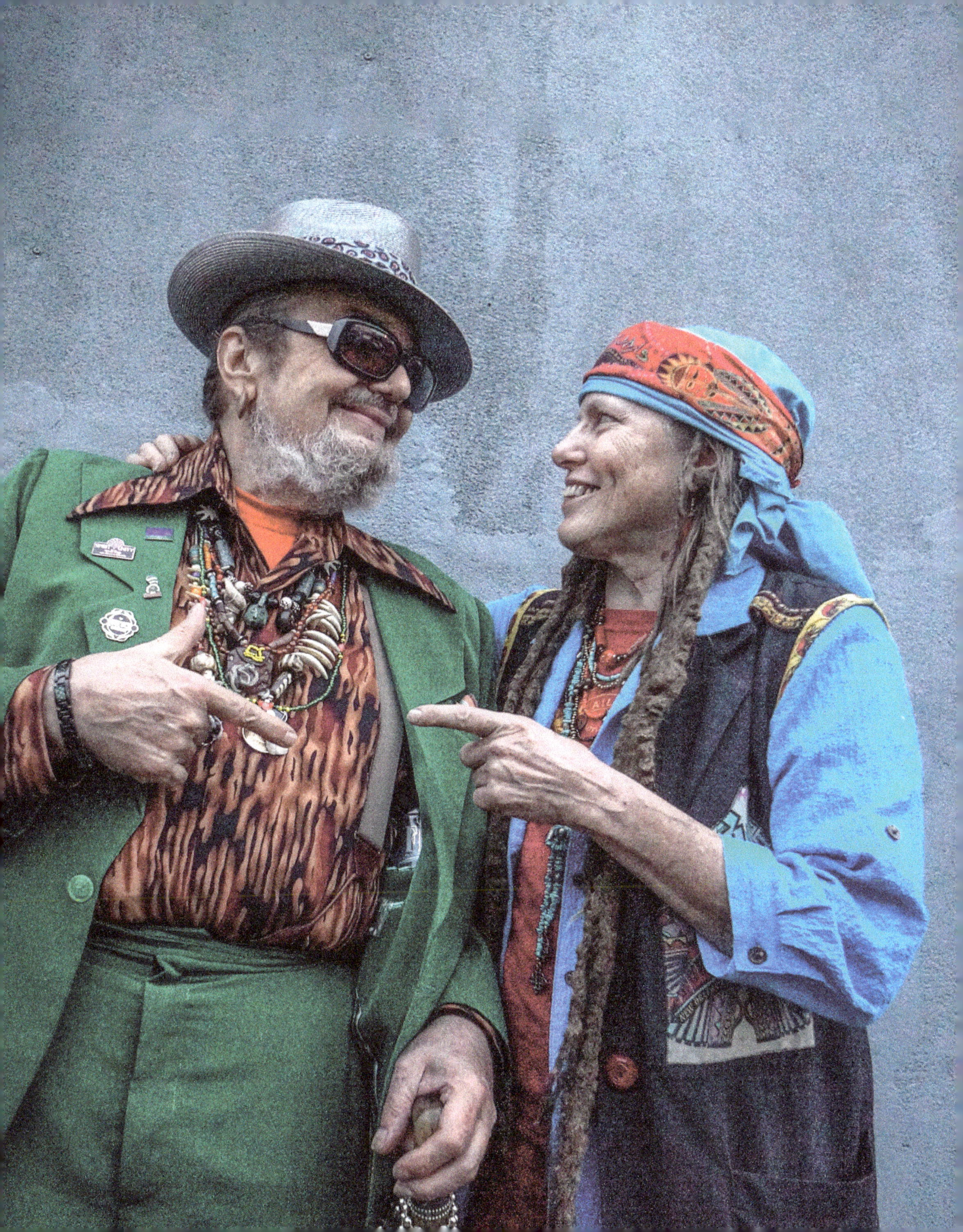

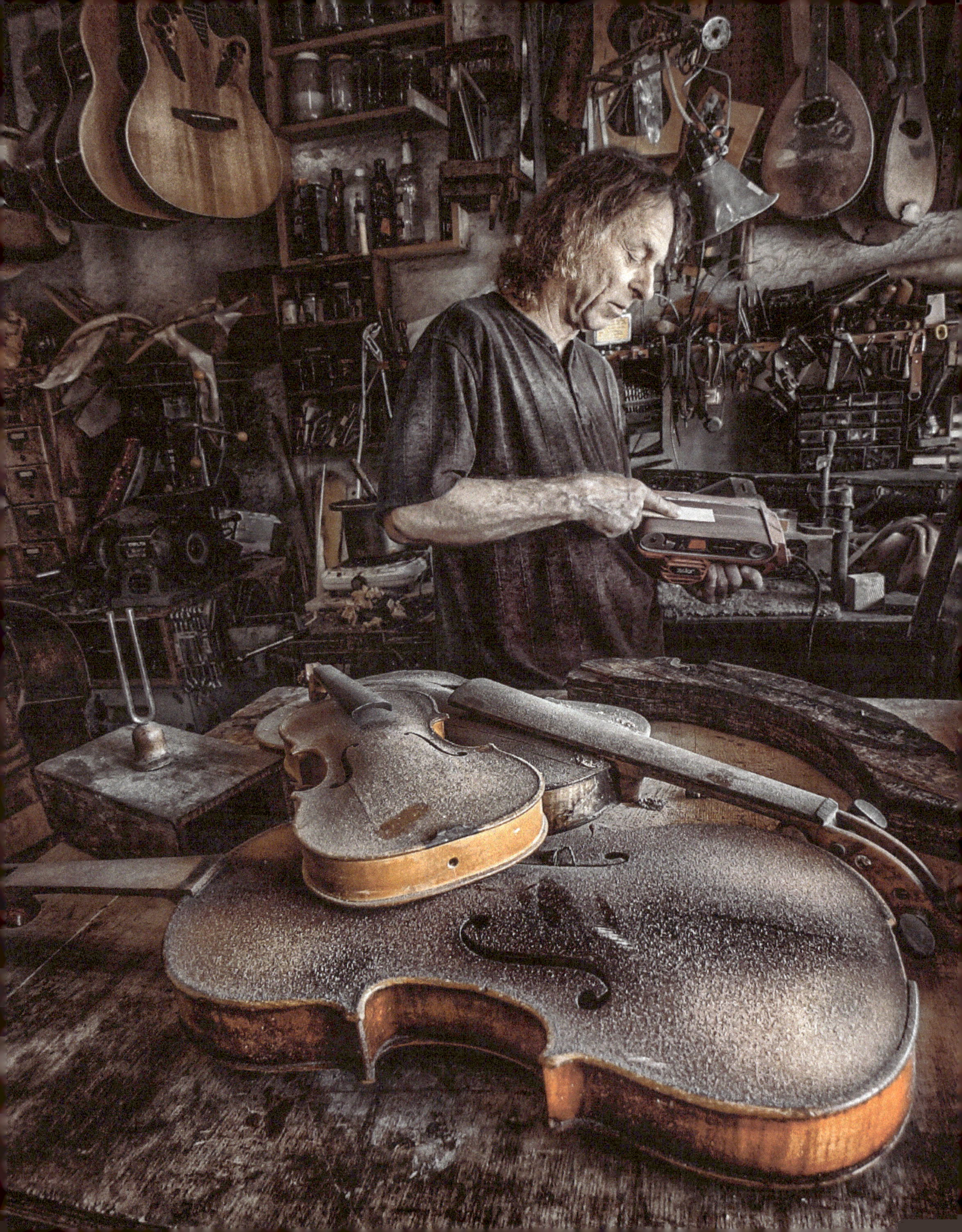

Salvador Giardina

Luthier—one who builds or repairs string instruments.

My feet were blistered and aching after two weeks of non-stop walking through the French Quarter. It was the last day of my stay in New Orleans. Salvador Giardina was on my long list of interesting characters to photograph for my book. A street musician known as The Bob Dylan Girl, told me, "One night I was on my bike headed home. My light was out. I got hit. I was okay, but my mandolin broke in half. Sal fixed it for a really good price."

I'd been wanting to meet Sal for a long time.

I dialed his number, half expecting to be put off and told to call back another time. Instead, Sal listened carefully, as I told him about my book project. He jumped in and said, "Come by any time. I go to lunch between noon and one o'clock."

Twenty minutes later, after a taxi ride up Canal Street into the Metaire, I found his tiny shop. As soon as I stepped through the door, I thought I might be on the set of *Storage Wars*—but in the 15th century Europe—in a room filled with piles of decaying wooden instruments, waiting to be restored by Sal. Violins, guitars, banjos, bases, ukuleles, even dulcimers were stacked everywhere. A few looked like works of art—others looked as if they'd just been rescued from a garbage can. I had to carefully pick my spot to stand in on a floor sprinkled with wood shavings. I tried to make sense of it all, scanning the walls where more violins, guitars and mandolins hung high above shelves piled with tools, bottles of glues, stains, and violin bows. Every inch of the place was covered in a gentle snow of fine Renaissance sawdust.

Sal greeted me with the warm sandpapered hand of a craftsman. He smiled, standing behind a cluttered counter, working on the bridge of a splintering bass, with the demeanor of a man who loves his work. Sal's weathered face and long hair reminded me a little of Neil Young, his skin a bit sepia-toned, aging like the rest of the stained orchestra lining the walls. Behind him was a workbench littered with a hodgepodge of tools from his trade mixed in with instrument parts and scraps of wood; all collected during nearly 40 years in business.

A boiled-over, gooey can of blackened glue sat on top of a rusting hotplate.

Sal grinned and confessed, "I'm an artist. One thing I'm not is neat. You can shoot as many photos as you like, but I gotta just keep working. I get so far behind try'n to get this stuff out. Customers come in and yell at me, 'You know how long you've had my instrument?! When is it going to be finished?!' I just tell 'em, 'It will be done when it's done.'" Then he shrugs, "I never know."

Sal paused, his hands struggled with a large bass, trying to wedge its bridge into place. "I don't own this shop. I don't run it. It runs me."

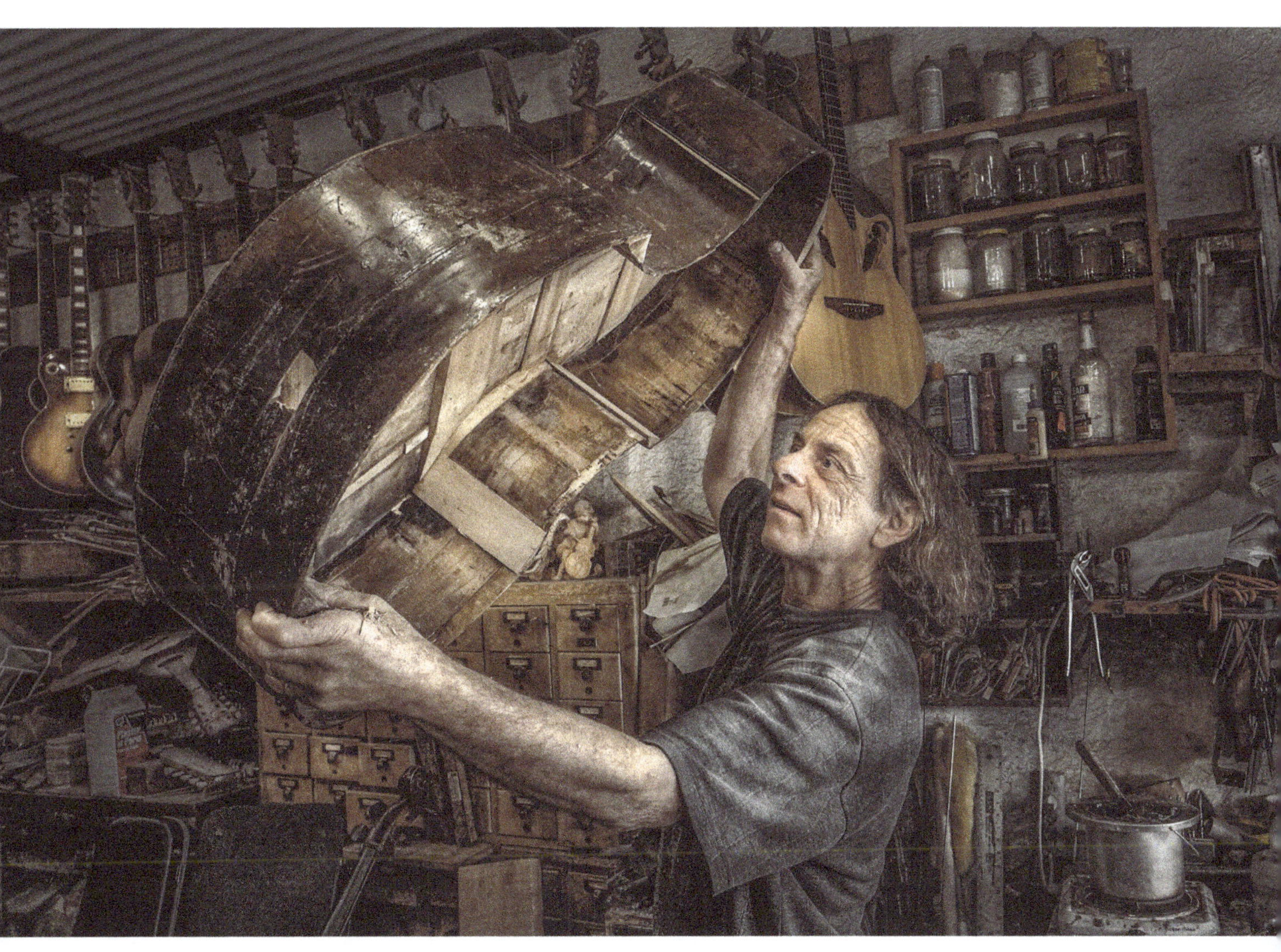

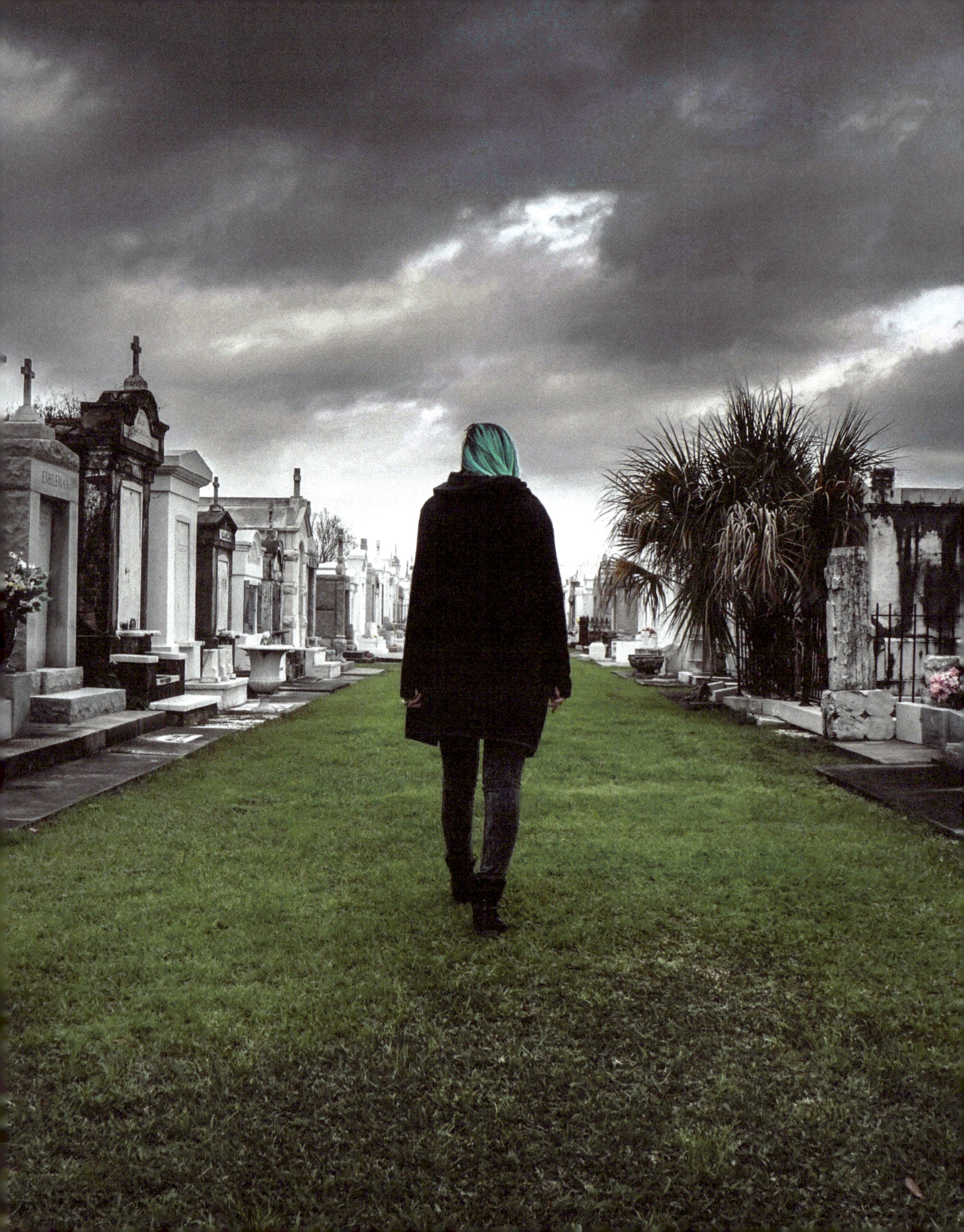

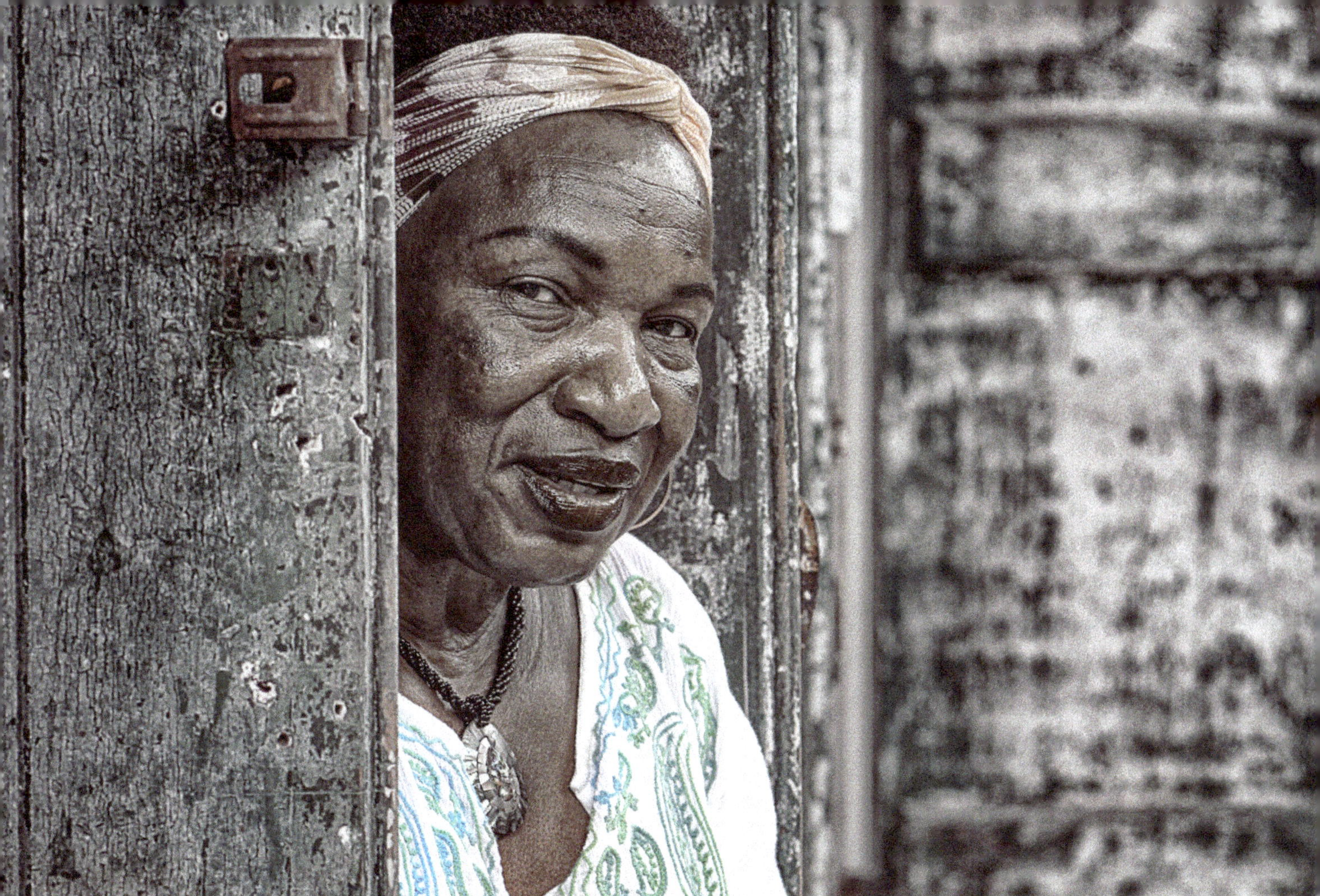

Priestess Miriam

Priestess Miriam says she has had visions and mystical experiences
since she was eleven. Once an operating room technician in
Chicago, she later became ordained as a bishop in the "Angel
All Nations Spiritual Church, then co-founded the New Orleans
Vodoo Spiritual Temple. Nicholas Cage invited her to perform a
blessing ceremony during his wedding to Lisa Marie Presley.

Darryl Young, AKA, Dancing Man 504

"After Hurricane Katrina, I needed to be healed. Everybody was yelling, 'Bring the music back! Bring the food back!'" Darryl noticed that many of the tourists were hesitant to interact with locals. "I started doing movement to feel better and to narrow the gap between the New Orleanians and visitors. Folks started calling me Dancing Man. I added the 504 (NOLA's area code) and it stuck.

"To me, Second Line is often a kind of structured chaos. It is also a form of medicine. When you're in a Second Line you don't worry about the bills, or about your relationship, of if your knee hurts, or if your head hurts. Once you are in that moment, everything seems to heal itself. Second Line dance steps adapt to the surfaces we move on. The streets here are all beat up and sideways. You gotta pick up you legs to get over the obstacles. We not only dance on the street, the sidewalk, the porch, but we sometimes even get up on someone's roof. If your car is parked in a Second Line, we may dance on top of your car."

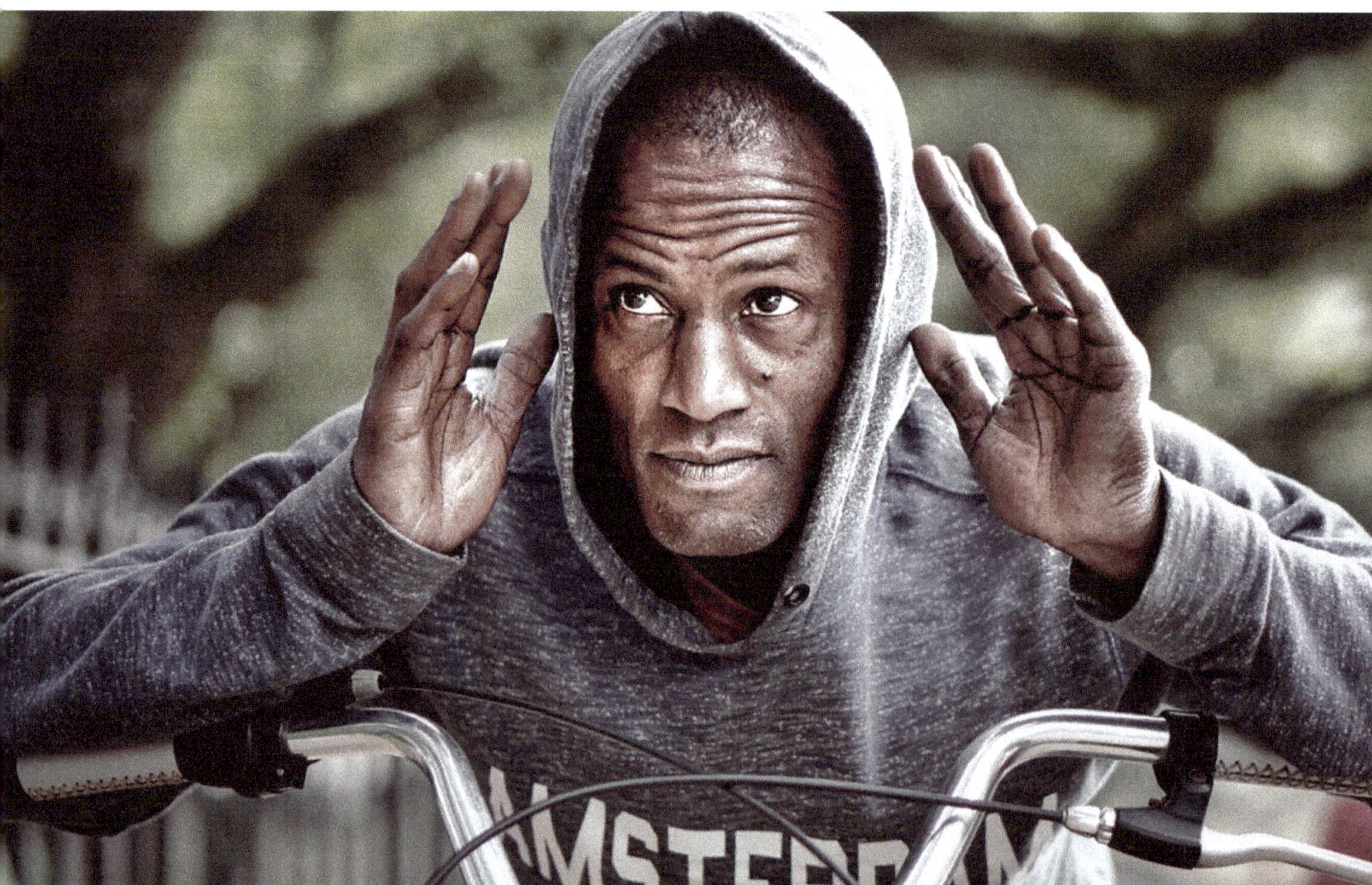

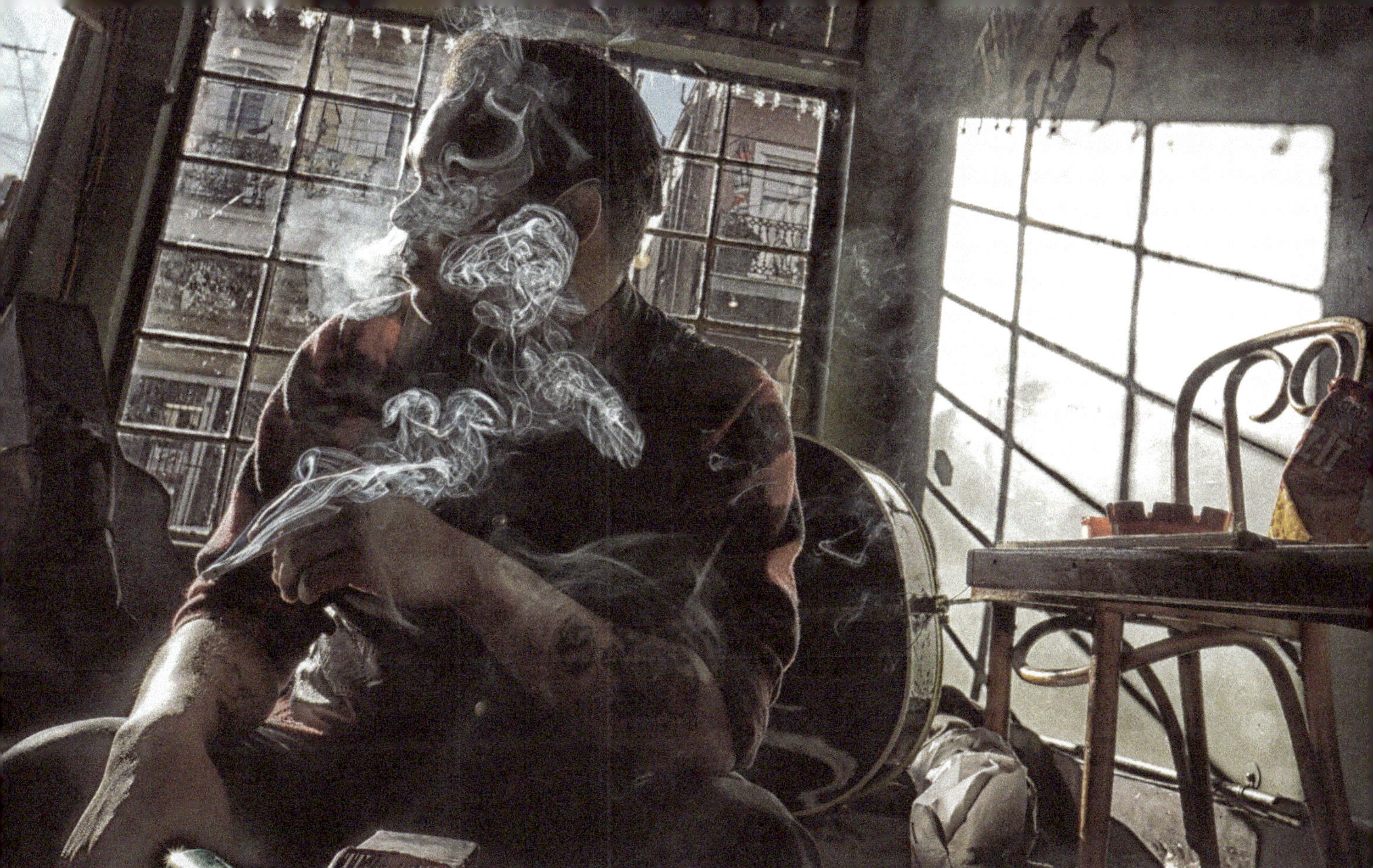

Dizzy Rucker, Bassist

"I came here from Southern California. For a while, I was so broke that I had to sleep under a freeway bridge. I couldn't even afford strings for my upright bass. I used Weed Wacker trimming line instead. Now, I play gigs nearly every night, often at The Spotted Cat. I have real strings and I don't sleep underneath a bridge anymore.

"If I was still in California, I'd be working at Target. Here in New Orleans, I can be who I was meant to be."

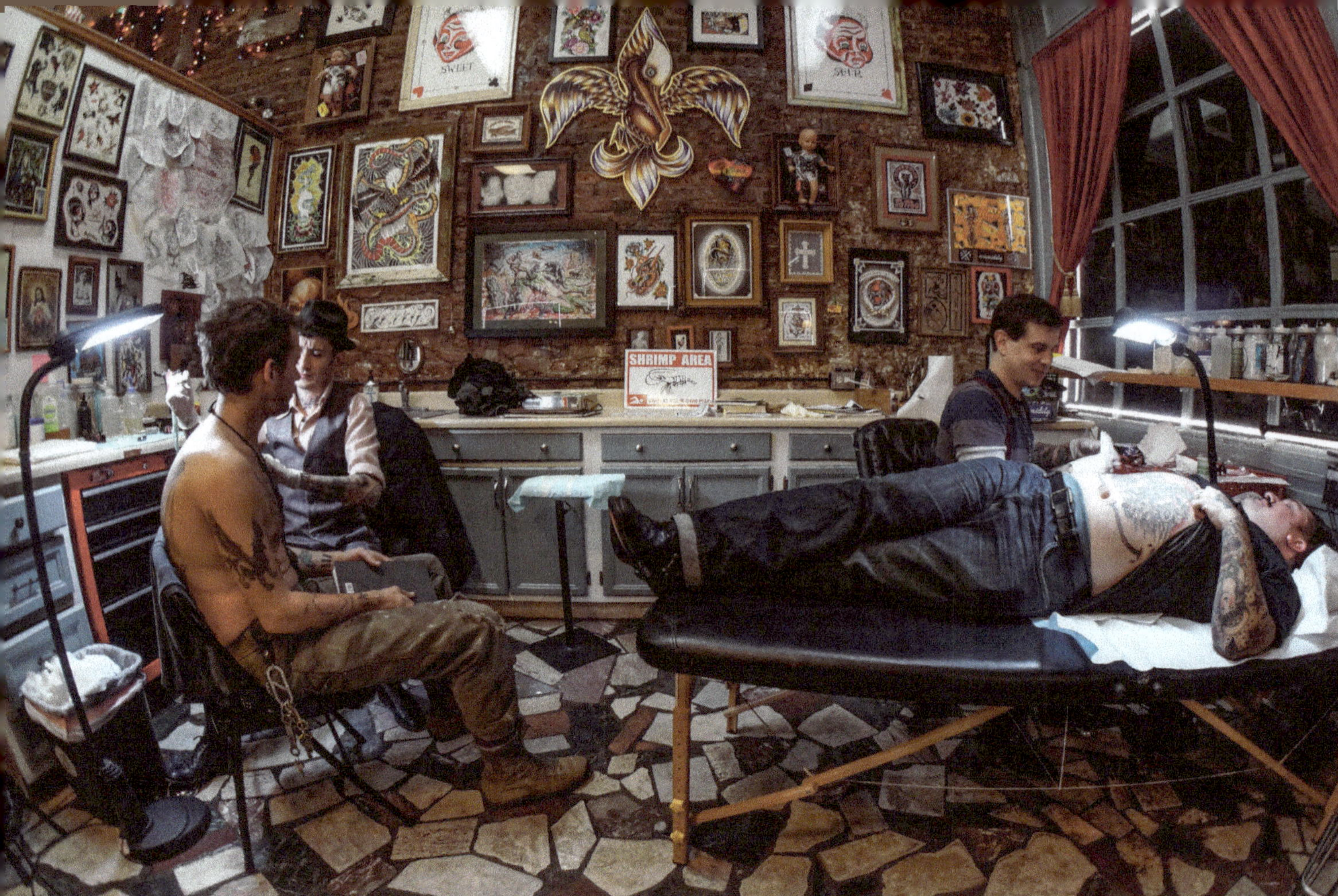

Pauly Lingerfelt, Tattoo Artist

"I got my first tattoo in my friend Nina's bedroom when I was 16. It made me feel like I was wearing armor all the time. Every tattoo I get becomes part of my life history.

"We get a lot of grandmas coming into the shop and they're fearless. They act like eighteen-year-olds, full of confidence. This one woman in her seventies wanted her first tattoo right between her breasts. I told her, 'Are you sure? This is your first tattoo, and that's a really painful spot.' But she wanted it there so I made her this pretty sizable fleur-de-lis.

"She didn't wink an eye; she just sat there like a champ. I see that a lot with women—they have no issues with the pain. And there's a patience that only women have, like no one else."

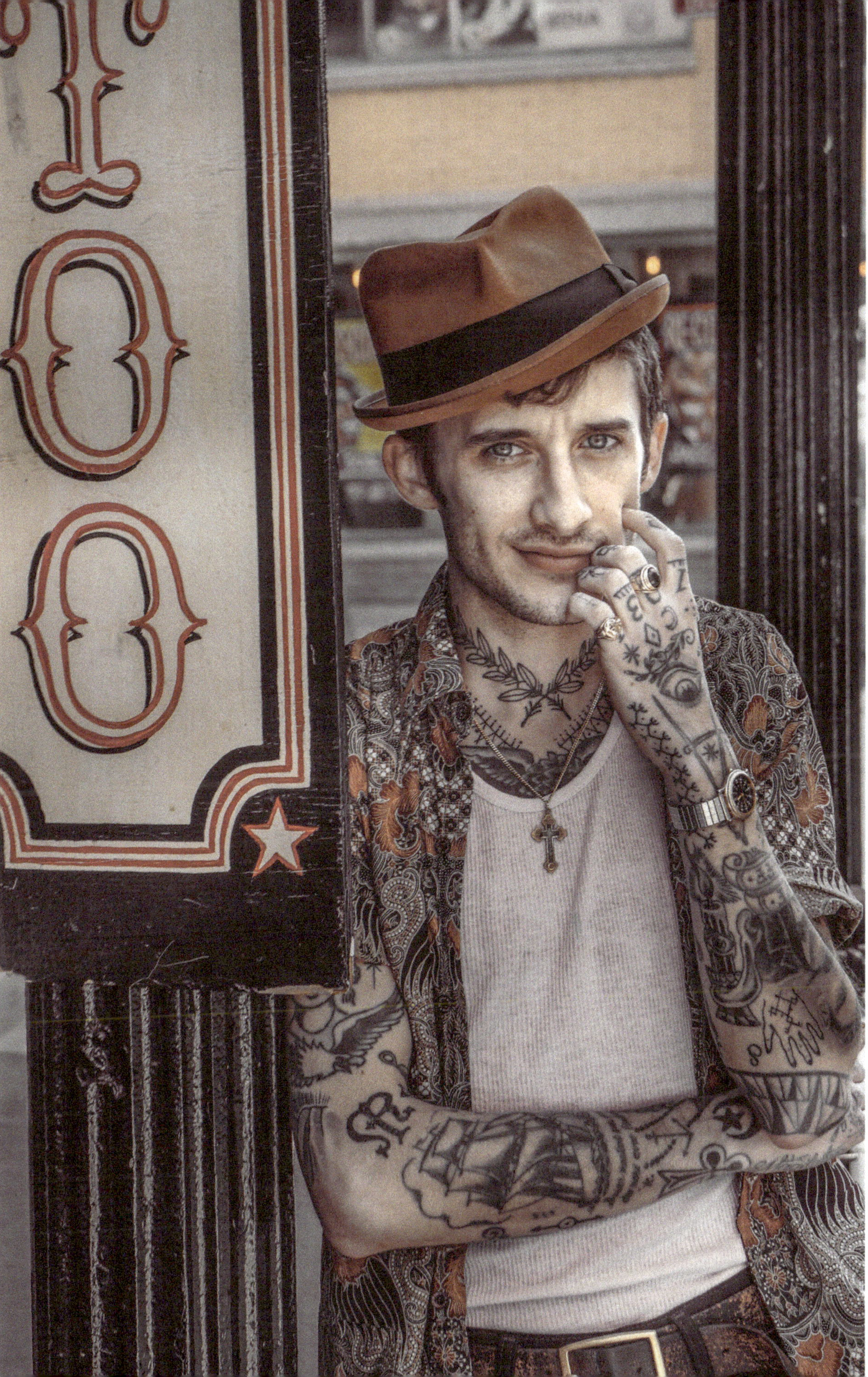

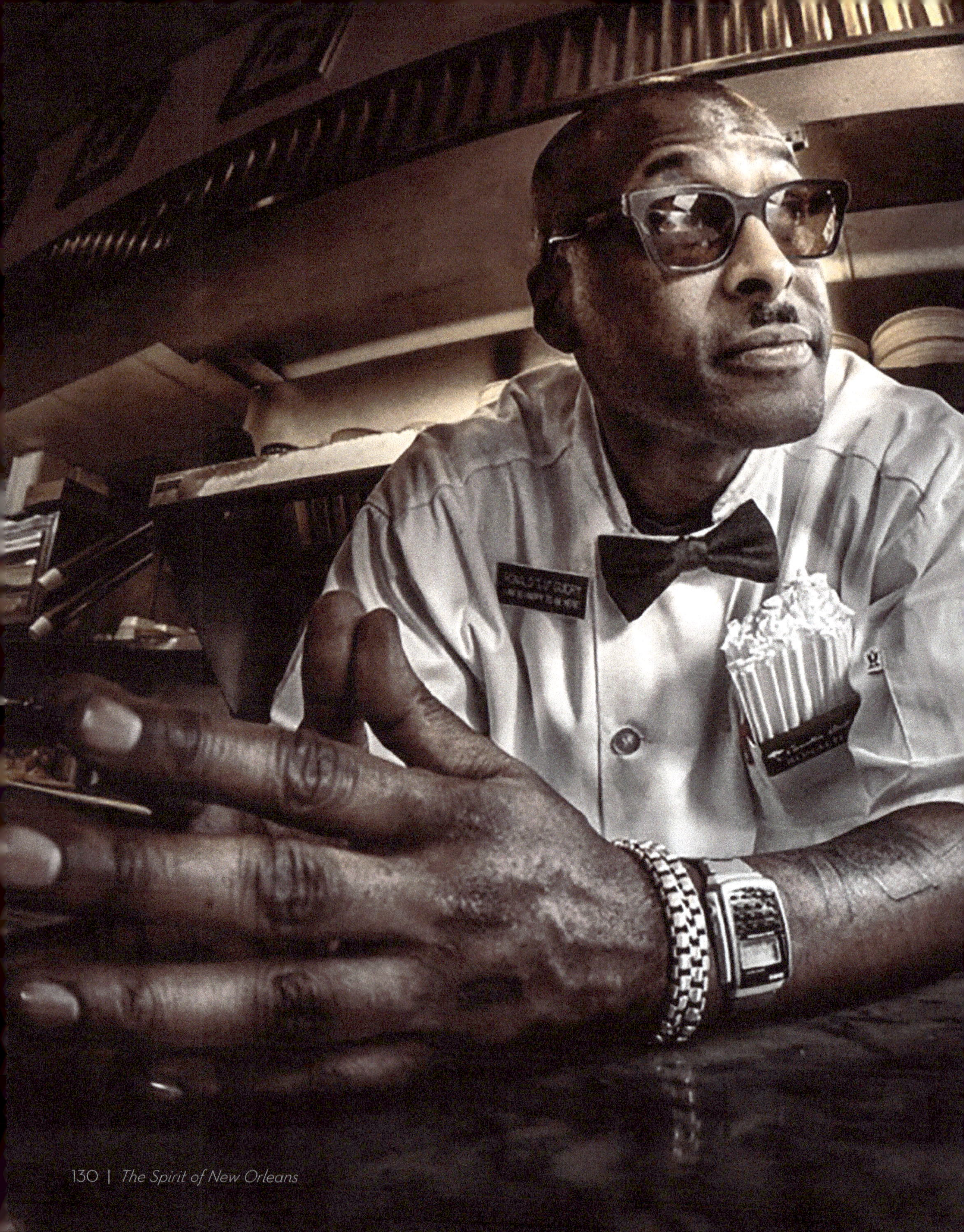

Passion at the Grill

The Camellia Grill stands at the corner of Charters and Toulouse in the New Orleans French Quarter. Seven days a week, it's packed with customers, all sitting on round metal swivel stools along a meandering Art Deco counter, seemingly unchanged since the 1950s—with lots of pink and chrome.

Smoke drifts off of the grill as it sizzles the sound of frying bacon and burgers. Lu—dressed in bleach white with a black bow tie—is the guy who is clearly in charge.

Watching Lu work the crowd of hungry diners is like watching a young James Earl Jones as a Shakespearean actor in the round. His passion for his work is enviable and his excitement rolls over me with the mixed aromas coming off the grill.

Lu booms orders at the two skinny black men anxiously working the grill, tapping their spatulas, arranging and re-arranging bacon, burger patties and hash browns like it's a fast game of Solitaire." Make that bacon well-done! Make it as dark as Wesley Snipes!"

With great attention to detail, Lu takes pride in placing knives, forks and spoons precisely, deliberately, on the shiny counter next to each bleach-white cloth napkin. Several papered straws are packed into his shirt pocket, as neat as new crayons on a box. His eye contact bounces back, "I like you, too." I glance at his name name tag. Ronald "Lu" Gudry. Under his name is inscribed his tag line: I am so happy to be here.

Lu greets tourists and locals alike with warmth and charm. Minutes later, he stops everyone mid-bite with his booming bass voice: "Clap your hands if you're happy!" A little red-headed boy, who looks like his name should be "Skippy", sits sandwiched at the counter between his mom and dad. He just stares up at Lu, not sure what the rules are. The kid's beef patty is about to dump its backend load onto his plate. Lu stops and insists again, "Clap your hands if you're happy!" Skippy glances sideways at dad, as if asking for permission and let's his burger down onto the plate. Then suddenly he smacks his greasy hands together. Lu lets out a laugh and shakes his head at the white customers who can't quite match his own passion. Lu gracefully moves back to work, He banters with the grill crew with the speed, rhythm and grace of the Harlem Globe Trotters. Part drill sergeant part cheerleader, Lu spins toward the grill man again, instructing, "Gim-me a one-eyed buck with cheese!" Like an air traffic controller he keeps an eye on the larger landscape of the room, remembering the details of every order as well as who's coming through the door.

When he brings my omelette, I motion for him to come in closer. In a near whisper I ask, "what's a one-eyed buck?" Lu explains a bit too loudly (to the stupid white guy) the facts of life. I use my hands to push down his voice, glancing sideways, afraid everyone else in class will laugh. "You crack the egg, you put the egg on the grill. It's look' up at you like a one-eyed buck. Then you put cheese on it."

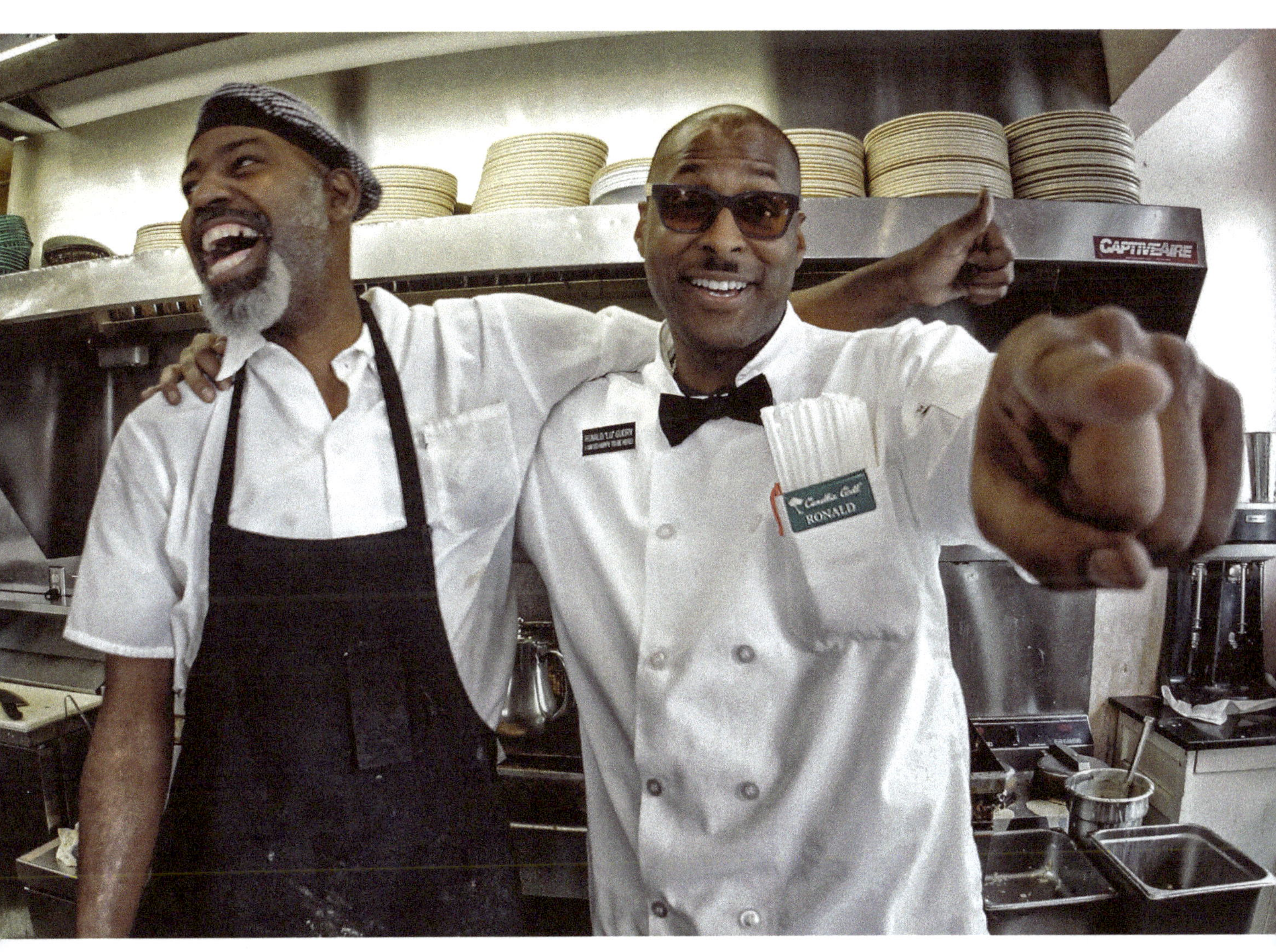

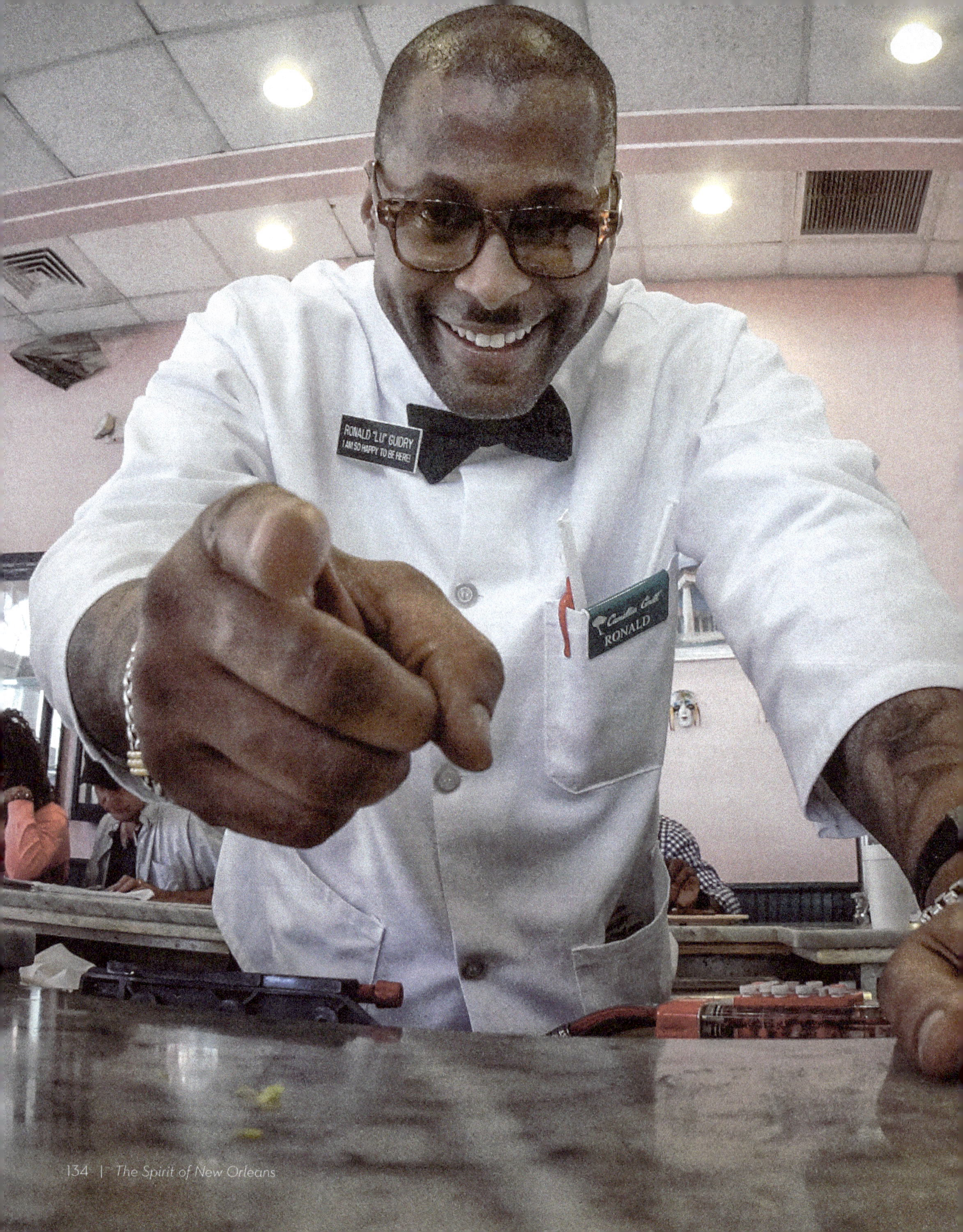
RONALD "LIL" GUIDRY
I AM SO HAPPY TO BE HERE!
Camellia Grill
RONALD

I knew that.

I glance at the face of a young boy inked into a long tattoo inside his forearm and ask him who the boy's is.

Lu tells me, "That's my son, Savoy, and slowly runs his fingers over the ink on his skin. I ask him more about his life. "I'm always excited to come to work." He goes on, "I like fine things. I'm touchy-feely. I love the company of women," he says in a deep, soulful voice, a blend of Barry White and Lou Rawls. He turns his head to look out the window and carefully studies the tourist-packed sidewalk. His sexual radar is scanning.

Lu notices some of his new fans are about to pay their bill at the front register. Little Skippy's mom asks to have a selfie taken with Lu and hands a cellphone to the cashier. Lu jumps in behind them and smiles like a movie star on Hollywood Boulevard. Without missing a beat, he moves on to a guy and his girlfriend about to leave. Lu smiles and wraps his arms around the girlfriend, enveloping her like a spider on a fly. Her blush confesses that she loves his attention. I fear she will melt on the spot and never want to leave.

A few more hungry customers crowd in from the street to wait for an empty stool.

Lu walks over and re-fills my coffee cup. He leans down onto the counter and confides in a whisper, "I could never get away with this shit at TGI Fridays."

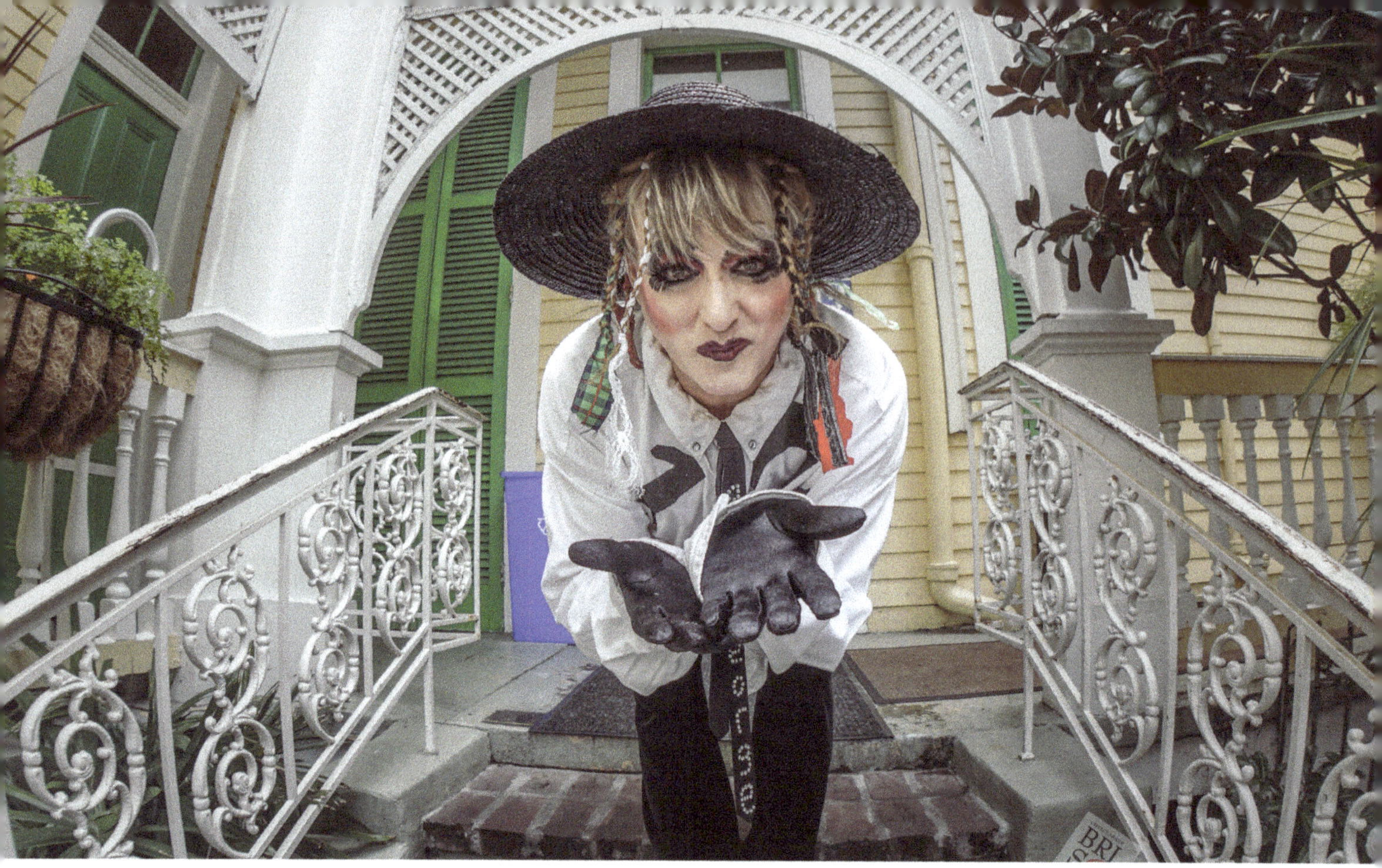

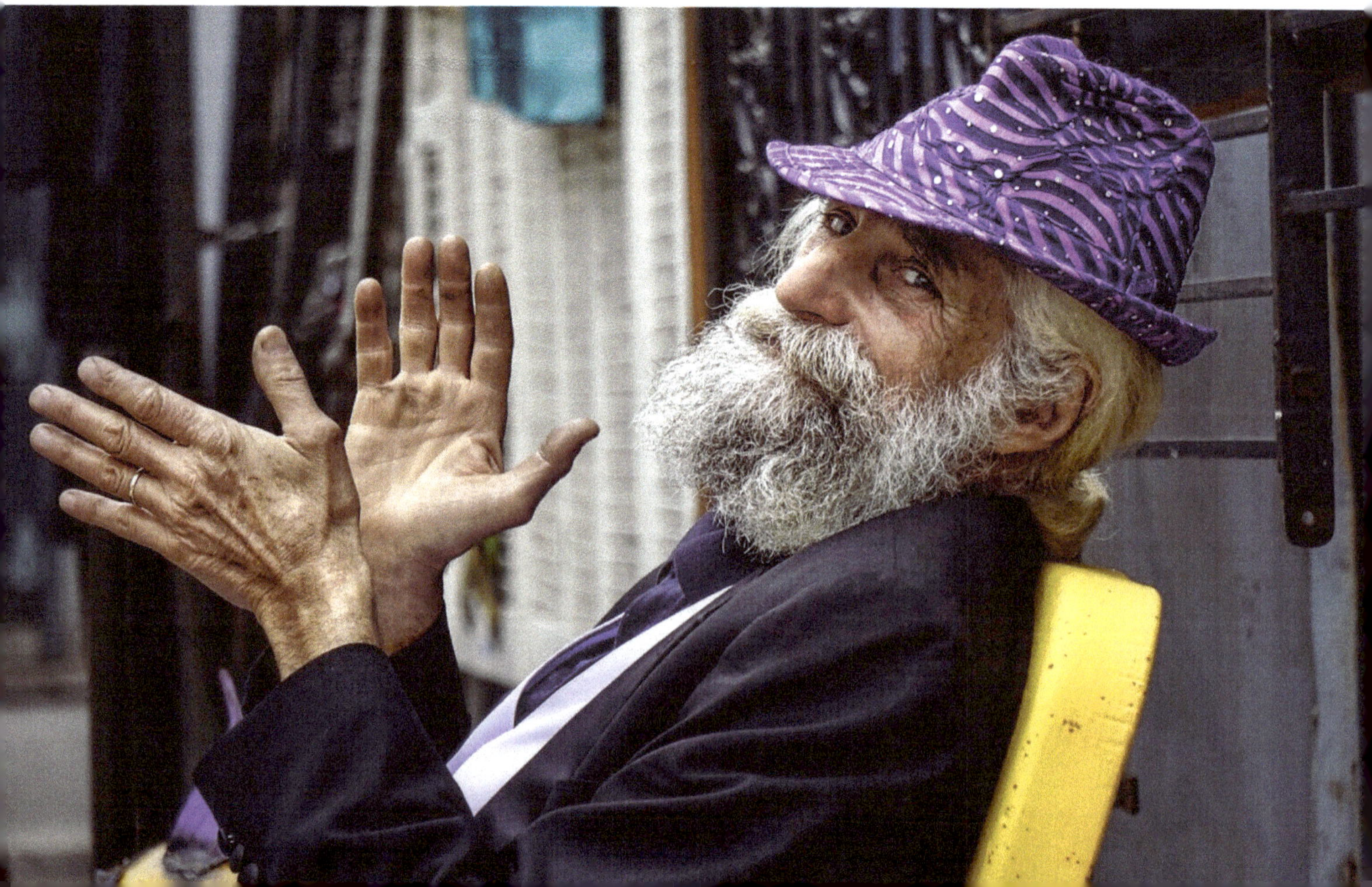

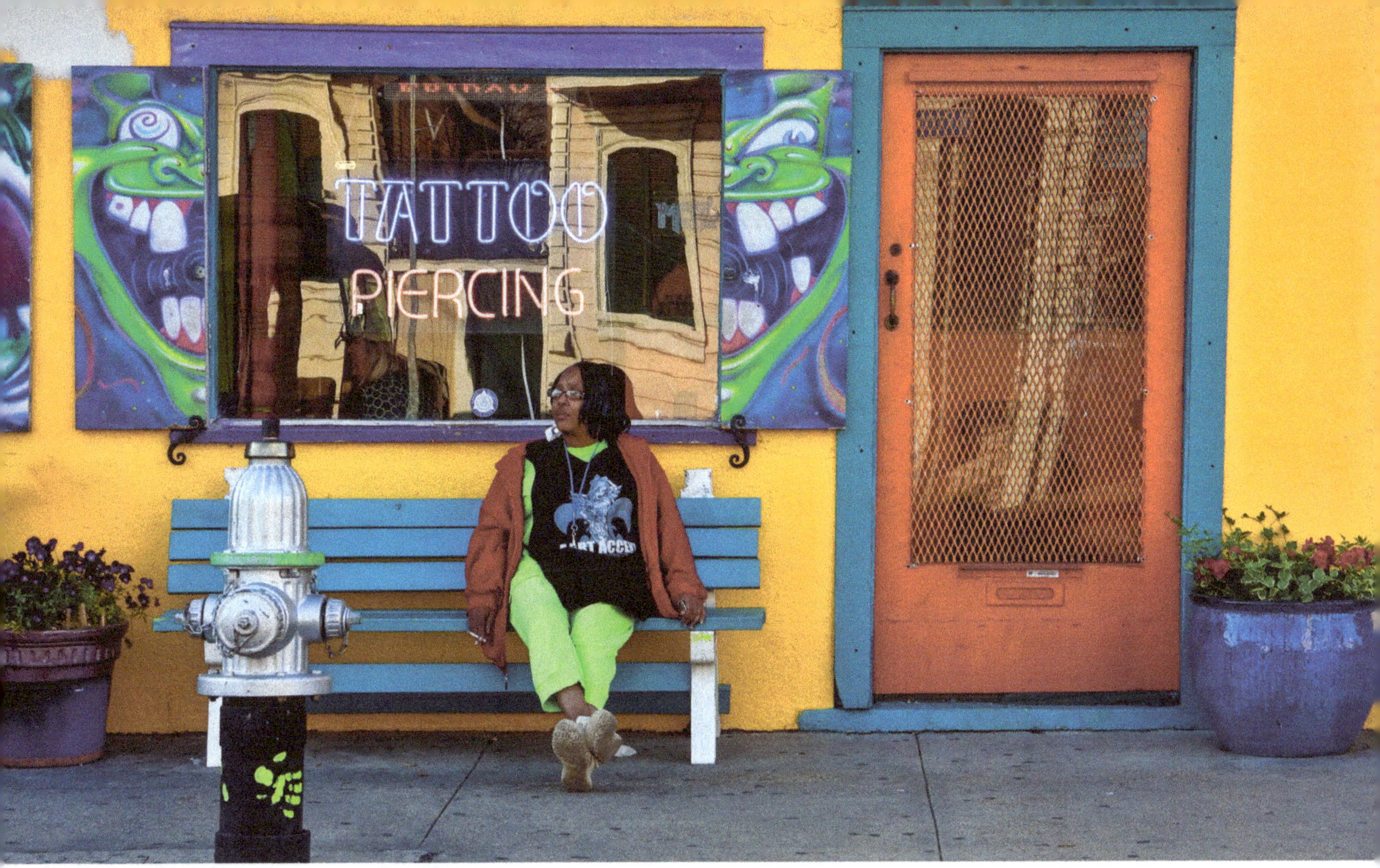

TATTOO

PIERCING

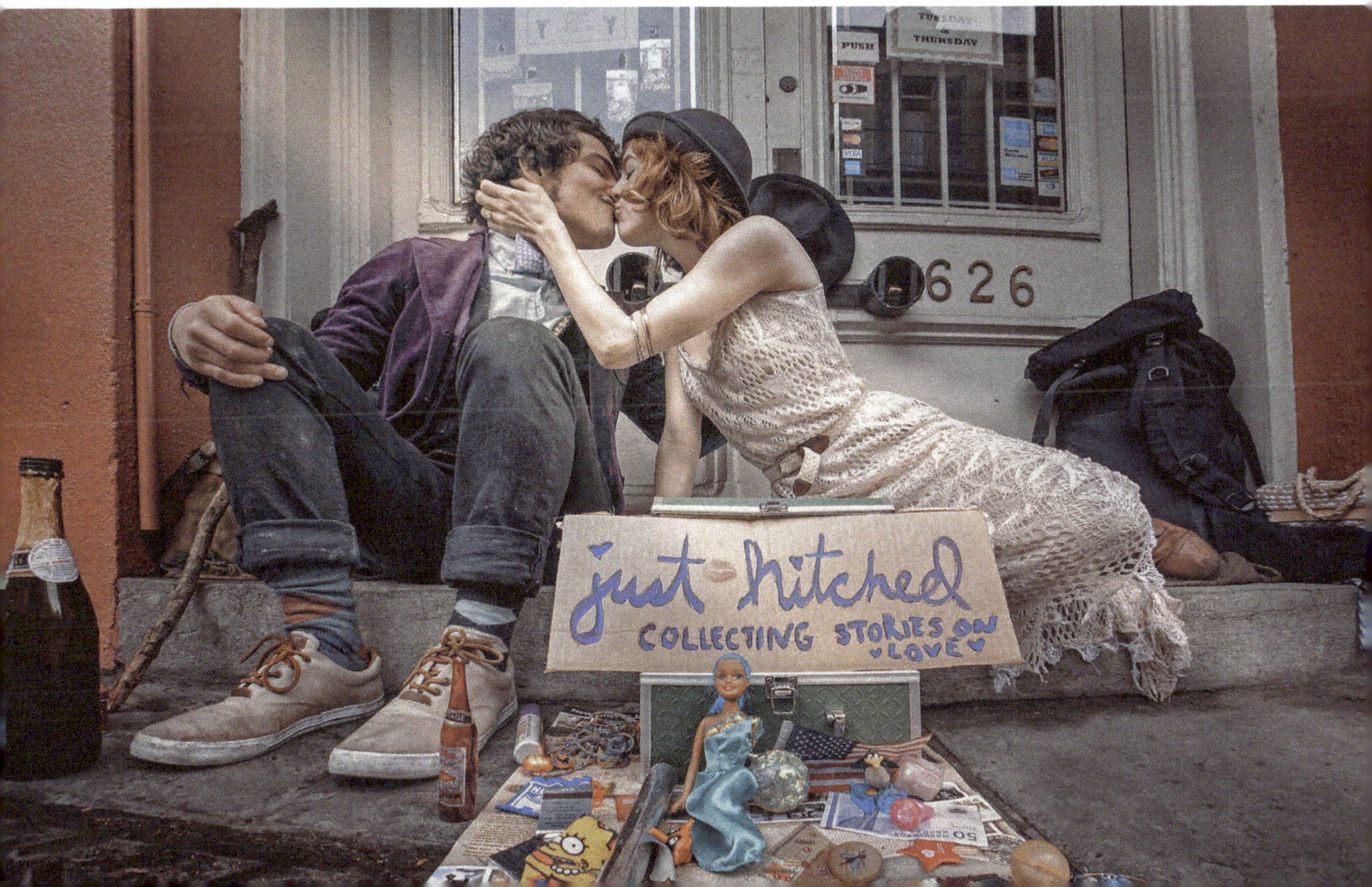

PUSH

THURSDAY

626

just hitched

COLLECTING STORIES ON LOVE

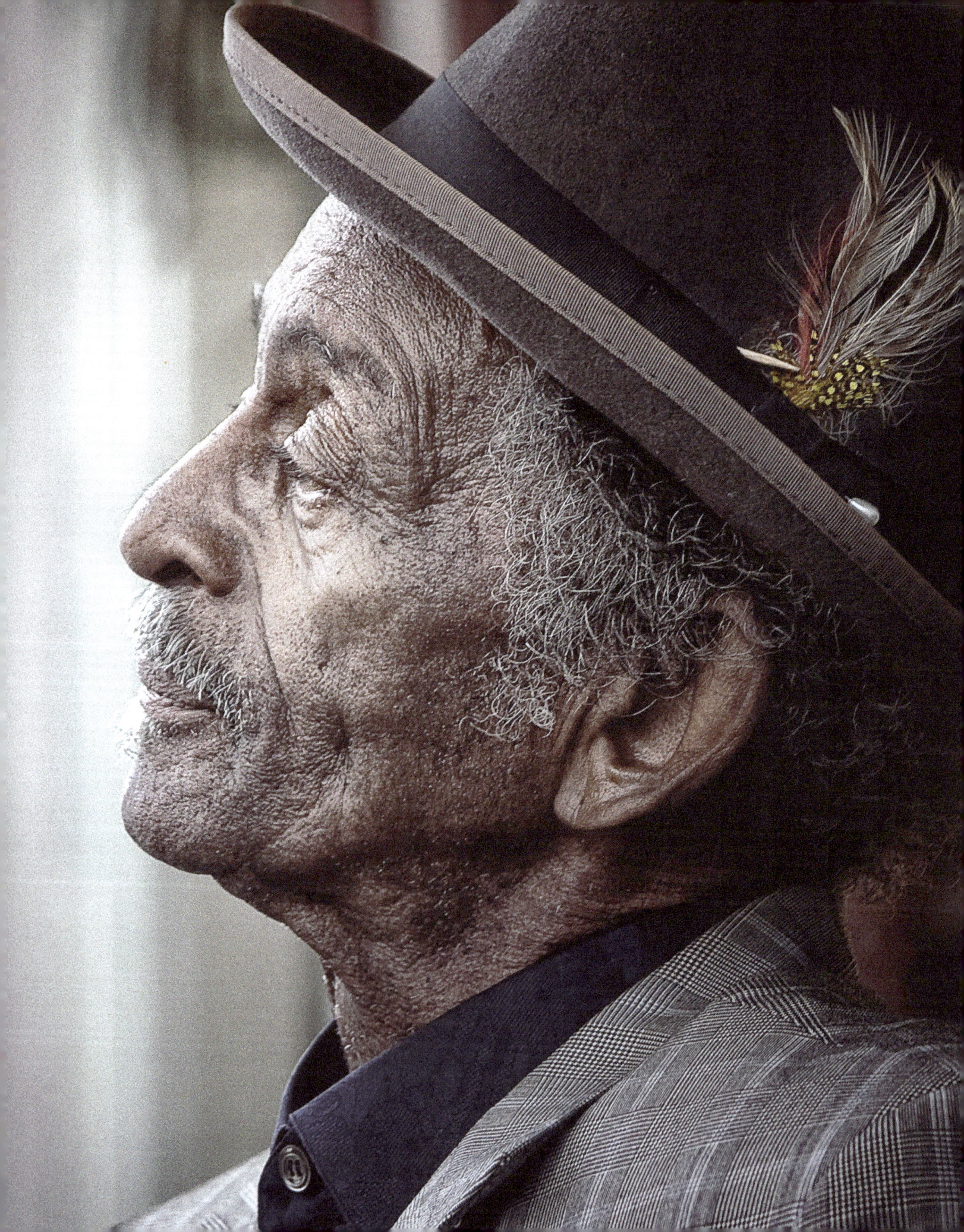

Lionel Paul Batiste, Sr. "Uncle Lionel"

"I was born in a neighborhood with a lot of famous musicians. I was surrounded by musicians such as Georgia Lewis, Alfonzo Cooper, Jim Robinson, Smile, Jim Crow, Slow Drag. All of them was in the neighborhood where I was born.

"In my house we had a lot of instruments. The only instrument my daddy didn't play was the horn. He didn't play in any nightclubs.

"My sister played guitar and drums. My two brothers played guitar. Daddy played all the instruments and my sister—she is 83 years old now—she went to school to learn to play. Everyone in the area had a piano in the house. In my backyard, I would grip something with my toes and it sounded like taps. Kids upstairs would take an aluminum cane and tap it on the steps and clap their hands.

"My mom used to take my little nieces and put them on their feet. If some did not participate she'd to ask 'em to leave. My brother would come over with his girlfriend and if she wouldn't do this or that, my mom would ask him to have her leave. Mama didn't want no wallflowers!

"I get music from things that happened to me in my life. In my music, the words to the song mean something. You either talkin' about someone you loved or something that was important in your life. I was always tryin' to learn more as a musician. Music is very textured. It's vibrating in your body."

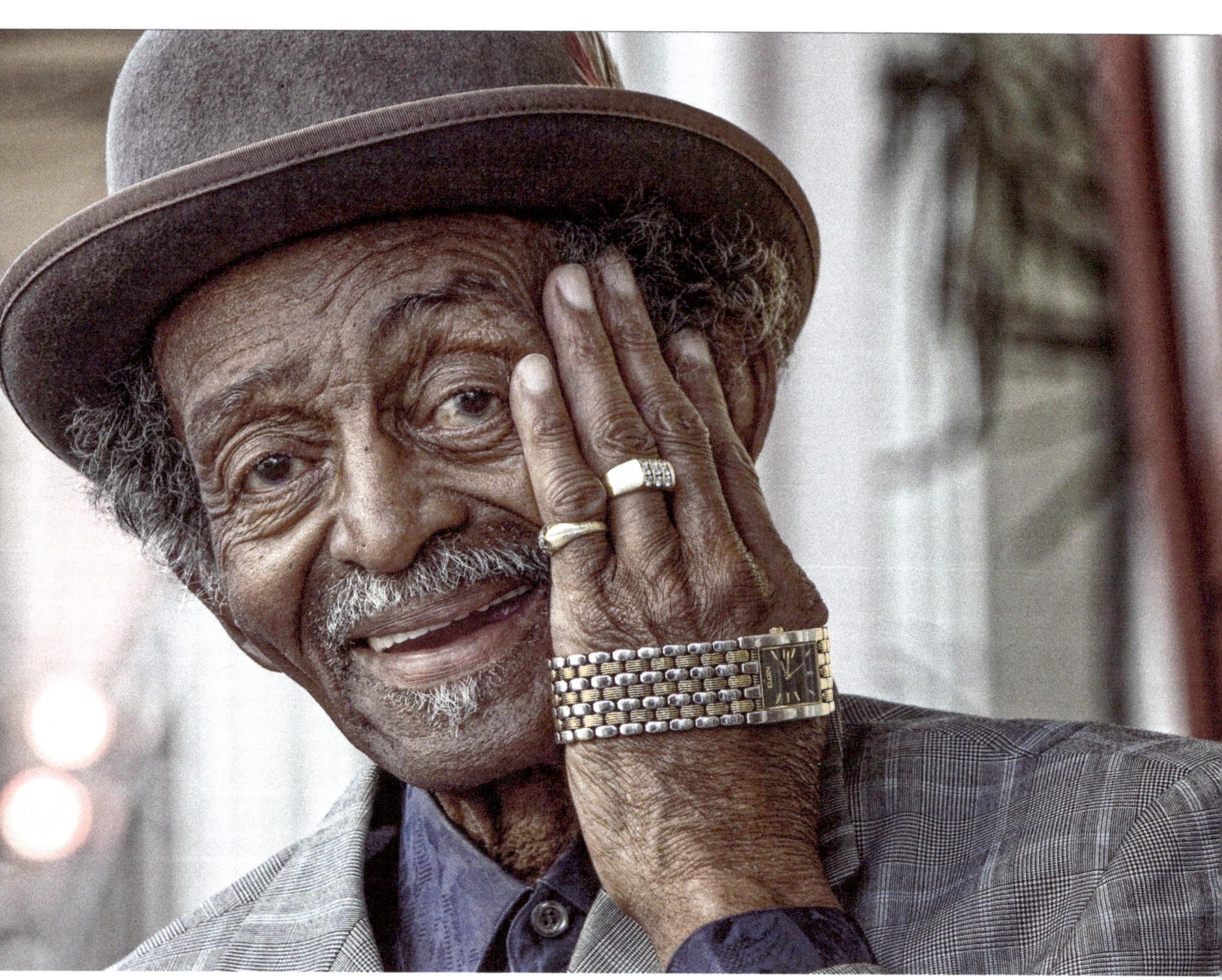

A Letter to Uncle Lionel

July 24, 2012

Dear Uncle Lionel,

On a sunny New Orleans afternoon, just a couple of years ago, I had the pleasure of spending time with you as we sipped coffee outside of a French Quarter cafe. You were kind enough to grant me an interview for my book, *Bathtub Blues.*

Of the many people I have photographed during my career, few have radiated the poise, grace, and kindness that you extended to me. You were dapper in a tailored pressed suit with a derby and high-shined shoes. (I read in *The New York Times* that you wrote the date you bought them on your soles. I also read that you made a pocket square from a snip of a necktie so you'd have a perfect match.) All of this was accented by several rings displayed on your fingers atop that beautiful cane. (Is the rumor true that you kept a dagger hidden in that cane?) I asked about the gold-banded watch always stretched across your palm. You laughed, "That way I'll always have time on my hands." Later, when I looked through my lens about to snap your photo, I felt as though I was in the presence of some kind of royalty.

I promised to send you a copy of my book when it was finished.

Then, last week, I was shocked to read... you died.

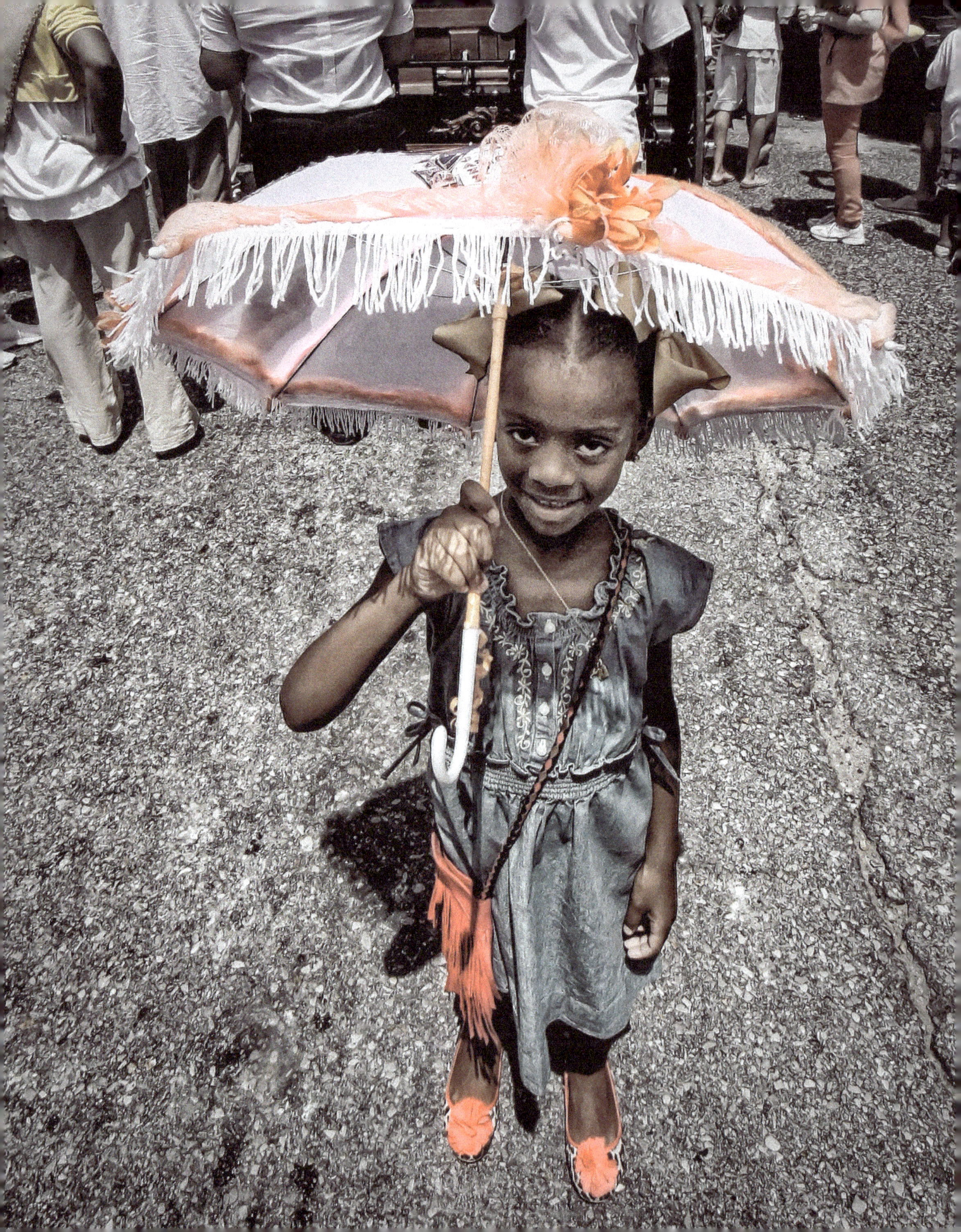

The news of your passing brought not one, but two levels of pain to me. The first was the shock and sorrow of having to say goodbye to such a kind, beautiful soul who had touched so many. The deeper pain was the guilt I felt upon realizing that I had taken something from you without returning the favor. I have been perfecting my book *Bathtub Blues* for two years, always planning to send you a copy once it was complete. I had written the "thank you" letter to you many times in my head, but never mailed it. You never saw any of the photographs I took of you that day. So many others have; my friends, my clients and my family. I promised you that I would send you a photograph and the book. I failed. I failed because of my habit of letting work pile up. I failed because of the way I procrastinate.

With a sense of confusion and frustration, I booked the next flight for New Orleans. I needed to say goodbye, and to finally give you the respect you deserved.

The first newspaper I spotted in The Louis Armstrong Airport was filled with photos and stories about you, predicting that yours would probably be the biggest Treme funeral ever. As it turned out, your city gave you two funerals. The first one was on a stormy Friday.

When my cab couldn't get through the crowd, I hopped out in the streaming rain and made my way through a parking lot jammed with well-wishers kept partially dry by the elevated, leaking Interstate 10. A loud Treme band marched and danced back and forth, up and down the paved area, celebrating your life, ready to send you home. Scores of friends, fellow musicians, and curious onlookers danced and moved along with the marching band. Barbecue and beer were on sale. A man advertised an autographed copy of a Jazz Fest Congo Square poster portraying you for $500. Another offered copies of a publication called *The Boulevard* with your image on its cover for $3.

At the last minute your burial had to be postponed. The cemetery was flooded. Nonetheless, the loud music, mainly drums and horns, continued and drifted down the side streets to where you stood upright in the funeral home near to your wooden coffin.

Keith Spera of *The Times-Picayune* quoted blues guitarist Little Freddie King, talking with a friend, drummer Waco-Wade Wright: "They've got him fixed up beautiful."

Wright agreed. "They've even got his watch on the mannequin's hand," he replied, referring to your lifelike figure standing in the funeral home's chapel.

"That wasn't a mannequin," King replied. "That's him."

The piece in *The Times-Picayune* continued: "In a send-off as unique as the man himself, Mr. Batiste wasn't lying in his cypress casket. Instead, his body was propped against a faux street lamp,

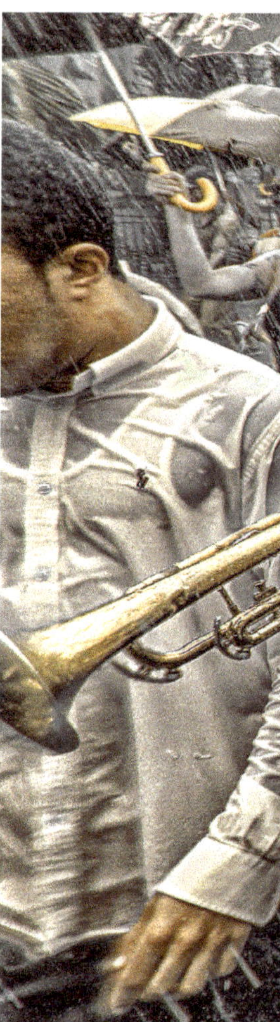

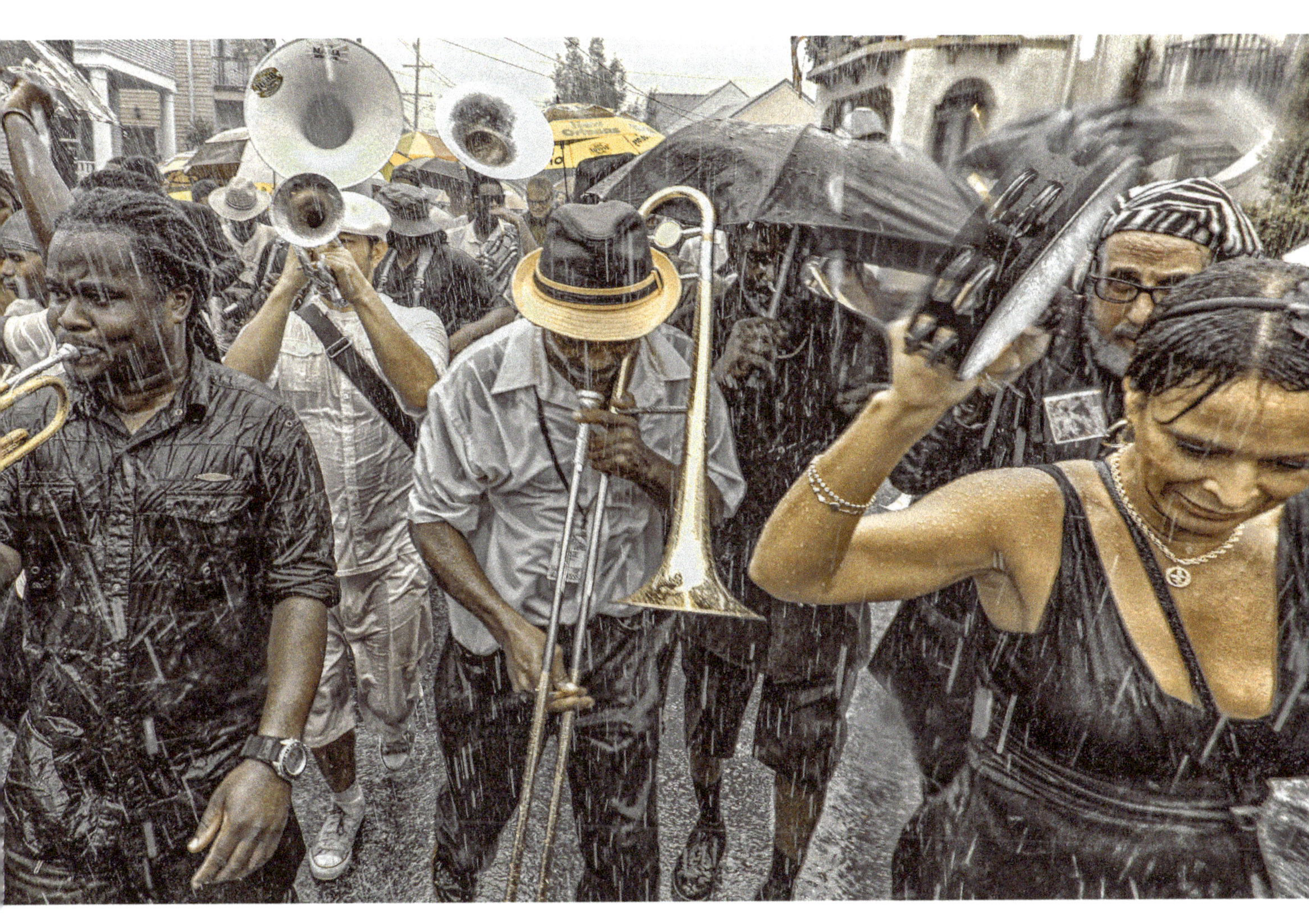

standing, decked out in his signature man-about-town finery. He wore a cream sport coat, beige slacks, tasseled loafers, ornate necktie and matching pocket square, bowler hat and sunglasses. His bass drum and his Treme Brass Band uniform were positioned nearby... His head was cocked slightly to the left. He appeared ready to step from behind the velvet rope and saunter off to Frenchmen Street, where he reveled in dancing and drinking beer."

Storyville Stompers tuba player Woody Penouilh remarked, "He looks better today than when I saw him the Thursday before he died. Heaven is agreeing with him."

Heaven may have been agreeing with you, Lionel, but as buckets of rain came down, some said that you just weren't ready to go.

It poured.

At the hint of a weather break, the procession made its way through the old neighborhoods in a sea of bright colors. There were top hats, suits, and Mardi Gras Indian costumes. Apparently, you instructed your daughter, "No dark colors, no crying." People stood on porches, some even on rooftops, all wanting to pay their respects. Uncle Lionel, your wake was a celebration like none other. This city loves you.

The heavens wept, then became a deluge. More than 11 inches fell by four o'clock in the afternoon. The parade barely slowed and kept going. One man in a tow truck pulled over, hopped out and just started dancing, soon completely soaked.

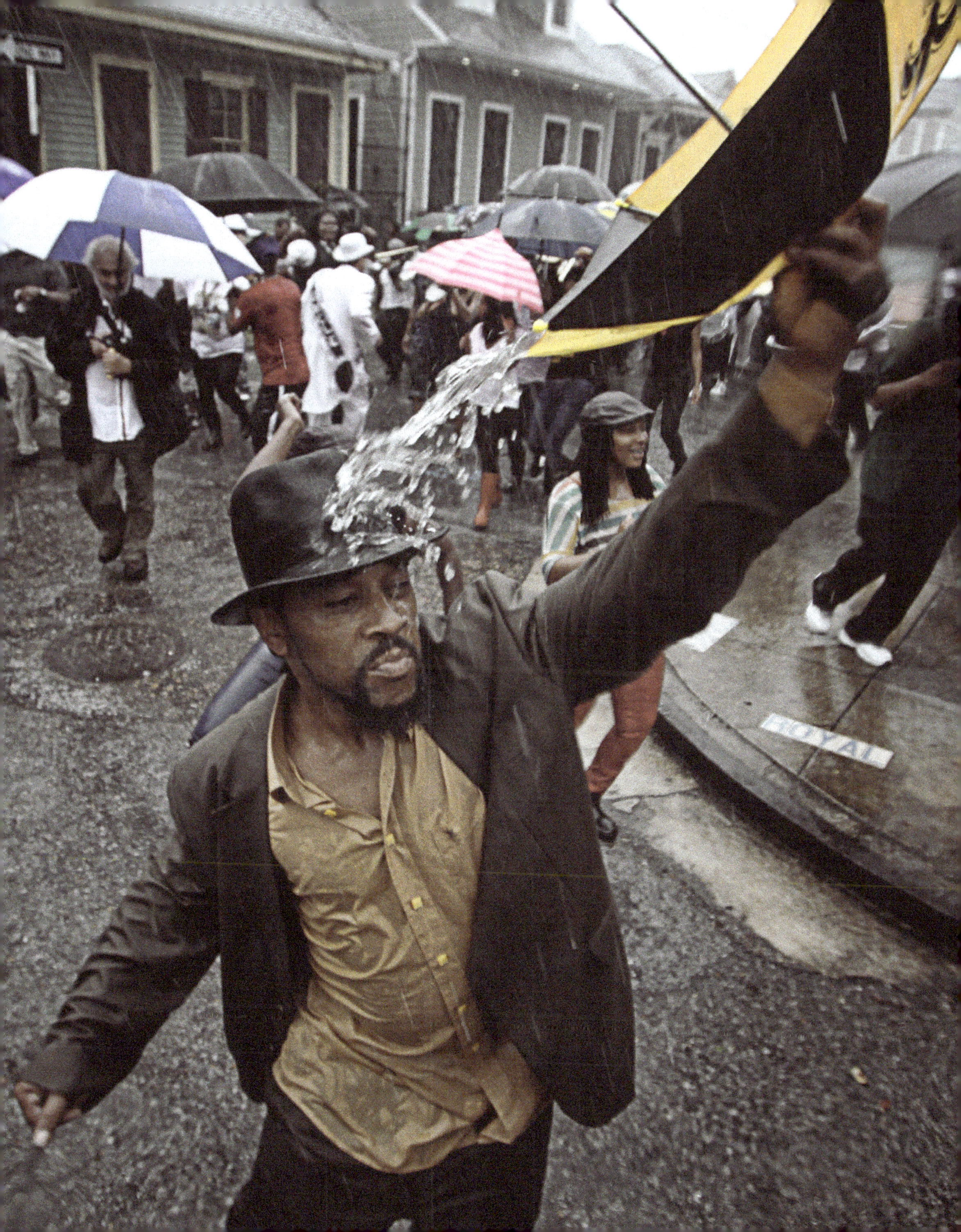

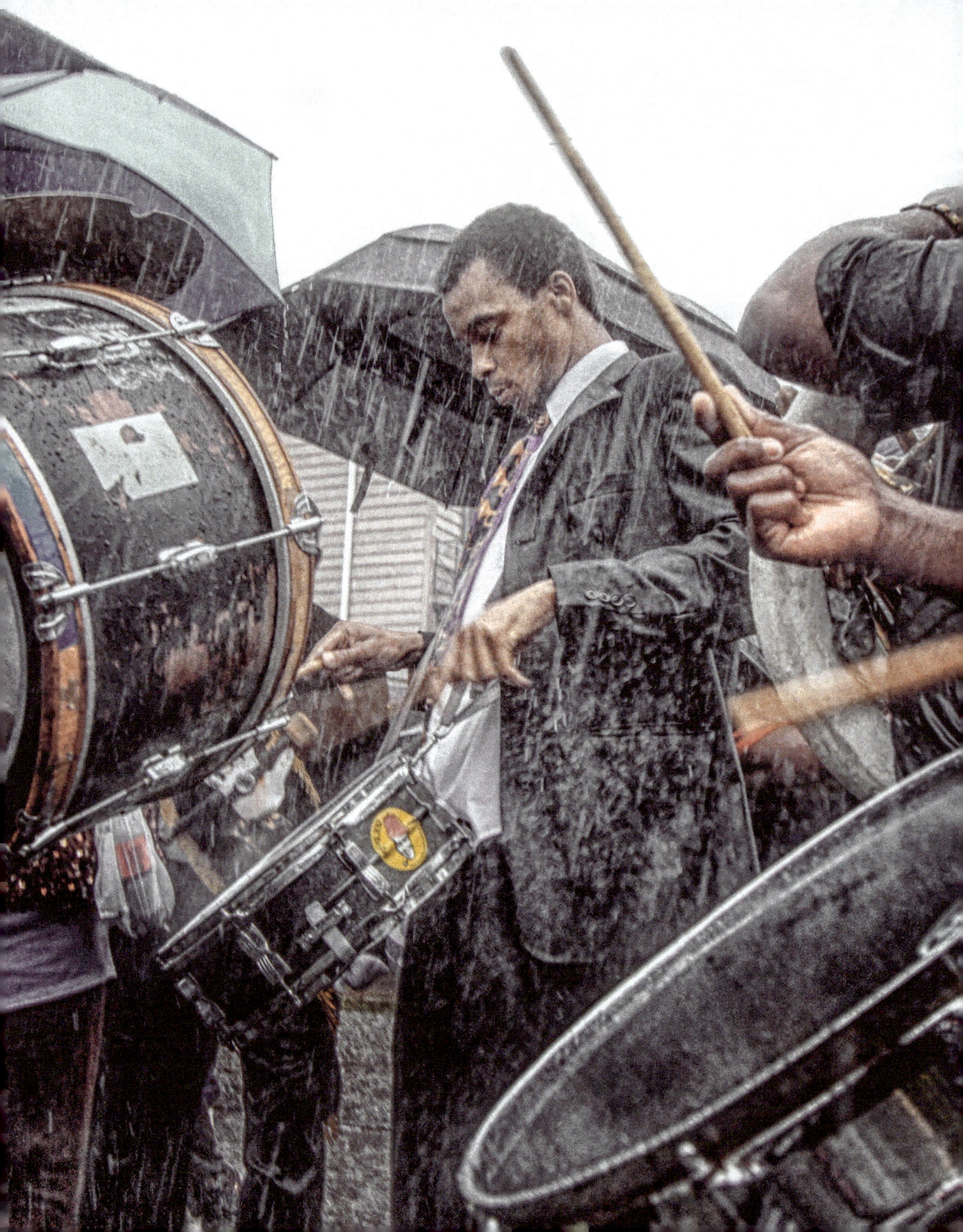

A fry cook stood outside of his cafe, drenched with his red bandana bleeding crimson down his white shirt. One partygoer, wading calf-deep in the flooded street, turned his small umbrella upside-down and held it high. After it quickly filled with water he dumped it over his head and kept dancing. Not even another Katrina could have kept your admirers from saying goodbye.

Your last funeral was the following Monday, this time in muggy 100 degree heat. Last Friday we were all drenched from rain; today we were all drenched from sweat. Four white horses pulled your casket toward the Mount Olivet Cemetery, weaving through every neighborhood along the way. I walked with you as the wooden wagon wheels crunched the pavement. Finally locating your son, Lionel Jr., I told him about meeting you and how sorry I was that you had not seen the book. Your son opened my package and gazed at your face on the cover. His eyes lit up like yours always did. He then smiled and thanked me. At last, I felt my mission was complete. I hailed a cab for the airport.

Thank you, Lionel, for your kindness and for allowing me to capture your beautiful grace.

Uncle Lionel, please forgive me.

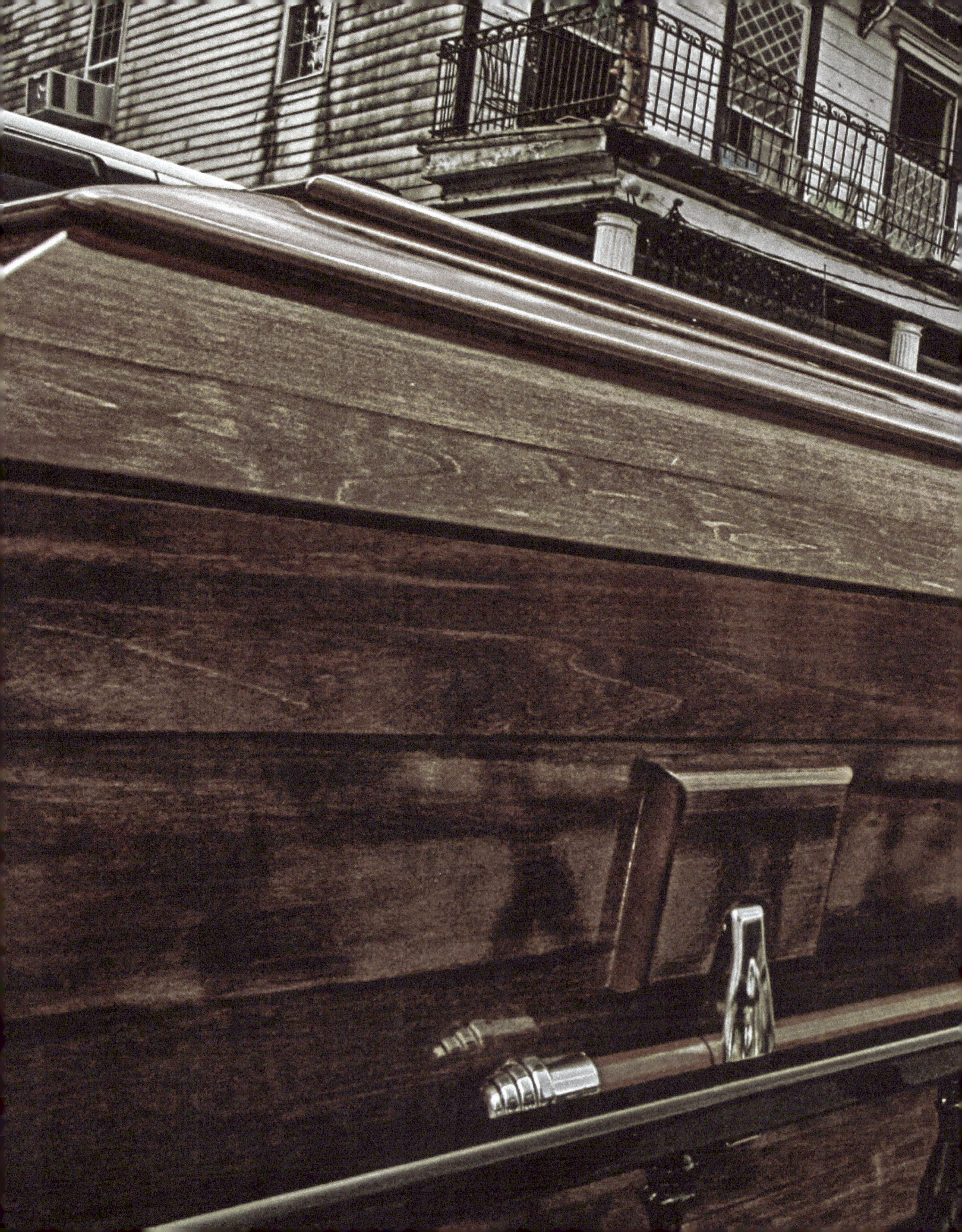

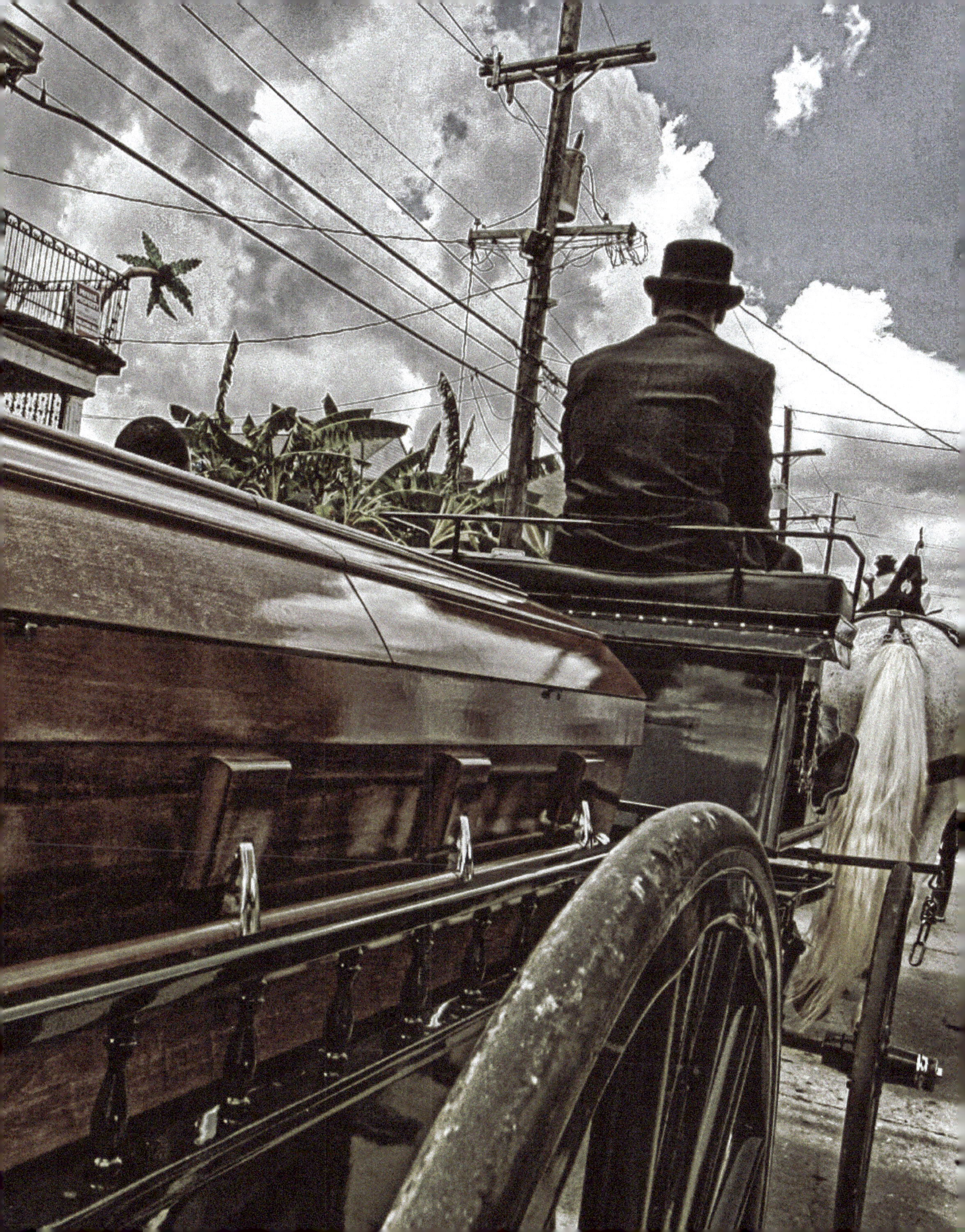

"One night I was layin' down,

"I hear Papa talkin' to Mama.

"I hear Papa say to let that
boy boogie-woogie.

"'Cause it's in him and it's
got to come out."

                **—John Lee Hooker,
                  "Boogie Chillen"**

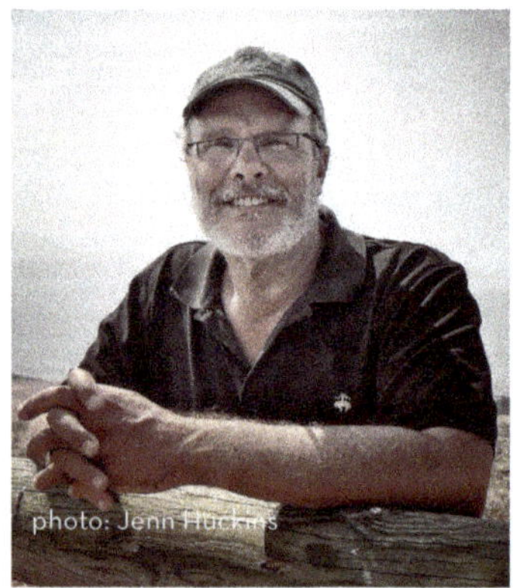

Christopher Briscoe can be reached through
www.ShiftingGearsPub.com.